ADVENTURES IN 3D PRINTING

ALSO AVAILABLE FROM CHRISTOPHER D. WINNAN

3D Printing: The Next Technology Gold Rush

ADVENTURES IN 3D PRINTING

Limitless Possibilities and Profit

CHRISTOPHER D. WINNAN

CONTENTS

PART I

PART II

PART I

1

Introduction

"Somewhere, something incredible is waiting to be known."
—Carl Sagan

Earlier this year, I self-published a very popular eBook entitled *3D Printing: The Next Technology Gold Rush - Future Factories and How to Capitalize on Distributed Manufacturing*. At more than 340 pages, it was an in-depth look into this fascinating new technology, and it very quickly received positive reviews from all sides of the Internet. Even so, due to the rapidly changing nature of the subject, many readers have been asking for an updated version. So here is an all new eBook on the subject. I hope that you enjoy reading it as much as I enjoyed conducting the research.

The first part of this eBook focuses specifically on the practicalities of turning a 3D printer into a money-making machine and is filled with tips and tricks that I have learned the hard way. Like many early adopters, I have been playing with a Makerbot for the last twelve months and I am pleased to share my hard-earned experience with you.

The second section goes on to discuss a selection of related developments that will be interesting to anybody with a fascination for 3D printing.

Of course, we are not the only ones who recognize the potential of 3D printers. The leading stocks in the field (3D Systems, Stratasys, and Proto Labs) are on aggregate, up an amazing 180 percent in a six-month comparison versus the S&P, the Dow Jones, and NASDAQ. 3D printing exhibitions have been taking place all over the world and governments are investing huge amounts into new additive manufacturing facilities. Venture capitalists are practically foaming at the mouth over these opportunities. Andreessen Horowitz, for example, injected an enormous $30 million into New York-based Shapeways (who are now printing more than a thousand items a day) while the Foundry Group ponied up another $10 million to get a share of Brooklyn-based Makerbot. Stratasys then upped the ante considerably by paying an enormous $403 million for that very same little manufacturer. We all know that there is rarely smoke without fire; these investors must think that they hold all the aces in order to be investing such enormous sums. It is no surprise that some of the most successful projects on crowd-funding sites such as Kickstarter and Indiegogo are regularly 3D printing related.

Fortunately for all of us, this technology is at such a nascent stage that almost anybody can still get in on the ground floor. Remember that it was university dropouts like Bill Gates, and unkempt, contemptuous nineteen-year-olds like Steve Jobs that helped make home computing part of the very fabric of today's society. If 3D printing lives up to its hype, then it may well be one of this eBook's readers that becomes the world's first trillionaire. Who was it that said that the geeks will inherit the earth?

Few people at the moment have any serious experience with 3D printers, let alone grasp the economic viability of manufacturing in 3D. The biggest hurdle to widespread consumer adoption at the moment is not in the technology, but in the content, a problem that Jon Buford of Makibox described most eloquently,

"If you ask someone if they think 3D printing is cool, they will say yes, but if you ask them what they would print, they don't know really what they would use it for."

This eBook has been written especially to address that problem. By the time you finish the last chapter of this eBook, my hope is that you will be overflowing with new product ideas, and ready to go and start printing ingenious objects straight away.

Figure 1. The author

Why Buy Your Own Printer

The media is filled with a growing number of pessimists asking why anybody would want to own a home 3D printer, just to make an iPhone case or some other useless doodad that will sit on a shelf and gather dust.

The truth is that the vast majority of people are simply not yet familiar with the advantages of this technology, and a few simply lack the imagination to find a use for it. One website contributor, who shall remain anonymous, recently wrote that he ran out of interesting things to print, something that I could not imagine happening for a very long time. He then went on to say that 3D printers are still lacking a practical application before they can really take off. Surely creating physical objects on your desktop is about as practical as anybody could ask for. Some people would not recognise a killer app if it smacked them right between the eyes. There might even be a more sinister explanation. Anything that comes along to upset an industry's business model is likely to be trashed by any means possible, from negative propaganda to using government lobbyists and the enactment of prohibitive regulations.

Most people are still very much in awe of this exciting technology and large swathes of us are enjoying an extended honeymoon period with 3D printing. Last year, we were all yawning at 3D TVs and yet another ultra thin laptop, but this year people are genuinely excited about 3D printing. Perhaps it is because so many of us now have a severe case of Facebook fatigue and want something more tangible than one more social media start up.

Of course, there are bound to be limitations at the early stage in any technology. I will be the first to admit that 3D printers are almost as over-hyped as cupcakes, royal babies, or Hollywood remakes. In many cases, the objects they create are about as functional as my great aunt's collection of Franklin Mint figurines, but that is totally missing the point. There are two kinds of people in this world: those who complain that something is utterly impossible and those who go ahead and do it anyway. The latter is what we commonly describe as progress.

Even now, there seem to be a great many self-proclaimed experts out there, intent on putting down the current generation of budget 3D printers as only capable of producing "cheap plastic crap." There is nothing easier than finding faults, but it is the visionaries that are staying focused on the positives and pushing forward. Use begets innovation, and innovation begets usefulness. If nobody starts buying and playing with these devices, then development and innovations which address many of the limitations that I have outlined below will not happen for decades to come.

Doubters and Defeatists

I am really looking forward to these so-called experts having to eat their own words. Just recently, Terry Guo, founder and chairman of the infamous Foxconn (Hon Hai) group, which manufacturers iPhones for Apple in distinctly dubious conditions, stated that 3D printing is little more than a gimmick. In one idiotic sentence, this fool has made himself immortal. The telegraph, telephone, airplane, car, and television were all dismissed as mere toys at their early stages of introduction. Their various naysayers are eagerly quoted decades later as examples of those unable or stubbornly unwilling to acknowledge the future. Bear in mind, this statement came from a man who earlier admitted "Hon Hai has a workforce of over one million worldwide, and as human beings are also animals, to manage one million animals gives me a headache."

Foxconn hit the news in 2010 when video of security guards beating workers was released on the Internet and a flurry of worker suicides highlighted human rights abuses and sweat shop labor practices. The company is a perfect example of the way many industrialists in China ruthlessly exploit the work force, in ways not seen since the beginning of the industrial age. Workers are merely meat robots, forced to do the most unimaginably soulless and demeaning tasks. This is monotonous work unfit for human beings, requiring no craftsmanship, incredibly extended hours, and little time off until the point of failure, when the workers are quickly discarded and replaced. Working conditions are so bad that a percentage of workers view death as a plausible means of escape. Guo's solution was not to improve their conditions, but to erect nets on their dormitories to stop them from jumping and killing themselves.

Ironically, Guo himself started out making plastic parts for television sets, but it has been the exploitation of cheap labor, a slack regulatory environment, and endemic corruption that has enabled him to amass a personal fortune of more than $5 billion. A report from a Hong Kong labor rights organization describes Foxconn as having a stifling corporate culture requiring absolute obedience, with strict rules and no means of addressing employees' grievances. Promised wage hikes have been diminished through reductions in subsidies and bonuses. Overtime working hours far exceed the legal maximum. Student interns are used extensively, while safety problems and accidents go unreported. It has long been clear that Guo has few skills beyond the exploitation of young and vulnerable workers, and is unable to recognise innovation and creativity as having intrinsic value. With such little imagination himself, it is hardly surprising that a twenty-first century robber baron like Guo cannot see any further than his own crass assembly lines. As Apple continues to slash iPhone production again this year, based on poor international sales, I wonder how long it will be before Guo realizes that it is, in fact, his factory that is churning out the soon to be forgotten gimmicks.

There are still folks out there claiming that there is little or no marketable benefit to 3D printing, and that it will always be cheaper to buy plastic widgets from China than to buy the ABS or PLA reels, and print your own. Thankfully, there is still an entire universe of new plastic widgets out there just waiting to be created. Chinese factories are generally not well-known for their imagination and creativity, and a 3D printer is simply an extension of the imagination. If that is limited, then the same will be true of your level of success with one of these machines. With a quality 3D printer, there is almost no end of things that can be created: parts for robotics, automated pan-tilt assemblies, custom gears, custom servo horns, project cases for gadgets, educational toys for our grandchildren—need I go on? The only alternative is to cut and drill pieces from stock plastic, and that is still a real pain, compared to custom forming things from a CAD drawing.

The window for a small entrepreneur shipping 3D printed goods to the end user will not last forever. Shapeways, Kraftwurx, and I.materialize are doing all they can to fill the high end of that space, and before too long most first-world folks are going to have 3D printers of their own, or at least easy access to them. In fact, once some young genius integrates model creation, slicing, and printer control software into a single package, this technology will suddenly become child's play for almost anyone to use, without any special knowledge or training. At the moment, 3D printing remains a challenge for the hard-core, but the same could be said for just about any new business. The entrepreneurs who succeed are those who push the envelope, not the ones who complain that there are too many difficulties.

In a recent report entitled, "How 3D Printing Disrupts Business and Creates New Opportunities," Pete Basiliere of Gartner Research said that enterprise-class 3D printers will be available for under $2,000 by 2016, and that the devices will soon be as common in homes as traditional 2D paper printers were ten years ago. He went on to say that if your business is not already investing in 3D printing, then it should be. And if you already have a 3D printer, he recommends that you should buy another.

At first, I was one of those guys who could not even get my ordinary ink jet printer to print out a resume without punching it a few times, so how on earth was I going to cope with one of these? I always thought that printers hated me and that I hated printers. When I first heard about 3D printers, the first thing that I wanted to print was somebody else's credit card. Once I realized that might not be a such a good idea, I thought that I might wait for a 4-D printer that would let me go back in time to 1983 and print stock certificates for Apple and Microsoft. Eventually I began to understand what the technology was all about and I finally got a 3D printer hoping that I would be able to do some on-demand printing of trinkets I could sell at conventions and on eBay.

Although 3D printing as a technology is definitely ready for consumer level, it does not automatically mean that it is suddenly a mainstream product. 3D printing is useful for people who know how to intelligently use it and already have a specific set of objectives in mind. Buying a 3D printer for a random statue, downloaded from the Internet is much more questionable. It should be an amazing boon to small inventors and one-person businesses, especially for those living in more remote areas. Anything that can be imagined can be printed, and so we can expect an explosion of new inventions being marketed, one unit at a time.

I personally was very happy with my Makerbot, but I would never recommend it to someone who isn't already a hacker. Not necessarily a hardware hacker or a coding wizard. These days the word hack has become much more mainstream and can be applied to all kinds of situations. A quick search on the net will reveal all kinds of life hacks, travel hacks, and even relationship hacks. Hacking is a can-do mentality that finds the most efficient and effective way of doing something. Turning this into a financial advantage might be a good definition of smart business practices.

Although many people are claiming that this technology is going to change the world, if you have the money and time to invest in a 3D printer, it will certainly change your life. You will start looking at things around the house and thinking "What can I print that will improve this?" or when something breaks, you will think "I can have a replacement printed out in an hour!" If you are a DIY person by nature, then this will feel like having Star Trek technology on your desk. If you have ever wanted to be an inventor, you can now go from idea to prototype in less than an hour, without leaving the house. At that stage, you realize that one small change in your life can actually change the world after all. Any replacement part that you design and share is something from which everybody on Earth can benefit. This is how civilization improves, one small step at a time.

Of course, some people simply enjoy the practice of creating things in and of itself. For these guys, building things is fun. If it is also significantly cheaper and nearly as good, why not learn something on the way? I know that there are also many "why build when I can buy" types out there, but those who ask this kind of question will probably never understand the answer anyway.

At this particular moment in time, we at the budget end of the spectrum are limited to two kinds of plastic, but that will not last for very long. There are so many open source projects out there, perfecting their designs at breathtaking speeds, that there will soon be an explosion in materials available for 3D printing, from ultraviolet stereolithography machines to full-fledged metalbots. For those of us already familiar with printing "plastic widgets," stepping up to the next generation of 3D printers is going to be so much easier than starting from scratch. Remember how basic the first dot matrix black and white printers were, and how the technology evolved slowly but surely. How many people remember Versatec wet printing, magnetic printing, spark printing, or electrolytic printing? Even though each of these played an important role in the evolution of 2D printing, the reality was that xerographic and ink jet technologies were simply better, and all the precursors were quickly forgotten. In comparison to those early attempts, the latest desktop laser jets look as though they have been teleported in from a different dimension. It is also important to remember that we went from clunky nine-needle matrix printers to full-color home laser printers in just two decades. The current discussions around 3D-printer improvements may soon seem terribly outdated, just like a debate on the relative merits of different brands of wax cylinder for recording sound.

At the moment, a great deal of 3D printing is still about as user-friendly as a junkyard pitbull or MS-DOS in 1987. Remember when dot-matrix printers could print only one font in one color? Right now, most budget 3D printers can produce plastic parts in only one color, but that will soon change. Few of the early inkjet printers could print photographs, despite being sold as "300 DPI." Resolution was grainy at best, and the matrix was clearly visible. The colors were off and the whole process took forever. The damn thing only did letter size, would jam constantly, and what you saw on screen was rarely what appeared on the paper. Ink was unreliable and moisture on a humid day would make it bleed all over the place. Any prints that I made back in those days have long since faded, bled, or color-morphed. I wonder how many of the ABS and PLA gewgaws that we are currently printing will still be around in five or ten years. Maybe by that time we will have recycled all of our earlier efforts, and will instead be focusing on exotic compound alloys with the latest metal laser sinterers.

Before we begin looking into the future, let's take a quick look at the recent past to see if it can give us any clues as to what might be coming next.

Figure 2.
A 5MB hard drive for the IBM 305 RAMAC
Supercomputer, built in 1956.

Early computer performance barely sits on the same scale as the power and speed that we take for granted today. A 3 Gigaherz multi-core CPU is commonplace for desktop machines today and yet the guidance computer used to coordinate the entire Apollo 11 mission ran at only 1.024 Megaherz. Since then, things have progressed exponentially until the average smart-phone can now outperform those early incarnations.

If we go back even further, we can extrapolate some even larger trends. Automobiles took just fifty years to go from insanely expensive toys for the super rich to affordable modes of daily transportation for the common man. Computers followed a similar trajectory, going from machines the size of entire buildings to ultra light notebooks like the one I am using to write this eBook. TVs and mobile phones were adopted at an even faster rate, within less than thirty years of their introduction. We now have many orders of magnitude more engineers and scientists, as well as a global Internet with which to collect and share data. We may only be at the stage of printing semi-crude modular components, but micron-detail prefabrication in a multitude of materials is coming, and it is coming soon.

Figure 3. "Thinking ahead for the 1980s."

If you still have any doubts that 3D printing will indeed be massive, then I suggest that you go and watch a few episodes of Star Trek that feature replicators. As has always been the case with everything from mobile phones to touch-screen interfaces, Star Trek invariably leads the way.

Figure 4. Star Trek is predictive if not prophetic.

Some readers may have seen a recent study conducted by researchers in the Materials Science and Engineering Department at the Michigan Technical University (MTU). The report was controversial to say the least, in that the team claimed that a RepRap open source 3D printer could save the average household as much as $2,000 annually and recoup the cost of the printer in under a year by printing out common household items. The group used $18 worth of plastic to print twenty items and then compared this to their retail costs on-line, which ranged from $312 to $1,943.

These days, mainstream media is full of poorly-reported scientific articles and press releases disguised as news. This particular story stinks of search engine optimisation. I find it suspicious that six out of the twenty items are overpriced Apple accessories (iPhone 5 dock, iPhone 4 dock, iPhone 5 case, iPad stand, Nano watchband, and an iPhone tripod), and this alone makes me wonder if it has been secretly commissioned by the Makerbot PR department in Brooklyn, to grab the attention of middle class American Internet users.

The full list of twenty items:

iPhone 5 dock	key hanger (3 hooks)
iPhone 4 dock	iPad stand
iPhone 4 dock	orthotic
iPhone tripod	safety razor
jewellery organizer	pickup
garlic press	train track toy
caliper	Nano watchband
Wall plate	paper towel holder
shower curtain rings (12)	pierogi mold
shower head	spoon holder

Some of these items are distinctly bogus. The shower head listed is priced at $437.22. If I were to buy a shower head that cost more than $400, I would expect it to come with a lifetime warranty, have a hundred different settings, and make coffee while I am lathering up. One of the items is a medical orthotic, the retail price of which they set at $800, significantly skewing the statistics. The majority of people in the world, without fallen arches or foot problems will never need one of these, and even those who do cannot print one on their home printer without expensive scanning equipment to ensure a custom fit. As for safety razors, they set the retail price for the safety razor at $78! I am pretty sure that for $78 there will be razors included, but the rep-rap certainly will not print any. Finally, in all of my years of eating, I never even realized I needed a "spoon holder."

Some of the statements from the original article are downright comical, and bring into question the academic rigor that takes place at MTU. "It blows my mind you can print your own shower curtain rings and beat the retail price," said Joshua Pearce, an associate professor in the Materials Science and Engineering Department. Obviously, the associate professors at MTU are quite easily impressed. He continues by stating unequivocally that, *"The unavoidable conclusion from this study is that the RepRap is an economically attractive investment for the average U.S. household already."*

I think that a more unavoidable conclusion is that these researchers are locked in the basement of an ivory tower, with only the vaguest conception of the outside world. They certainly have little idea of what the average householder uses on a annual basis, and are financially inept when it comes to where and how to shop for said items. It seems to me that the only way this study could apply would be if you were to seek out the most expensive way possible to buy things—the equivalent of buying a soda at 1,200 percent markup in a movie theater. I realize that people do actually buy soda at the movie theaters, but I would not use it as a benchmark for drink prices. Unfortunately, this study only convinces me that it is easier to fabricate the results of a study than it is to fabricate anything on a 3D printer, and a probably lot cheaper, too.

Comparing the cost of the raw material of a 3D printer to finished factory goods that have likely traveled halfway around the globe is simply not a reasonable comparison. These low-end printers are not supposed to be left unattended while operating, so at an estimate of four hours per object created—assuming each design is perfectly designed and there is no clean up time—that is an eighty–hour investment. If you estimate that your time is worth only $10 per hour, it's still an additional $800 of cost. Those shower curtain hooks may only cost $0.005 worth of plastic, but what about the $40 of your time, not to mention the time involved in sitting down and designing all of the stuff you want to print? When I buy something, I do not insist that the item pay for itself in a specified amount of time, I just need it to improve my life. Nobody buys a smartphone with Google maps in order to save enough gas to pay for the phone. They buy it to reduce the amount of time that they have to sit in traffic.

The one thing that we can all learn from this study is that although plastic filament is still dirt cheap compared to ink, it still does not make the 3D printing of commodity items cost effective. However, for making replacement and custom parts, these machines can be a godsend. We can now easily repair all those things that would otherwise be "broken," those items that only have one small plastic piece inside that needs replacing, such as cheap but otherwise good toys, or those little battery covers that seem to disappear like single socks.

I do not want to generalize here, as it is just too easy to argue the case either way. Just as an ink jet printer can be used to print out messages to go on the fridge or the next multi-million dollar bestselling novel, a 3D printer is just as flexible. Instead, I want to look at the actual capabilities and performance of the current generation of FDM printers and then, in the next chapter, discuss how to leverage these abilities in an optimal fashion.

Limitations and Opportunities

I will be the first to admit that, as it currently stands, it is not easy to produce parts that do not look like rejects from the Lego factory. I will also accept that we cannot just print anything and expect it to look fantastic. That is the main reason why I am writing this eBook, so you will know which early opportunities exist and which areas are still fraught with difficulty. Overhangs, for example, still need support material and the skill to deal with removing them cleanly. If an object does not require support material (all of the overhangs are all under a reasonable angle), and the slices do not contain more than one connected surface, then even an entry level printer will produce a very respectable looking model. Items that have more than one surface per slice will have to deal with stringing, especially if the surfaces are close together. This shows that there are clear limitations to plastic extrusion printers today, but these can be taken into account when designing models in the first place. First of all, I will explain some of the most significant constraints.

Limitations:

Unrealistic expectations

To some extent, the name "3D printing" is a misnomer. It makes the whole process sound ridiculously easy. The term "rapid prototyping" is far more accurate, but, unfortunately, does not have that all-important media buzz to it. Much of the mainstream is claiming that 3D printers can make anything on the desktop, which is just not true. Anybody that has seen a very expensive, high-end machine on TV, which uses lasers or resins, is liable to be disappointed once they take their Makerbot level machine out of the box for the very first time. Budget 3D printers are not Star Trek replicators or all-in-one fabricators, but if we respect their current limitations and try to work within those limits then we will soon find new and unexpected uses for this exciting technology.

Figure 5. The hard disk you've been waiting for.

It is important to realize that we are still in the early stages with 3D printers, but that things will change rapidly over the next few years. Back in 1983, I purchased a 10Mb hard disk for US$500. Today I can purchase a 1Tb hard disk for a tenth of that price. This means that cost per megabyte has been reduced by a factor of five hundred thousand in about thirty years. It is for this reason that I am confident that we will see at least a 10x or 100x improvement in cost of 3D printing in the next couple of years. This laptop that I am writing on will play full 1080 high-definition video with eight speaker surround sound, something that would have been unthinkable with the early model PCs. Those early machines were like dinosaurs in comparison, but that did not stop us from finding reasonable uses that matched their nascent abilities.

User friendliness

The current crop of printers are fiddly and comparatively user unfriendly. It is possible to print out decent objects, but it requires tuning and maintaining both the printer and the software. It's a solution for tinkerers, not for Joe Average. As a comparison, anybody can grill a burger, but it takes an experienced chef with skill and motivation to create cordon bleu cuisine.

Few of us built our own video recorders, cell phones, or PCs, but that did not stop us from becoming early adopters. Recall for a moment how many people were stumped when it came to programming their VCRs with the remote control. In comparison, a DIY built 3D printer means having to properly integrate an Arduino Mega2560 controller board with RAMPS 1.4 and LCD/encoder/SD card reader and Marlin firmware just to have the compiler run correctly. How many average users are willing to struggle with the fact that Marlin was developed using an old version of the Arduino-0023 IDE and cannot be compiled on the latest Arduino IDE? The old IDE attempts to define the "round" math function that is already defined in the AVR-GCC compiler, so it will not run unless you comment out the "round" function definition in the old Arduino-0023 IDE. Unless the previous sentence is painfully obvious to you, then I strongly suggest that you do as I did, and buy a fully assembled machine. Even when the machine is up and running, there are about fifty variables in the firmware that can be used to fine tune its performance, each one needing to be individually identified and assessed in how it affects the print results. It needs to know things like steps/mm in each axis, size of the print bed, etc. A good operator should have a knowledge of the printer's mechanical, electrical, and thermal characteristics to get maximum quality results. If there was a simple ten page manual, then this eBook would be completely unnecessary.

These first home 3D printers have been compared to early TV sets. Our parents will probably recall that the early black and whites worked fine part of the time, but there were other times when it was necessary to spend a half hour tinkering with the dials, wiggling the antenna and smacking them on the side, just to get that snowy mess to turn into a picture everyone could enjoy. The same was undoubtedly true for early wirelesses and gramophones, and will probably be true for innovative new devices for centuries to come.

As a Makerbot owner, I quickly discovered that very small details make a huge difference on print quality. It is possible to achieve some really astounding quality out of a Makerbot level machine, but it can take a while to print, and simply printing again will not always yield the same quality as it did the first time. Most people will not want to wait hours for $2 curtain rings, and they certainly won't want to tinker with the machine's software for an hour before printing or, indeed, put up with failed prints.

Because of the relatively high chance of errors, many users develop a complex range of preflight checks to try to mitigate the likelihood of failure on any given print.

These often include the following:

1. Use ReplicatorG to preheat the extruder to be used to ~235 degrees Celsius.
2. Detach the filament guide tube from the extruder and remove the filament from the tube.
3. Manually apply pressure to the filament to push it through the extruder.
4. If plastic thread is emitted from the extruder nozzle, proceed to step #5. Otherwise, turn off the MakerBot, disassemble the extruder apparatus, clean off any plastic buildup from the components, reassemble the extruder apparatus, and start over at step #1.
5. Ensure that plastic is being extruded from the MakerBot nozzle and check that the MakerBot can automatically extrude plastic by itself without manually jamming it through the machine. In ReplicatorG, click the "forward" button next to "motor control" to initiate a feed through the extruder. If plastic does not feed through automatically, return to step #3. Otherwise, continue on to step #6.
6. Click "Build" and pray.

Going through this entire preflight process, which takes anywhere from ten to ninety minutes decreases the likelihood of a printer failure, but only in a very inconsistent fashion, sometimes only one or two percent. It is difficulties like these that are much larger deterrent then cost or time or effort. Unless you want to spend a lot of time tinkering, look for a 3D printer that is easy to use. Ideally this means downloading a design, checking to see that it is the correct model, printing it out, and brushing it up.

Strength

3D-printed parts are not as strong as traditionally-manufactured parts. In injection molding, strength is even across the part, as the material is of a relatively consistent material structure. In 3D printing, layers are built up. This means that the part has laminate weaknesses, as the layers do not bond as well in the Z-axis as they do in the X- and Y-plane. In layman's terms, the layers separate relatively easily. This is comparable to a Lego wall: place all the bricks on top of each other, and press down: feels strong, but push the wall from the side and it breaks easily. The fusion between the layers of the model is a weak point. In two dimensions the product is reasonably strong, but in the vertical or z-axis, damage can generally be caused using just the strength of human fingers. Even though a particular type of plastic might possess decent strength qualities, this does not mean that the inherent strength of the material will be retained if it is extruded through a 3D printer. The strength of a product has more to do with how the product is formed than it does with the base material.

One main problem is that the time between one layer and the next being laid down has too much effect on the weld quality. When trying to weld a hot thing to a cold thing, there are inevitably going to be some problems. A solution would be to heat the layer below just before the weld takes place with a small wattage laser or a hot air jet, but this would mean having to enclose and interlock the build area, as with a laser cutter. While it is true that the low-end plastic extruder approach has some fundamental flaws, I challenge anybody to name even a single technology that cannot be improved, and that has already reached the peak of perfection. Fortunately, the problems of cold solder joints and bad welds are much less pronounced on small objects, where the previous layer does not have time to cool completely. This is one reason why I have put so much emphasis on printing small and miniature items.

For reference, here is a PLA object that was left outside for about a year, but the effect was nearly as bad as we would have expected: http://www.protoparadigm.com/blog /2013/06/weathering-of-3d-printed-pla-objects/. Although PLA is described as bio-degradable, it really needs to be ground up very finely and composted in a very

specific manner.
http://www.protoparadigm.com/blog/2013/06/weathering-of-3d-printed-pla-objects/

Surface finish

When people hear about printing in plastic, they visualise a finished item that is glossy and smooth. They do not visualise a matt finish with rough layer lines. Parts can be post-processed, but this generally involves labor and unpleasant chemicals such as acetone, often losing detail and tolerance on parts. Bear in mind that many of the artistic looking prints coming off the more expensive enterprise level machines have been meticulously post-processed for hours, or even days, sometimes at great expense by highly-trained professionals. Often, there are supporting structures that need to be snapped off and rough spots to be sanded. In many cases, the printed product is made of a semi-porous plastic, which can be very difficult to cover or paint. Sometimes, finishing will therefore involve undercoating, before final painting can be attempted by the end customer. At the moment, only a few plastics can be used by home based printers and the results can be quite rough. The current batch of extruders have limited accuracy in terms of layer thickness and level of detail. In the future, we will be able to lay down a myriad of materials with micron precision, interlacing the various materials which will be differing plastics including conducting metallic ones, some flexible, some transparent, some structural, some soft and pliable. Home 3D printing is not yet at the stage where the finished object magically appears at the push of a button, looking like it came out of an injection molding factory, but it is not too far away. At the moment, 3D printer output is only comparable to 60 percent or 80 percent of an injection mold, but this is still very useful for improvised devices and design prototypes.

Cost

Cost for printed items is based on the material used, so larger items are obviously more expensive while smaller ones are cheaper. Cost is not related to complexity, or the number of parts or expensive tooling. Even so, the materials are still much more expensive than buying just raw material, with the cheapest being about $20 to $50 per kg, and ranging up to $500 for some of the more complex resins.

In reality, it is just bulk plastic and should be priced nearer fifty kilograms per dollar than $50 per kilo.

There was a significant drop in printer prices several years ago as startups such as MakerBot began introducing the former commercial technology to a do-it-yourself crowd. A 3D printer went from costing tens of thousands of dollars to just a few thousand dollars. More recently, machines that used to cost $20,000 have dropped to as low as $300 to $500. Despite this, in some areas, the trend has seemed to have reversed. MakerBot's Thing-O-Matic (which buyers had to order as a kit that needed assembly) went for $1,225 two years ago; its current entry-level printer, the Replicator 2, goes for $2,199.

If personal 3D printing has been moving closer to mass adoption, why haven't manufacturers been able to bring the price of 3D printers down? One problem is that many of the companies are newly established startups or began as Kickstarter campaigns. This kind of bootstrap operation does not have the manufacturing processes or facilities to begin taking advantage of economies of scale. MakerBot opened a new factory in June 2012, but still builds each 3D printer by hand. That means a significant assembly cost and little economy of scale. As orders increase, the company has to hire more assemblers. The sudden demand from 3D printing has dramatically driven up the price of components such as multiple NEMA motors that used to be relatively cheap. 3D Systems is an established, high-volume manufacturer, and that's undoubtedly one reason why its consumer level printer costs $1,000 less than the new MakerBot. That price, combined with the ability to actually mass produce, is why there are 3D Systems printers on retail shelves at stores such as Staples.

Manufacturers are now scrambling to address the limitations of 3D printers, and that development is also making the products more expensive. The latest consumer 3D printers may not cost any less than those available two years ago, but they are capable of printing much bigger objects with far greater levels of detail. They are more user-friendly and they have started to show advanced capabilities such as printing with multiple colors.

Speed

For small-scale manufacturers or crafters, 3D printers can be used as part of the manufacturing process, but they are still relatively slow, and this makes them unsuitable for manufacturing large quantities. At the moment, 3D printing is far from instant. Printing an object the size of a normal cigarette packet still takes about two hours. The process can be sped up by making the layers thicker, but then surface finish quality suffers. Materials such as ABS and PLA are limited by their chemical properties and can only be extruded so fast before their structure begins to suffer. Unfortunately, we live in an age of instant gratification. ("You mean I have to wait five seconds for that web page to load? Screw dat!")

Failure rates

3D printing currently presents the same level of difficulty to hobbyists as computers did in the eighties. Loading an early BBC Micro from an old audio tape recorder failed on average 30–50 percent of the time. The key trick in those days to pushing reliability closer to four out of five was to mark the position of the volume knob with a pen. I remember when CD writers were like this too. About 25–33 percent of new burns quickly became drinks coasters, simply because the machine could not keep the write buffer full. CD burning was a delicate balancing act of setting it to burn, not touching absolutely anything, and hoping to god that it did not spit out a failure error. CD/DVD burners are now so dirt cheap and reliable that it is hard to imagine the days when they were so extremely sensitive. In just a few short years, 3D printers will become similarly reliable and mainstream. They will continue to fall in price, until people are churning out all kinds of crazy creations without giving it a second thought.

In the meantime, print failures remain a fact of life, especially when you leave the machine unattended. It might have something to do with the nearby body heat, or maybe a hidden camera that verifies a person is in the proximity, or maybe just pissed off little gremlins that cannot stand to be lonely, but most printers still need babysitting. This could be proof that machines are malign intelligences intent on maximizing human misery, which would also explain traffic light timing and photocopier jams. Slightly more worrying than the risk of spaghetti prints is the fact that the cheap ramps-based printers have very little internal protections beside some code on the Atmel micro-controller. If the Atmel hangs with the heater on, then it will continue until it fries something, and it is this that prevents me from leaving my printer running unattended when going to work.

Figure 6. Look at what you could have won!
One of the General's many early failures.

I would estimate that my MakerBot's early failure rate fell in the range of 25–33 percent. Some of these glitches could be attributed to human error. For example, forgetting to configure the energy saver settings properly on the laptop feeding data to MakerBot via USB, and then the laptop going to sleep causes MakerBot to time out as well. Neglecting to set the temperature of the MakerBot platform high enough can lead to the plastic, partway through the print, to stop sticking to it, potentially causing the model to tip over and/or spray a bird's-nest jumble of plastic thread over it. Hopefully prior knowledge will help you avoid such problems.

Computer Assisted Design (CAD).

3D CAD software is a disorganized mess. Simple programs are far too simple: even basic users will quickly run into the limitations of programs such as Sketchup and AutoCAD 123D. Complex programs are expensive and require extensive training. Even those that are free, such as Blender, require significant time investments in software familiarisation. Designing a 3D object on a 2D screen with 2D controls (i.e. a mouse) has always been a major challenge, but having experience in drawing or creating objects (sculpting, model building, anything) certainly helps. Each of the different programs have their own idiosyncrasies, quirks, and limitations. Something as simple as subtracting two shapes from each other can quickly become a nightmare in some programs. Sometimes it works without any effort at all, but other subtractions convert the model into a horrible mess of triangular fragments that can take hours to correct.

All too often, CAD programs cannot even create a true arc or circle, only approximate them with lots of straight line segments. Some experts say that there are a whole category of surface modelling programs that you should never use because they create lots of problems when preparing the CAD file for 3D printing. Pioneers in the field, on the other hand, such as Bathsheba, describe specialist software such as Surface Modeller as her secret weapon. The results of her positivity are visibly clear.

Figure 7. Just a tiny selection of Bathsheba's geometric designs.

For the time being, one of the easiest solutions is simply to print out other people's designs. There are superbly talented designers all over the world, and the Internet makes collaborating with them as easy as making a phone call. For those willing to invest their time in a particular program, the rewards are enormous. Seeing a 3D drawing created completely from scratch manifest as a plastic object is extremely satisfying, despite the process being an exasperatingly steep hill to climb.

Word processing made the business of writing letters and reports a hundred times easier than before, but that process is still not instantaneous. Users cannot just click "print," and expect a finished report to emerge. Words have to be typed, paragraphs crafted, and then the whole thing needs to be checked for mistakes. In 3D printing, a digital model must first be designed and created. That model then needs to be optimised for a particular printer. The main problem at the moment is that for most of us, creating a digital model is still an awful lot harder than writing a letter.

Recall for a moment how difficult it used to be to become a published writer. Before the Internet, first-time authors had to go to a publisher and practically beg to obtain the investment required. Nowadays, eBooks or blogs have dramatically reduced those costs and, at the same time, democratized writing.

Even better news is that new 3D model libraries are opening up all the time. The downside is that many of these new sites are soon inundated with the same 3D files that are featured on all the other sites. Many are entirely unmoderated, meaning that their models are not even guaranteed to be 3D printable. Many of them are made for animation/rendering and are flat surfaces with images projected onto them, making them definitely unprintable. Even the major 3D printing libraries are filled with files that contain horrible errors and that have been designed with little respect to the capabilities and cost of 3D printers. The quality of the model has as much to do with the outcome as the printer itself. Garbage in, garbage out.

Materials

Enterprise level machines can 3D print in hundreds of different materials, but for home use, most of us are still limited to either ABS or PLA. The good news is that these are relatively safe compounds that cool quickly, meaning the parts are safe to touch straight off the machine, and leave little in the way of mess. This is certainly not true for any other type of printer. Resins, though higher detail, are still messy and expensive; powder-based printers are even more messy, and sometimes explosive to boot. Others operate at ridiculously high temperatures or produce mountains of waste. This means that FDM (Fused Deposition Modelling) is as yet the only really suitable technology for the home.

Unfortunately, most items in the house are made up from multiple materials, and most of them are both metal and plastic. Those two cannot be made together as their melting temperatures are hundreds, if not thousands of degrees apart. Furnace temperature smelting is not a process that many people would be happy to see in their living rooms.

ABS plastic is relatively safe, but not food safe. PLA plastic is somewhat more food safe and biodegradable (it is produced from plant starches), but can be difficult to work with. Of course, for printers that have no heated bed, PLA is the only option. Laser sintering for nylon or titanium still costs more than a Ferrari, so until we have Jay Leno's budget, we had better learn to love ABS and PLA.

The good news is that injection molders have literally thousands of plastics to choose from for their products, each one with unique properties optimized for different types of applications, UV resistance, shatter resistance, flexibility, etc. Some plastic products even have fibers molded into them to make them stronger. This is what we can look forward to in the near future.

Size

Most budget-level 3D printers have a print bed area a little over twelve centimetres in size. A few printers have larger capabilities, but not much. Once the print area is broadened, other issues such as heat stability and platform evenness begin to become much more complicated. In addition, complex objects still need to be printed in pieces before being assembled. Of course, this is a drawback that has been overcome many times in the past. Back in 1886, the gargantuan Bartholdi Lady Liberty was assembled from more than three hundred separate crates and, before that, the pyramids were built using more than a million individual blocks of limestone.

Another common misconception is that any object can simply be scaled down and printed in a miniature version. Actually, neither scaling up nor down can be achieved without a significant amount of digital rework. Besides, the fact that it has to "work" (wall thickness, assembly of the pieces of the kit), it also has to look in balance. If, in reality, a piece of steel plate has a thickness of 10mm, it would become 0.11 in 1:87 (a popular model car scale). This means that the scale version would require artificial thickening, and also the skill to ensure that it still fits in visually. This is clearly where artistry and craftsmanship become involved and this becomes more than a simple manufacturing process.

Opportunities:

It is clear that the current generation of extrusion printers come with their fair share of liabilities and limitations, but it is important to be aware of these before jumping in feet first. The good news is that 3D printing represents many advances that simply have not been previously available to artists, hobbyists, and inventors. If we look back at the history of art, almost everything was subtractive. Renaissance artists tried to recreate 3D images using 2D paints, while sculptors were restricted to very time consuming reductive techniques. From this perspective, additive plastic is a completely new medium for an emerging class of creatives. The most successful users will be those who not only recognize these opportunities, but are able to take fullest advantage of them.

Reduced costs

Aside from the initial investment in the printer and materials, the costs associated with 3D printing are relatively low when undertaken by individuals. This is equally true for even the largest corporations. Airbus designers recently reported that 3D printing brackets used in ailerons from sintered titanium halved both the weight and cost of trying to machine the same part. 3D printing allows the placing of material only in the key loading directions where the part has to be rather than where it does not.

iMakr charges $15 an hour to run its machines while Shapeways charges roughly $3 per cubic centimeter when the plastic itself costs less than $0.05. However, when you factor in shipping and turnaround time, you see the real advantage of having a desktop printer nearby.

Ordinary people are becoming frighteningly industrious and making things that conventional manufacturers would never have thought to make, leading to an explosion of unparalleled creativity and facilitating entrepreneurship for the masses. This is a designer's dream, a way of experimenting, exploring, and, most importantly, not going bankrupt in the process. Current bottlenecks in manufacturing are not due to a lack of ideas, but accessing the funds needed to make those ideas reality. We can dream up countless amazing things all day long, but none of them will come to fruition if we do not own a factory capable of producing them.

This is a brave new world where imagination has no boundaries. Not only will it allow a lot more ideas to come to life than are possible with the current greed-based business culture, but it will enable whole new forms of business and a totally different type of economics. We can look forward to a resource-rich, idea-rich economy, rather than the artificial scarcities of "supply and demand."

This is going to have an incredible impact on amateur inventors. Canadian TV has a popular show entitled *Backyard Inventors*. What always amazes me when I watch this program is how much money people have spent to develop their ingenious new products. Figures such as $40,000, $60,000, and $80,000 are regularly quoted when guests on the show state how much they have spent thus far on their projects. In the last episode I saw, one woman claimed that she had spent more than $120,000 to create a beverage-cooling cup, something I can find dozens of in my local high street. Suddenly, 3D printing is set to reduce these ridiculous costs, as well as break the stranglehold that big business holds over these creative geniuses. No longer do they have to add 50–100 percent markups for manufacturers, retailers, and assorted other middle men. Now they can simply print their product and market it on-line.

Customisation

Reductive manufacturing requires extensive modification and recalibration of machine tools, making it very expensive to customize. With a 3D printer, it is suddenly possible to create a different object every time you hit the print button. Self-replication is a fine goal, but rapid manufacturing techniques should be used to build one of something, not an army of something. Using rapid prototyping for production is by definition a mistake. If you want ten or ten thousand identical things, it is much better to use a production system. 3D printing is designed for people who want just one thing that is unique to them. Even the original inventor of FDM printing Scott Crump said, "The main draw of 3D printing is to build custom or low-volume items that aren't being mass manufactured."

What is the point in printing something as boringly ubiquitous as an iPhone cover? Not only are you going up against some of the biggest factories in China, but you are looking at a market that is almost saturated by big business. The beauty of a 3D printer is that you can print something straight out of your imagination in just a matter of minutes. Dig deep and come up with a product that meets the needs of a market of one. If you try and take on the big boys at their own game, do not be surprised if you end up as entrepreneurial roadkill. If you insist on doing iPhone covers, then make sure that they match up to imagination of Oscar Blanco.

Figure 8. The amazing work of Oscar Blanco

This freedom of being able to manipulate every object that we own will bring back an old-time craftsmanship that has almost disappeared. Just as your grandfather made his own furniture, with all those details that he loved so much, the coming generation can use computer power to create anything virtually, and then create it using some kind of 3D printer. It allows electronics engineers, for example, to release their inner artist and gives them the opportunity to present their prototypes or demo boards in a much more attractive way.

Creativity

With 3D printing, I finally have a tool that can actually keep up with my imagination. Taking weeks or months off the traditional design process enables fully-fledged capitalism with very little capital required. The experience of starting out with nothing more than a digital file and then just moments later having a physical object is truly amazing. In the past, this would have required a workshop with a vast range of tools, a team of designers, artists, sculptors, and god knows how many other expensive, fully-trained artisans. Thanks to my 3D printer, I can go from image to object in just a matter of minutes. The consequences of failure are almost non-existent when using these tools as compared to situations where a craftsman has to work with less forgiving materials. This allows for hacking in a very real sense and creates an opportunity to invent new intricate machines and design their shape in any way at all. We may well see an explosion of steam punk contraptions or arcane paraphernalia designed by retired tattoo artists and mad toymakers. Every single item we own has been designed by somebody. This new production regime means the financial costs are reduced, so designers can take more risks with design. Innovation can hit warp speed. Expensive market research and endless focus groups are no longer required for businesses that have something to sell, but are not sure about its future performance. Now they can simply create two or three and see how orders go.

Figure 9. Creativity without limitation

The thought of producing something out of additive plastic means people come at the same problem from a completely different angle. As the barrier to entry is lowered, this will inspire a whole new generation of CAD artisans and bring fresh blood to the industry.

Time to market

One of the most important advantages of 3D printing is that it finally puts the rapid into rapid prototyping. At the moment this is still the bread and butter of the industry. Rather than having to design a conceptual model and then source the materials and equipment necessary to create a physical prototype, small businesses can simply design the model digitally and print it out. More traditional methods of turning graphic designs into working models, such as creating wax prototypes with a milling machine, would cost $60 to $100 per design compared to just $3 for a 3D-printed prototype. Whenever there is a new idea for an original product, there is no longer the need to contact an injection molding factory in China, attend endless negotiation meetings, cough up $5,000 for a sample, another $5,000 for a finished product, and then go through the nightmare of trying to ensure quality control over a process that is taking place ten thousand miles away, in a completely alien culture.

Suddenly, a 3D printer does away with all the expense and hassle. You have an idea, and then within a few hours you have a prototype product. Being able to transform a thought into a tactile object that you can hold in your hand within just a few hours is an incredibly gratifying experience for any designer. This certainly makes up for the relatively slow speeds of 3D printing, especially when compared to conventional CNC methods, let alone hand fabrication. Ordinary people wanting to make prototypes of objects could, until recently, only do so with the help of people who owned factories. Prototyping has always been a notoriously slow process, regardless of the technology used, but that is changing very quickly. This significantly reduces business startup costs and product development time cycle in the manufacturing and engineering fields. Things that took weeks or even months to design, test, and implement can now be completed in a matter of days or even hours. The cost savings and competitive edge that these devices bring are amazing. One designer described his Cupcake 3D printer as a "bone maker" in the larger ecosystem of rapid prototyping technologies. He uses it for prototyping ideas and making the scaffolding around which to wrap skins with more finish.

Component complexity

3D printing is in some ways a wish-fulfilment technology in that it allows artists and engineers to dream up any design and then make that object, often using shapes that are simply not possible with any other technology.

Intricate assemblies are extremely labor intensive and expensive in a reductive manufacturing world. Most of the work done in China for example is assembly, taking advantage of what was, until recently, very cheap labor. In the future, additive manufacturing (with metals, plastics, glasses, and the ability to insert and build around third party components) will reduce the cost of complexity.

Think of a metal part containing hollow, honeycomb-like structures, such as the valve body of the transmission for example. These control valves are extremely complex central nerve systems that tell the transmissions what to do and when. At the moment, these complicated arrangements of spring-loaded valves, check balls, servo pistons, and fluid passages are built using metal casting methods. 3D printing would make design and construction of such housing much more simple and efficient, and could be applied to other kinds of complex heat sinks, pumps, or air ducts.

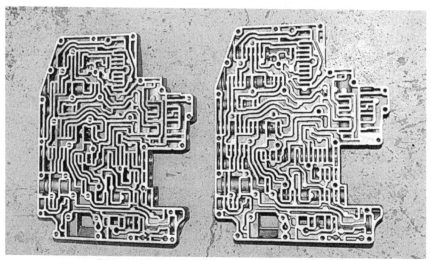

Figure 10. A fearfully complex component

Now that we have looked at some of the advantages and disadvantages of the technology, we will spend the next chapter looking at the machines themselves in more detail. Once we are more familiar with the current crop of machines, we will go on to think about what we should actually be printing.

Choosing a Printer

Thanks to an upsurge in consumer interest, there are now 3D printers available at a vast range of prices, many having plummeted in the last few years. Six years ago, a 3D printer cost between $60,000 and $500,000. These days they range from just a few hundred dollars for a basic open source model to hundreds of thousands of dollars for a high-end machine capable of printing artificial body parts. Unless you have recently inherited a large fortune, I would advise you to minimize your investment at this early stage of the game. Remember that the real beauty of these machines is that they are being built with the eventual aim of self-replication. That means that as soon as you have your 3D printer up and running, the first thing that you will be able to print are the components for a better 3D printer. This in itself is a major game changer.

I personally have (or at least I did have) an original Makerbot clone churning out ingenious little plastic products, and there are a number of reasons that I chose this particular machine. The first and most important of these is that it was open source, unlike the more recent machines unveiled by the fast-growing Makerbot company.

There is a popular belief in the West that competition and economic incentive drive diversity in the marketplace. What the open source and RepRap movements have continuously shown is that in the modern interconnected world, this is patently untrue. In fact, it would seem that diversity occurs more quickly and with fewer constraints in the open source community. RepRaps are proliferating in an eclectic assortment and some observers have likened this process to the amazing birds-of-paradise of Papua New Guinea or the strange marsupials of Australasia.

Thanks to the internet and open source, almost every 3D tinkerer and experimenter on the planet is now part of my R&D team. It also means that my machine was significantly cheaper than the new Makerbot Replicator 2, which now has to fund hefty executive salaries in New York, metropolitan property rentals, pay back $10 million in venture capital and justify another $400 million that Stratasys recently shelled out to buy the firm. Makerbot's first product, the CupCake, was launched with a price tag of $1,000 that later fell to $450. Next up, the Thing-O-Matic kit came out at $1,200. Then the Replicator launched with a $1,750 price tag, and the latest incarnations, the Replicator 2 and 2X, now sell for $2,200 and $2,800, respectively. I paid the equivalent of just $800 for my Makerbot clone, fully assembled.

As big business moves into this area, it would seem that stockholder demands are pushing up prices across the industry. 3D Systems launched the original Cube with a $1,300 price tag. The latest generation, CubeX, sells for $2,500 to $4,000 despite locked-down functionality, an overpriced model store, and proprietary cartridges. (The Cube is obviously intended to generate ongoing revenue through sales of raw materials.) A single cartridge is $49 (the company does offer bulk discounts) and the cartridge is a sealed unit with a chip. In fact, some cynics have added that the only thing missing is an Apple logo. Customers are now paying for stylish designs and custom cabinetry over the simple laser-cut panels of the more basic models. To me this is irrelevant. My Makerbot sat locked away from prying eyes, printing out useful products in the spare bedroom. The neighbors were aware that I had some sort of machine delivered to the apartment, but for all they knew it could have been an oversized microwave or a dish washer. I did not buy it to drive around the city centre on Saturday night, in order to pick up girls. How it looked was of little importance to me. What really matters is how much it costs and how it performs. Even when I am ready to upgrade, my next purchase decision will be based on print speed and reliability, not aesthetic appearance.

It is the open source movement that has bought this technology down to the level where we ordinary 99-percenters can afford it, and it will be the open source movement that will make the largest strides forward in the near future. This is as good a place as any for a novice to begin their relationship with 3D printing. When teaching a child to ride a bicycle, we do not go out and immediately buy them a custom built, carbon fibre, professional racing frame. I learned to ride on a Raleigh Chopper which barely even resembled a normal bicycle, but it did not stop me from mastering the basic skills of balance and road safety.

It is very much like buying a Tandy computer in the early 80s. As steep as that learning curve was, there were unequivocal benefits and advantages realized by getting in on the ground floor and growing with it. Like the personal computer, 3D printers do not come without growing pains for home users and early adopters.

Whatever you decide to buy, choose carefully and you may have a valuable antique on your hands in twenty or thirty years' time. A case in point is the Apple-1 that recently sold at auction in Germany for a jaw-dropping $671,400. It was one of the original computers that was built by Steve Wozniak back in 1976, in Steve Jobs' parents' garage. The retail price for the Apple-1 at the time was $666.66. In a way I wish I could have afforded it, if only for a chance to harass The Woz for tech support.

Before we look at the printers themselves, let's take a quick look at some of the individual parts (sometimes known as the vitamins) with which you will need to become familiar. This knowledge will be essential if you are planning to assemble or build your own printer from scratch. The less adventurous of you can skip to the section on pre-assembled machines, followed by a brief introduction to materials.

Platforms

The build platform is the moving surface on which your model is layered. Platform material varies, and some are heated to help prevent the ABS from warping as it cools. If the build platform is wonky, then so is your model. Most printers require manual leveling, but we are starting to see automatic leveling features on some of the newest machines.

There are basically two types of platforms: heated and non-heated. Heated beds are usually made from a simple PCB with a maze of traces etched onto the surface to create resistance. This is topped by a 1/8-inch thick sheet of borosilicate glass that is covered in high-temperature tape, as they can often reach temperatures of 140 degrees. Their main advantages are that they improve print adhesion and reduce warping and splitting. Non-heated beds are produced from laser-etched acrylic and tend to require large amounts of rafting. Both types will benefit from a covering of high temperature tape, such as Kapton or Polymide or 3M's PET-based tape. Being able to adjust the bed adjustability is a major factor in print quality. Some utilize a fixed mounting solution while others are adjustable with a spring under each mounting bolt, allowing users to level the bed by tweaking each individual corner to obtain a perfectly flat surface.

Electronics

At the moment, most open source 3D printer electronics are

based on the Arduino and a few even come as shields that that go directly on top of an Arduino Mega. Listed below are four of the most popular controller boards currently available.

Sanguinololu

Originally designed and developed by Zach Smith, while he was still at the RepRap Research Foundation, this is a relatively simple single-board design that is based around the Sanguino (an Arduino compatible board) with an almost entirely through-hole design, which makes hand soldering convenient and easy. As with the RAMPS, it has headers for modular Pololu stepper motor drivers, but it can only run five stepper motors and two heated assemblies, which means it is out of the question for dual extruder machines.

RepRap Arduino Mega Pololu Shield (RAMPS)

Using the micro-controller's IO pins to control the actuators of the stepper motors draws a great deal of power and so A4982 driver chips have been utilized in a compact circuit called the Pololu stepstick. The only Arduino that could handle the multitude of tasks was the Arduino Mega 2560 and so the RAMPS was born. The 1.4 version of the "RAMPS" requires a 12V power source with a minimum current rating of 20 amps. Many scratch builders have scavenged standard 300 watt power supplies from old PCs to power this board. It features controls for three heated assemblies (one bed and two extruders), but I am still somewhat puzzled as to why it would have connections for up to six extruders. For ease of maintenance, the Pololu stepper motor drivers are individually plugged into header pins, just in case one should unexpectedly burn out.

RepRap Gen 7

The generation 7 electronics from the RepRap project are an entirely DIY project, which means they are aimed at the most mechanically and electronically minded. That is the bad news. The good news is that every component is through-hole for easy soldering, and the PCB features a single-sided design for ease of home etching. Like the previous two boards, this also utilizes the modular stepper drivers from Pololu. If you do find that you have bitten off more than you can chew, then there is a very useful Gen 7

RepRap Wiki page as well as the RepRap IRC and forums.

RAMBo

Designed by Johnny R. from Ultimachine, this is one of the newest controller boards and, as an all-in-one "RepRap motherboard," it is considered by many to be the Rolls Royce of 3D printer electronics. It features an Arduino MEGA compatible Atmega2560 and Atmega32u2 processors that are compatible with all RAMPS class firmwares. Housing five PWM outputs and five on-board stepper motor drivers, it can handle up to three heated assemblies via three independent power rails.

Extruders

An extruder is the business end of a 3D printer that deposits the filament and is therefore perhaps the most important part of the whole set up. It is made up of a feeder, a motor drive, and a hot end nozzle that melts the plastic filament and squeezes it out in the form of hot, toxic toothpaste.

Makerbot StepStruder

The StepStruder MK7 first shipped with the Thing-O-Matic, and both the Replicator 1 and 2 had this identical component with only a slight variation in the nozzle, something that their marketing department failed to mention in their glowing write ups. It utilizes a built-in heat sink and fan to keep the filament cool until the heat chamber, instead of a plastic-based thermal transition barrier. There has been a minor modification in the way the thermocouple and heater cartridge are attached and the Rep 2 also sports a secondary fan for the blower. The blower helps to reduce warping when printing with PLA, but is not really an innovation or a noteworthy change. The latest version of the Rep 2 includes the MKV J-Head and a RepRap MK2 Improved Heat Bed. The J-head has undergone numerous iterations and is now a much more stable design and also has a 0.40 mm nozzle option.

Makergear Stepper Plastruder with Makergear GrooveMount HotEnd

This rather bulky extruder differs from the MK7 in that it utilizes a plastic insulator between the hot end and the filament feed to prevent the kind of filament preheating that can often cause jams. It also features a gear reduced stepper motor that provides additional torque to feed filament into the hot end. Even so, many users feel that its nichrome wire heating method is messy, antiquated, and unreliable.

The Wades Extruder is still very much a work in progress that is regularly modified by users. It features a nema 17 stepper motor and user-created 3D printed gears, such as the Parametric Herringbone Gears by Scribble J. The Wade Reloaded design features a spring tensioned filament system, instead of the rubber O-rings on the MK7, which makes changing filament and cleaning blockages much easier.

Different users prefer different hot ends, but there are three popular options.

The Arcol V3 features machined aluminium cooling fins to prevent the feeder from acting as a heat sink and is therefore a good choice for plastics, such as nylon and wood-infused plastics, which require extreme temperatures. The Reifsnyder Precision Works J Head has a machined design that is able to dissipate excess heat while allowing for faster head travel and a longer lifespan. It is a good choice for the more exotic, high-temperature plastics. Like the Arcol, its only downside is that its nozzle diameter is fixed and cannot easily be swapped out. Perhaps the best of the bunch is the prewired Lulzbot Budaschnozzle 1.3, based on the Arcol, but with the removable design of the MK7. This combines reliability with accuracy and is able to print well beyond the 0.25 mm limit of other nozzles.

Firmware Packages

There are three main firmware packages. Marlin, also known as Sprinter, is the RepRap default, Teacup is written in C rather than C++ making it much smaller. Sailfish (previously known as Jetty) is built on generation 4 Makerbot and MightyBoard firmwares, with added acceleration features from Marlin. Although it adds a number of improvements, such as the asymmetric JKN Advance algorithm, the "Yet Another Jerk" jerk control and fixed-point computations for added speed, Makerbot has updated it to further reduce the amount of support and raft material required.

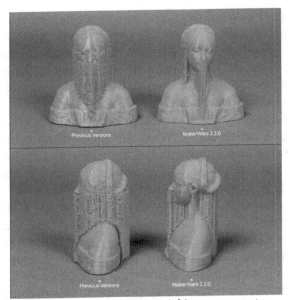

Figure 11. Support material improvements.

Control Software

This is the code that slices up STLs into wafer thin horizontal layers, generates toolpaths, and then calculates the amount of material to be extruded There are two common variants. Slic3r is bundled with most firmware while Skeinforge uses Python scripts to create G-Code instructions, which are then converted to .x3g or .s3g for execution. It has a whole host of manual settings that can be edited to optimize the printing operation, so much so that it can seem quite daunting in the beginning.

In addition, there are three main print control programs. Printrun quickly became the default open source choice for the majority of DIY enthusiasts. It comes pre-packaged with Slic3r and works well with all RepRap and Makerbot based 3D printers. The Repetier-Host package is a relatively new comer and requires a full installation of the host client firmware. Replicator G has long been the Makerbot default, but has recently been superseded by Makerware which features a new slicing engine, said to be up to twenty times faster than Skeinforge and a powerful interface that allows users to move, rotate, and scale multiple models in the virtual build space. The downside is that unlike Zach's Replicator G, this new software is completely closed source.

Microsoft has recently added an API that provides native 3D

printer support in Windows 8.1, allowing developers wishing to build 3D printing capabilities into their applications to do so, attracting developers who are interested in 3D printing to the Windows software. It is hoped that printing 3D objects will soon be as easy and seamless as operating 2D ink-jet and laser printers, but there are a number of obvious drawbacks.

Many of the existing 3D formats such as STL are unsuitable for streaming processing by the Windows spooler and print pipeline as well as missing important features like color and material support. Therefore, the company has introduced the 3D Manufacturing Format, or 3MF, a new file format is based on XML.

While designers tend to use Macs, most CAD/CAM and engineering software is only available for Windows. Thus, there is a ready-made audience for these printers in the hard sciences and, more importantly, an opportunity for Microsoft to grab that market share while maintaining an air of technical advancement.

The company also wanted to provide uniform compatibility for 3D printers that exist both today and in the future, and define a feature set for 3D printing that represents the capabilities of current and upcoming 3D printers as well as other manufacturing devices such as water jet cutters and CNC milling machines.

Some enthusiasts have accused the company of creating another proprietary API in order to lock out competitors. Microsoft has a history of adding Windows-only software and, considering the company remains one of the largest proponents of DRM, this has a lot of people very worried. The other factor is that while Windows 8 is still so unpopular, the whole thing might just be ignored anyway.

DIY Printers

If you have ever built your own computer, then I would encourage you to save some extra money and buy a 3D printer kit. For the confident, there are now hundreds of 3D printer kits available, although in many ways they are often essentially the same kit with the same parts, but being sold by different sellers. According to Wohlers' Associates, the number of units sold in 2011 in the United States alone was more than 23,000. In percentage terms this equates to a 35,000 percent increase since 2007, when just sixty-six units were sold in this bracket. This is perhaps one of the most rapid markets ever to be developed.

Make sure that your seller has already purchased all the

necessary parts, otherwise it could be weeks or even months before your kit will arrive. Try to ensure that the kit is complete and that it includes all the key components including printed or laser cut parts, extruder parts, and guide rods. Furthermore, buyers must decide whether they are going to build from a kit or completely from scratch.

If you are the DIY type, then building from scratch is a great way to cut down on costs and, of course, the very best way to properly understand something is to build it yourself. There is certainly a great deal to be said for the kind of intimate knowledge that derives from knowing every nut, bolt, and quirk. Even so, the main headache for scratch builders is the amount of time that it takes to source everything. There are hundreds of nuts, bolts, wires, belts pulleys, and more to find, purchase order, and inventory before the build can even begin. This is fine if you are based somewhere in the Guangzhou-Shenzhen-Hong Kong megalopolis of the Pearl River Delta, and there is good reason why pioneers like Zach Smith and Jon Buford have relocated here. Zach literally orders custom circuit boards in the same way that you and I order pizza. Being located right at the very epicentre of the Pieris Population Circle also means being smack in the centre of what we now term the workshop of the world, and has some very distinct advantages. Even when all the hardware has been sourced, a controller board will still need to be selected and purchased or, depending on your skill level, designed and built. As for me, I am going to stick to ordering pizza.

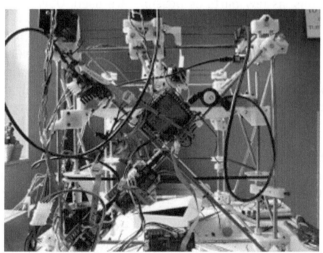

Figure 12. 3D printer or deuterium centrifuge?
Only the builder knows for sure

Fortunately, many of the current entry-level 3D printers are built around designs and technology that is derived from the RepRap project. This is great news for scratch builders as the community that has developed around the RepRap is very similar to the early home-brew computer club, but far more widespread and well-established. In addition to the valuable on-line source of technical support, the RepRap project is fully open source, so that all of the design files, hardware bills of materials, and software are free for anyone to download, modify, and use however they wish. Of course, assembling a 3D printer is not putting a satellite into orbit, and there is a wealth of on-line of help available. There are example videos on YouTube, as well as countless support groups and community forums. If you have a local hackerspace, then try taking your box of components down there, and see everybody's face light up when you ask for their help in assembling your latest acquisition.

Nearly all the entry-level printers available at the moment are fused filament machines, which means that they employ additive deposition techniques usually based on either PLA or ABS. I personally am a big fan of the Mendel design, especially the Mendel Max as it is so robust, reliable, and easy to set up and tune. Of course, these are not the only 3D printers that can be built from scratch, but with the Mendel variants or one of the Prusa designs, there will always be somebody willing to help in the various forums or IRC chat.

The open air style frame is popular on cheaper kits where, for cost reasons, as few parts as possible are used. Obviously, this can effect machine rigidity and print accuracy.

A large majority of current commercial printers employ a box type frame, sometimes of laser cut acrylic or even CNC machined wood. The advantage of this is that the boxes provide a solid rigid frame, but the downside is that the internals are relatively difficult to access, causing problems if the machine needs fine tuning or repairs of some kind.

The RepRap Mendel Style is based on a wedge shape design that is constructed from printed parts and threaded rods. While this design allows for easy access, inexperienced users may have some initial troubles matching up all the threaded rods perfectly. The RepRap Mendel Max Style, on the other hand, has a frame constructed from 20 mm aluminium extrusions, held together by printed connector plates. Building a well-tested, open source Prusa Mendel will cost about $300 to $400, self sourced.

RepRap Mendel

The RepRap Mendel is a second generation 3D printer from the RepRap project utilizing a wedge design. It is small enough to fit onto a desk, but with a print volume large enough to experiment on quite large items. Much of the machine is printable and the rest can be sourced from local suppliers and on-line.

Prusa Mendel V2

The Prusa Mendel V2 is a very popular derivation of the RepRap 3D printer due to its simplicity and small number of parts. It improves on previous designs in many ways such as using printed bushings instead of regular bearings, though options to substitute inexpensive LM8UU linear bearings or other types of bearings or bushings are available.

Mendel Max

Designed by Maxbots in December 2011, the Mendel Max incorporates printed brackets and inexpensive aluminium extrusions instead of threaded rods for the structural elements. For an extra $80 more than the standard Prusa Mendel, this gives a huge increase in rigidity. It is also much easier to assemble than a standard Prusa. Even an inexperienced builder should have no trouble building the whole frame in an evening, two at most. Others have described it one of the most hackable 3D printers, with just about any part being removable with just a few screws.

Morgan RepRap

Named after the biologist Thomas Hunt Morgan, famous for studying the genetics of the fruit fly, drosophila melanogaster, this interpretation has a CNC base, printed frame, and jointed extruder design, as well as a moving print bed that distinguishes it from its metal, rectangular ancestors. I have written much more about this derivation in the second section.

Kit Builds

If you happen to live in South America rather than Shenzhen, or Guilford rather than Guangzhou, then a kit built 3D printer will still enable you to save money without having to go through all the hassle of sourcing parts, and then modifying them to fit together. Purchasing a pre-assembled DIY kit removes a lot of the custom modification work, but you still must be able to assemble things using screwdrivers, wrenches, and other hand tools. There are many manufacturers selling kits with "easy-to-assemble" instructions included, but you definitely need to be mechanically inclined and able to understand basic geometry. Some come with already finished electronics while others will need a soldering iron to populate the PCBs. Just as with a scratch build, there will still be the need to spend hours adjusting, calibrating, and configuring things before the machine is printing at an acceptable quality level. This usually involves seemingly endless tweaking of the axis position and threaded rod positions.

Self-Assembly Kits

Josef Průša, designer of the Prusa i3, has written a very useful book called *Getting Started with RepRap* in addition to running workshops and offering 3D printing consulting. In fact, many fab labs and hackerspaces now run "Build Your Own 3D Printer" workshops and are great places to learn how to wield dangerous industrial tools like hex keys and tweezers.

Prusa Mendel Kit from Maker Farm is a $550 kit that features Greg's Accessible Extruder and V2 Linear Bearings which have almost no resistance and slide like butter, unlike the printed bushings or bronze bushings found in other kits. This makes for better prints and easier assembly. The kit includes almost everything from printed parts to hardware to electronics—but not the threaded and smooth rods or a PC power supply. Additionally, you'll need to purchase a sheet of glass for the heated bed.

The Prusa 8" i3 kit from Maker Farm is a laser cut 8x8x7.25 inch i3 kit, priced at $560, that is said to be very easy to build. It includes everything except for an ATX power unit and a pane of glass for the build platform. The Prusa i3 from Prague-based Josef Průša boasts a build volume 20 percent larger than the Replicator 2. While Prusa i3 is not strictly a RepRap machine—as it requires parts that need additional processing i.e. the laser-cut frame—it does still utilize 3D printed parts. Take this into account when buying your parts as a warped or incorrectly calibrated print made by an amateur may not work.

Figure 13. The Prusa i3

Printrbot LC and PrintrBot Plus

PrintrBot was based on a very successful Kickstarter campaign. They offer four different models covering a range of build volumes and budgets. Each kit comes with everything required to start printing, including easy to understand build instructions and documentation. The Printrbot LC (Laser Cut) features a 6x6x6 inch build envelope, but is a little more expensive at $649. The Printrbot LC PrintrBot PLUS features a slightly larger build envelope of 8x8x8 inch. The Printrbot Jr. and PrintrBot Simple feature 4.5x5.5x4 inch envelopes, and are only able to print in PLA, although this is compensated by the low price of $399.

TeraWatt Industries offers a Mendel Max version 1.5 kit, with a build volume of 8x7.5x4 inch, but without a glass plate or an ATX power supply, for $1,225. The Mendel Max is a popular favorite among Reprap hobbyists due to its relatively speedy printing and rigid frame which equates to better quality prints. Makers Tool Works goes one step further, offering a full Mendel Max 2.0 kit, the next generation of open source printers with an impressive 9x10x7 inch build envelope for just $1,495. The kit is fully inclusive, but is, at the time of writing, in its beta stages and the documentation is still being put together.

MakiBox

Deep in the heart of the Hong Kong New Territories, Atlanta-born Jon Buford makes the MakiBox a6, a 3D printer that is as easy to assemble as a piece of Ikea furniture, and sells for around $300 plus $50 for international shipping. It is a largely original design with certain parts based on other open-source projects, with assembly time taking around four hours, and there is very little calibration required to get started. The basic kit includes all MakiBox parts with electronics and power supply and so no soldering irons are required and 1 kg of plastic (2 x ½ kg spools of ABS). No software is included, but there are plenty of open-source solutions such as ReplicatorG (http://replicat.org/). The MakiBox uses trapezoidal drive shafts that provide 8 mm/revolution travel. Print speed should be around 60-80 mm/second with 1.8 deg. steppers. The consumable material is typically 1 mm ABS plastic which MakiBot will sell for $20USD/kg in ½ kg spools, but there is also a new extruder design that allows plastic pellet feed. Filament typically costs between $25 and $40 a kilogram while pellets sell wholesale for less than $5 a kilogram.

At last we have commercial 3D printers reaching the price point where I can successfully hide them from the girlfriend.

Figure 14. The Makibox

Deltas

Deltas, also known as Rostocks, were first developed by Johann C. Rocholl and there are now many different variants put together by other users and developers. Even Johann has a new design (Kossel Wiki here: http://reprap.org/wiki/Kossel) based on the open-beam aluminium construction.

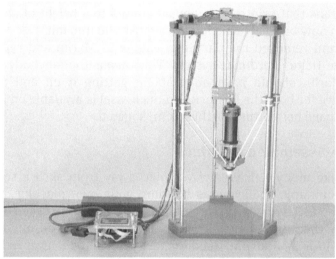

Figure 15. The Deltamaker

Deltas have a number of advantages including speed, stability, and agility. Industrial pick and place robots use this architecture because relatively small motions of the three actuators translate to large motions in the effector. There is also the benefit of modularity; each actuator is the same, which eases manufacture. The universal joints can be a little tricky to print, but can be achieved with a 0.5 mm or 0.4 mm nozzle. In robotics, Deltas are used for speed—since the travel is the result of combined efforts of all three motors. It is also very stable, since the part count is much lower and the motors are stored within the base.

Deltas are fascinating to watch, but can be a real pain to calibrate. In regular Cartesian printers, axis travel accuracy depends on the quality of the rails and bearings, and so good rails equate to perfectly linear travel. With Deltas, the situation is much more complex. Linkage and joint tolerances, the motor non-linearities, and even rate of acceleration can all have a real impact. While some of these obscure engineering problems can be a real headache, at least most of us tend to know plenty about our own joint tolerances well in advance.

Perhaps the main advantage is that all the axes are equal, instead of having two axes on belt drive and one on a threaded rod. The main downside is that twice the machine height is required for the print area, This is due to the fact that the push-rods are required to be moved vertically to position the nozzle in X and Y directions. This also means that printers previously limited to a height of about 145 mm can now build objects that are almost 400 mm tall.

Johann removed the Cartesian engine in Marlin and replaced it with the Delta coordinate system. This means that anybody familiar with Marlin should have no problem getting it up and running. Firmware for both the Rostock and the Kossel is available on Johann's Github page here https://github.com/koggdal.

Pre-Assembled Machines

If, like me, you have always shied away from such a seemingly insurmountable challenge as building your own machine, I would recommend buying a pre-assembled machine. I returned home at 6:00 pm the day that my Makerbot clone was delivered, and I was up and printing by 8:00 pm. Needless to say, I did not stagger to bed that evening until well after 2:00 am, and at least a half a dozen prints later.

Ensure that you have all the necessary wires and attachments when you purchase your machine, and ask them to throw in a couple of rolls of filament to get you up and running. Any business that is unwilling to make such a minor concession is unlikely to be of any great assistance should the machine suffer technical difficulties at a later stage. We made sure to do a couple of test prints at the sales office, just to make sure everything was functioning well, and so that we could go through the process a couple of times with an expert on hand to show us exactly what to do.

Now that the market is primed to hit the mainstream, there are new printers coming out all the time, and so the bad news is that whatever you buy is might be out of date in twelve months time. For that reason alone, I would recommend that you start off as I did, with a basic model such as a Reprap or a Makerbot. The good news is that, as of yet, the consumer 3D industry is too small for the Googles and Apples of this world to take notice. And this is exactly why it is so exciting. This is a brand new industry with no breakout stars and no foregone conclusions. Ultimately, success and the financial rewards that come with it are there for the taking.

I do not want to take up too much space here with endless printer reviews. This task has already been well executed by the editors of *Make:* magazine in their excellent book, 'Make: Ultimate Guide to 3D Printing'.

The Buccaneer

Figure 16. The Buccaneer

Kickstarter has been flooded this year with 3D printers. The Buccaneer raised $100,000 in just ten minutes, and eventually $1,438,765 in thirty days, more than 1,400 percent of their initial goal. It was initiated by three Singaporean university graduates who decided to base their project in the US mainly because Kickstarter does not support projects in Asia. Among the features promised include support for both ABS and PLA, an all metal hot end, a heated bed, and the ability to print from a mobile using cloud printing. Pirate3D, as they are calling themselves, have slated delivery for February 2014, with a few hundred pre-production units to be released to backers in December 2013 for public testing.

Cubify Cube

If Apple made a 3D printer it would look and function like Cubify's Cube. It was voted by *Make:* magazine as the "easiest to use" and the "most reliable" 3D printer, although other reviewers have reported that the software is clunky, and that there is no software to help you design 3D models. The body of Cube has a surprisingly small physical footprint and comes in five different colors to suit your tastes. The printer prints in both ABS and PLA, but can only print with one material at a time and only in one color. The filament also has to come from the company that makes the printer, so it is not just a case of popping to the shops and buying a budget replacement cartridge.

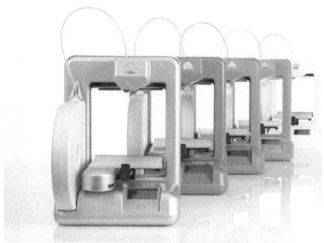

Figure 17. The Cube 3D

The CubeX has a larger 275 x265 x 240 mm build platform, big enough to print basketball-size objects and includes dual extruders, allowing for multicolor prints or ABS/PLA combinations to create easily-removable supports. It incorporates a touchscreen, allowing quick and easy set up, especially as it has the ability to print from a USB stick. Even so, the supplied software is disappointing in that it lacks control over essential settings, such as the number of shells (the thickness of the outer layers). 3D Systems has promised an update, and some users reportedly had more success with third-party software, but for this price, we expect everything to run smoothly the first time. The proprietary cartridge approach is another off-putting factor. While dual extruders are touted as a major advancement, each extruder is heated independently making the print process slow and frustrating.

The Replicator 2

The Replicator 2 is the latest 3D printer from Makerbot. This fourth generation machine has a powder-coated steel chassis, and boasts a resolution of just 100 microns, allowing users to print sheets of plastic as thin as standard copy paper, with a maximum 155 x 285 x 153 mm build volume. The thick, clear acrylic build platform works best when covered with a layer of kapton tape. Be aware, though, that there are numerous variations of RepRaps that have accomplished a similarly large print volume at 100 microns. Another useful innovation is the three bed levelling screws that make it quicker and easier to calibrate the Z-axis height. There is even an automatic script built into the control panel to help with this process. On-board controls are provided via a simple four-line alphanumeric LCD screen, with straightforward menus and a conversational tone. The included Makerware software is easy to use with plenty of options, and prints can be sent directly to Makerbot via USB or by slotting in an SD card.

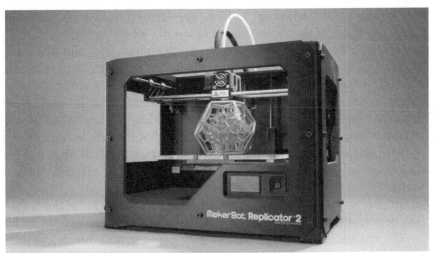

Figure 18. The Makerbot replicator 2

Even so, this "higher performance" comes at a very definite cost. It means that they are much more finicky and require extensive calibration and tweaking. They tend to get slightly jostled in transit, and having moving parts off by even a fraction can severely impact the final result. In reality, there are plenty of printers that offer the exact same and even experience, but cost $1,000 less. Much of this difference is probably going towards high-rental costs of assembling the machines in Brooklyn, as well as making a return on the enormous cash injections that they have received.

Makerbot can now afford a very strong marketing team that has managed to brand the company as the industry leader. Much of the media coverage describes the Replicator 2 as being a solid machine that requires little or no maintenance. User experiences are so far telling quite a different story, a fact that is sadly true of all 3D printers on the market at the moment. Some even accuse it of being falsely advertised, even of being put on a pedestal where the hype has become the selling point, rather than the printer itself. It is not a revolutionary printer in the same way a DLP or Rostock is, and it has not innovated significantly, even though the design aesthetic is a big improvement. On this version, users can even change the Alienware-esque platform illumination hue.

Many users have reported more time spent calibrating and repairing than actually printing, along with a lot of torture testing to learn the machine's ins and outs. Some of the many issues that have been documented so far include a tendency for the bolts to unscrew themselves when running Sailfish accelerated firmware. Another issue is that Makerware tends to fail when starting certain background processes, referred to as the conveyor, and the only known fix (and this is straight from Makerbot Support) is to reinstall. This can happen quite often, so be sure not to delete your install file. Other users have reported repeated extruder jams and even problems loading and unloading filament. This can cause the nozzle to jam. When this happened to me, I found that the whole head needs to be dismantled and cleaned out using an electric drill. It is quite a daunting task the first time round, but is actually simpler than it looks.

http://www.instructables.com/id/Clogged-MakerBotMakerbot-Nozzle/

On earlier models, the Delrin plunger, a small, black cylinder whose purpose is to apply pressure against the molten plastic thread and force it through the extruder nozzle, tends to wear out due to a grinding process. The Makerbot store did have replacement Delrins for sale at only $6, but they often go out of stock.

Although the Replicator 2 is marketed at beginners, it can often take quite a bit of knowledge and experience to figure out what is wrong and how to best fix it. One very useful tip is to put together an over-the-top spool holder that will prevent tangling and allow quick changes between filaments. Last but not least, due to its popularity, there is still a six week waiting list for overseas deliveries.

Makerbot Machinations

Makerbot was founded in 2009 by Adam Mayer, Zach Smith, and Bre Pettis, but four short years later, only Pettis remains. The company was an early champion of the open-source model, but reversed this attitude by applying for three patents last year with patent applications 20120046779, 20120059503, and 20120059504.

Stratasys has already patented the concept of an enclosed build envelope in a temperature-controlled chamber, but people are getting around it, and it was probably over-reaching, because the final paragraph attempts to apply it to all kinds of AM, including non-FDM processes that already existed. Remember also that these were the folks that repossessed Cody Wilson's machine simply because they did not agree with what he was doing with it. This has already alienated a large number of potential customers who will now be boycotting Makerbot for this reason alone.

Just two years ago, Makerbot received $10 million in funding from Foundry Group, Bezos Expeditions, True Ventures, RRE, and a handful of angel investors. Keen to maximize the return on their investment, they recently negotiated a buyout by Stratasys at $403 million, well above its Wall Street Journal estimated valuation of $300 million. To say that the company achieved phenomenal growth would be an understatement. They went from start up to 25 percent market share in just a few short years. Opinion is mixed as to why Stratasys paid such an enormous sum for Makerbot. Some claim that is was to do with patents, but if this were true then they would have to buy 99 percent of the personal 3D printer companies out there, along with 3D Systems, which they certainly cannot afford. Others have postulated that the decision was based on the fact that they currently have no personal 3D printer of their own, while 3D Systems has the Cube and CubeX, both of which are FFF personal class printers, one of which is now sold in Staples stores. This is a very attractive niche where Makerbot will generate $50 million in revenue this year. Others claim that consolidation at such an early stage in the industry life cycle usually means the market is not big enough or growing fast enough to support all of the existing firms. The reality is that the average personal 3D printer needs to become as easy to use as a Stratasys Mojo, which currently costs $10,000. But what incentive does the company have to make a $2,000 printer work as well as their $10,000 printer?

Ultimaker 2

Ultimaker 2 is a Dutch-built, open-source, self-funded 3D printer which was rated "Most Accurate," "Fastest," and "Best Open Hardware" in *Make:* magazine's latest of fifteen 3D printers. Using its own Cura software (for Mac, PC, and Linux) enables it to pre-process 3D files sixty times faster than typical slicing engines, a process that can otherwise take upwards of an hour. There is also an interesting draft mode to print a quick prototype at lower quality if necessary.

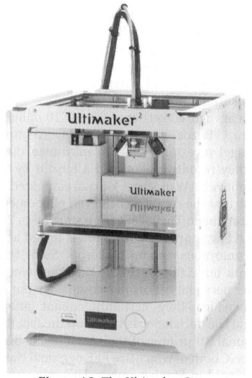

Figure 19. The Ultimaker 2

The Ultimaker 2 has the same external dimensions as its predecessor, but a larger print envelope of 22.5 x 22.5 x 20.5 cm inside. Improvements have also been made to the extruder, which is now made almost entirely of metal, and is therefore much less likely to melt than before. The machine is Wi-Fi enabled and surprisingly quiet compared to others in its class. It is definitely a good choice for enthusiasts in Europe who want to get started in 3D printing.

LulzBot TAZ 3D Printer

For an even larger print envelope (298 mm long x 275 mm wide x 250 mm high), the LulzBot TAZ 1.0 is a no-frills RepRap-style 3D printer for just under $5,000. LulzBot's fourth generation printer uses the company's sixth generation hot-end that can print layer heights from 75 to 300 microns at a speed of up to 200 mm/second.

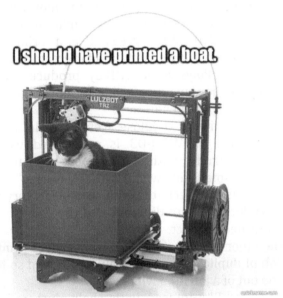

Figure 20. The LulzBot TAZ 3D

The Libre Hardware and open-source software allows customization to the finest detail. Slic3r and Pronterface (the printer interface) can tweak everything from deposition layer height to model solidity, and even has options for the pattern of the inside support structure. Users report that the machine can easily handle very large models as long as an ABS slurry is used on the platform to keep the prints well rooted in place. LulzBot is now offering an array of interesting materials. Apart from ABS and PLA, it also supplies polycarbonate, HIPS (High-Impact Polystyrene plastic), nylon, and even a wood fiber filament.

Printing Materials

ABS (Acrylonitrile Butadiene Styrene) and PLA (Polylactic Acid) are the main 3D printer plastics. ABS is tough, but prone to shrinkage, while the slightly weaker PLA is the eco-friendly choice. When printing for outdoor use, be sure to include multiple overlapping perimeters and ensure a good bonding between traces to keep dirt and moisture out. PLA does not like enclosed areas that get particularly hot, such as cars left in the sun, and if left in them, will likely suffer print deformation.

For clear prints, 1.75 mm PET (PolyEthylene Terephthalate) filament can be printed on plain aluminium without warping or breaking loose using print settings similar to PLA, with a nozzle temperature of 210–220 degrees. Use a print speed of 20–40 mm/second and set 100 percent infill for greatest clarity.

High Impact Polystyrene (HIPS) produces relatively smooth objects and has the same dissolvable support qualities of PVA. It can be dissolved with Limonene.

As an alternative to cellulose acetate, lignin and other forms of wood composite, LAYWOO-D3 is a recycled wood and binding polymer that extrudes with settings very similar to PLA. It looks, feels, and even smells like wood, with a "layering" effect that gives it an authentic carved effect. It is even possible to vary the temperature of the extruder to obtain different and the "burning" in of patterns onto the finished product.

On the other hand, there is no way a plastics printer can really do a good job of duplicating a nice maple grain and so Matthias Wandel will not be out of a job for a while yet.

Laybrick, is PLA-infused with chalk dust to emulate a stone texture and feels like a very fine-grained sandstone, but without the coolness of authentic stone.

Recycled Materials

The Filamaker is a prototype recycler created by Marek Senicky, who demoed the machine at the Rome Maker Faire, and is an interesting competitor to the filabot. It works by grinding down and melting old print jobs and then extruding fresh strings of cooled filament at a rate of about three feet per minute. Senicky hopes to improve the speed before releasing a for-sale version at about $680. Hopefully, these machines will mature and become capable of recycling more varieties of plastic. Being able to toss in an actual food container, for example, could completely change how people recycle and 3D print.

There are basically two main types of plastic: thermoplastic and thermoset. Thermoplastics can be re-molded and therefore re-purposed while thermosets are more problematic. Even the recycling of thermosplastics is not strictly true. It can be re-purposed, or mixed with new plastic, but it is not like a metal which will retain its properties after recycling, and so 100 percent recycled plastic is a bit of a misnomer.

Perhaps the closest we can come at the moment is HDPE milk jugs, which are shredded into flakes and then augured out into extruded filament. Details of the process can be found at fabbersuw.blogspot.com.

Even so, HDPE does have a few drawbacks. The first of these is poor adhesion. HDPE does not like to stick to a lot of things, but when it does (for example, to heated steel), it becomes very difficult to remove. Secondly, HDPE's thermal expansion coefficient is almost like twice that of ABS (2 percent for milk bottle HDPE compared to 1.1 percent for ABS and around 0.6 percent for PLA. This level of shrinkage becomes more of a problem on larger items, but not on smaller parts. The third problem is viscosity. Milk jug HDPE is manufactured for blow molding and has a melt flow index of around 0.55 to 0.7. The melt flow index of HDPE used in injection molding (which is similar to a 3D printer extrusion) is more like 6 or 7. The higher number means that it flows much easier, and so milk jug HDPE needs a high torque motor push to overcome the back pressure. Fortunately, none of these problems are insurmountable.

In the very near future we can look forward to seeing a great many more materials for 3D printers. Some brave entrepreneurs are even talking about re-purposing old supertankers to sit out in the ocean garbage gyre, powered by solar and wind power, to suck up and filter out the small bits of polymer and turn it back into base plastic pellets.

In addition, the localised aspect of 3D printing will have an effect on manufactured materials. Previously, manufacturers had to meet just a few government requirements for sustainability. In the future, it will be necessary to satisfy millions of earth-conscious consumers who will demand that their products do not simply end up in the landfill. More things will be made new out of materials that can upcycle, recycle, or simply disappear when they are worn out, broken, or obsolete. Once we get on to 3D printing metals and other more robust materials, we may even manage to fill in some of the gaps on the periodic table.

2

Getting Started

Remember that if you are buying a 3D printer to make money, you will want to retain a competitive advantage over every other Tom, Dick, and Harry for at least a few months. I would therefore suggest that you refrain from telling everybody and their dog that you have a Makerbot or an Ultimaker at home, earning you hundreds of dollars a week. For the time being, resist the urge to broadcast the news to all and sundry, at least until you have made your first million anyway.

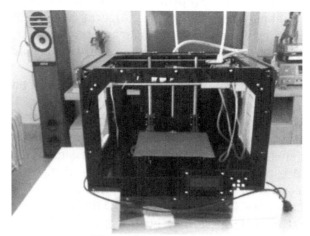

Figure 21. The General

My own Makerbot was quickly named "The General," after the much maligned General Ludd, the standard bearer of artisans and craftsmen everywhere. If those Duke boys can name their Dodge Charger after a confederate general, I see no reason why I cannot take inspiration from a hero of the working classes. The General Lee had her doors welded shut and we always felt that we were climbing in out of our Makerbot in order to get to the build plate. Still, our machine does not have Confederate naval jack and we have not had the steppers singing the "Dixie" melody yet. I somehow doubt that it jumps over patrol cars quite as easily either.

Despite all the propaganda, the original General Ludd represented a hatred for injustice and wanted to restore balance to an uncaring kingdom by setting ordinary working people free from the oppressor's yoke. Branded as an anti-technologist, Ludd was actually a rallying point for traditional craftsmen, such as wainwrights and blacksmiths, who were being reduced to menial labor and "wage-slavery."

Our General spent his first couple of months hidden away in a spare bedroom, well away from prying eyes. Occasionally, he came out with me to assist in giving a presentation on this revolutionary new technology, but most of the time he sat all by his lonesome, chugging away, helping to pay for my next travel adventure.

I paid the Yuan equivalent of just under $800 for my fully-assembled Makerbot clone and he was worth every last Renminbi. Actually, I only really paid half of this, as I was able to convince a good friend to go halves with me, so that he too could experience this exciting new technology for himself. I would recommend this as a good way to go for anybody else that is considering purchasing a 3D printer. See if you can persuade a couple of interested friends to work together and offset the initial investment. You can always start printing off more printer parts, to make sure that everybody in the group has their own machine.

For the time being, I still think that a 3D printer is a great investment. If nothing else, they can still be sold second-hand without anything like the kind of depreciation suffered by a new car. An average new car loses around $5,000 in its first year alone. I am confident that many 3D printers will sell for only a little less than their purchase prices in twelve months time. Demand remains high for these machines, and because of all the VC money that is being invested, if anything, prices are going up for some models, rather than down.

When you buy your first machine, if possible do at least one test run at the shop. In our case we used the snake design on Thingiverse by Zombee, as it is quite simple but will highlight problems such as curling or lack of base adhesion straight away. We spent about an hour with the vendor, having him show us how to do everything from the very beginning, from turning the machine on, to setting it up to print. Once the machine was under way, we went out for some lunch and a smoke, and came back to a finished print. By that time we were happy to box the thing up and have it delivered to our address just down the road. If a test really is impossible then do not worry too much, as there is plenty of help out there on the forums, and plenty of videos showing how to get the thing up and running.

Once we had The General powered up and ready to run, I quickly began to realize that this was much more of a contraption than a machine, and that I was going to have to play the role of eminent gizmologist in order to simply resist the temptation to defenestrate the entire device, including the lower thrunge plate. In somewhat less technical terms, I soon discovered that I was tinkering rather than operating, and that such breakthrough technology could quite easily drive the owner to toss it out the window in complete frustration. Actually, I really enjoy that feeling of being a digital explorer, pulling together a range of disparate technologies into one groundbreaking convergence point, and I am sure that you will too. Operating a 3D printer is much more like experimenting with some exotic laboratory equipment than simply using a PC, and you might soon find yourself slipping into a slightly steampunk vernacular.

I have no doubt that you will have similar teething troubles on your first few printing attempts, but, in all honesty, this is part of the learning curve, and is an essential part of the experience. The truth is that spending that first night familiarising myself with The General's intricacies, I realized that I had not had so much fun with a computer since a similar evening some twenty years prior, when a friend and I tried to connect our early model laptops together, so that we could play multi-player Doom. Anybody new to 3D printing will likely recall their first experience with Windows in 1988, or low-cost digital cellphones in 1996, or Google search in 1999. This feels like the same kind of transformative technology. While most of us have read extensively about 3D printers, it usually takes that first personal experience to have a creative epiphany. Suddenly, there is a realization that it is now possible to make almost anything that you can imagine and that you can do so in just a fraction of the time that it would have taken before.

Some of the obstacles that I had to overcome at the beginning included the following: ensuring that .STL files were copied into the correct program file location, so that the software would generate proper G-Code; tampering with the machine settings, so that the bed heated up to a mere 70 degrees rather than going up all the way to 120, and then having to cool down again; correctly fitting the plastic spool at the rear so that the feed did not entangle itself and stop the entire process at a suitably critical juncture. New reels of spool are sometimes slightly wider at the very end than the main thread. Nobody warned me about this and, as a result, I spent about half an hour wondering why The General was refusing to print before I finally realized what was happening. I simply cut about half a centimetre off the end. The extruder then gripped it firmly and we were away.

Some people claim that the process is slow, but once you get to know your printer well, it is relatively easy to print at speeds up to 300 mm/s and still obtain a decent level of quality. On earlier models like mine, it is still frustrating when the print head trundles around for ages before doing any printing and then both the extruder and the bed have to reheat independently again before it starts. It would have been nice if both could have been kept up to temperature, but these are minor software niggles and will probably be fixed by the time you buy your own printer.

Figure 22. Keeping The General happy

Your own stumbling points may differ slightly from my own and they will seem extremely frustrating at the time, but I can assure you that they will seem trivial just a few moments later. In hindsight, I found that pulling lots of strange Emmett Brown-type facial expressions certainly seemed to help, and if I were to do it all again, I would probably wear a white lab coat, just to make sure that I felt more like a groundbreaking inventor rather than a fiddling factotum.

Once I had ironed out most of the basic kinks and The General was settling into his stride, I found myself almost hypnotized by the musical sounds of his X- and Y-axes while he was printing truly organic shapes. This is not immediately noticeable when printing largely geometric items such as the above-mentioned snake. The machine sounds very much like a machine as it lays down filament in straight, angular lines, but once it begins printing anatomical and biological patterns, it develops a silvery, almost euphonious tone. The printing process is strangely hypnotic, and I could sit for hours watching it compile matter before my very eyes. Each print is sliced slightly differently and every time the parameters are tweaked, it slices differently again.

I know that I am not the only user who experiences this

mesmerising musical phenomena, as I recently read about some Lulzbot owners who hacked together a Python script that parsed a MIDI file to output a G-code equivalent that caused the stepper motor to produce frequencies and modulations that were actually musical. A quick search on the hackaday site will reveal a small library of classical music that can now be played on a Cupcake, Thingomatic, and Ultimaker. How long it is before somebody assembles a complete orchestra of laser cutters, routers, and CNC machines, though, remains to be seen. While I appreciate their creativity, I found that The General had some specific preferences when it came background music. Whether he ran more reliably with a certain selection of musical accompaniment, I cannot be sure, but it certainly seemed that way at the time. I have included The General's personal playlist in the appendices, in the hope that it will inspire you to have some musical fun and find a top ten for your own 3D printer.

While it is clearly wise to read up in advance, the niggles, nuisances, and assorted pettifoggery that you will experience are likely to be quite different from my own. And yet, I would still advise you to prepare yourself for as many of these minor setbacks as possible, simply to avoid a first evening of petty discomposure, disgruntlement, and vexation. If you are proceeding correctly, you should even find yourself slipping into eccentric inventor's jargon, as I occasionally do.

Although I had planned to make that first evening highly productive by immediately printing out a full set of parts for a better, more advanced Deltabot, I actually found myself experimenting with all the different machine settings and printing out a fair few unrecognizable items that were headed straight for the waste bin. This is the point where you learn firsthand about the difficulty of printing items that require extensive support material, and that sometimes it is simply easier to turn the thing upside down rather than struggle with extensive overhangs. You will discover that positioning on the heat bed can often be critical, and that printing in an aligned fashion to the X- and Y-axes can be much faster than making the extruder dance in difficult diagonal fandangos. The machine will likely be set at a fill rate of 10 percent, but this can quickly be lowered to a small fraction of that to save on filament. In fact, the strength of both PLA and ABS means that for most items, this can often be dropped right down to zero. It is worthwhile to spend some time exploring the properties of extruded plastic. Spend some time learning firsthand about the necessity of raft, the thin foundation of extruded material that helps objects stick to the build plate during a print, keeping it level and secure. It is also interesting to discover how a surprising number of things can snap together, or bend along a perforated or thin seam.

When I first took delivery of The General, my average print size was about three cubic centimetres that took about fifteen minutes to print. A spool of filament cost about $30 and weighed a couple of kilos. The average weight of one of my prints was a couple of grams, meaning that the cost per print was mere pennies. The filament is actually much thicker than the extruded plastic so a single centimeter of filament equals eight or ten centimeters of extruded plastic. It literally took dozens of prints before I could tell that there was any filament missing from the spool. Prior to this, everything had to be sculpted by hand, used to create a rubber mold, and then cast in resin. The 3D printing process immediately puts you at the stage of producing the item, saving hours of work, and dropping the cost by a factor of almost ten.

One of my fellow printers described the experience this way:

> *It was life changing for me, and I immediately bought one. I still, after about a year, feel it was a really important purchase. I use it all the time. I used it yesterday and I will use it tonight. Those who say they find 3D printers a novelty have not learned to wield the technology.*

It has been suggested that much of 3D printing's popularity can be attributed to the fact that we currently have a massive glut of geeks who desperately want to make things, but who never had access to a workshop in school or at home. Things were quite different for the previous generation when apprenticeships and domestic blue-collar production meant that a much larger proportion of society had engineering and practical woodworking skills. Now that a large part of the West is focussed on a service economy, the emphasis is now on financial tools and computer skills, rather than any practical "making stuff with your hands" kind of work. In many cases, a far greater number of fathers that worked in offices rather than factories just a generation before meant that many youngsters simply had no one to teach them anything about manufacturing. In my own situation, my father was a very skilled craftsman who started out as a fully apprenticed boat builder and eventually ended up as a work study engineer and consulting troubleshooter. Like many of his peers, his work responsibilities shifted quickly from making products to writing reports. During his working life, so much factory production was off-shored to Asia that he and other experienced engineers had no choice but to retool and retrain. When I was younger, he had a garage full of all kinds of weird and wonderful tools with which he could have a go at making just about anything. These days he has a handful of household power tools, but certainly no machine tools.

Therefore, perhaps this fascination with the new possibilities of distributed manufacturing is simply meeting a need from those of us who never had the opportunity to study in a machine shop and make things with our own hands.

Just to prove that I am not some slack jawed 3D-printing groupie, below I am reproducing the comments of a fellow 3D printer that works at Google, no less.

What is it like to use a 3D printer?

It's life changing because of all the small things. I need a paddle for my new paddle board . . . I could spend $50–$150 or I could print the handle, laser cut the paddle, and buy a wood rod at Home Depot for $5. I now have a good looking paddle for ~$5 rather than spending $50-150 that is as good as my other paddles. Now that I have the cad files I can also make them for friends for about $5.

Another example: I recently bought a bunch of shirts only to realize that they were air dry only. Where to hang all these shirts while they dry? Sure, I could hang them in the shower (awkward), or get a clothesline. I could also make a custom retractable clothes rod that sits over my dryer. It costs nothing and is exactly what I needed. Nothing like it exists, but it does exactly what I needed.

My wife and I have trouble hauling several large paddle boards . . . No problem, I can just print out the parts to make a rolling carrier. I figured out how to build it by the end of breakfast, and next time I go out, I won't have to carry our boards, I can use the carrier.

I could list dozens of other cases where I was able to build something custom to fulfill a weird need like the ones above.

It's awkwardly slow since you usually expect a printer to be fast. At first, it's really cool to watch it work, but the outcome is amazing. I'm hoping that eventually technology is developed to use different materials (besides plastic) to print with.

Here is a small selection of what I have printed so far:

1. A settlers of Catan 3D board game
2. Handle for a SUP paddle
3. Custom retractable rack for hanging clothes
4. A rig for carrying three paddle boards
5. A prototype self-watering pot for plants
6. Parts for my printer
7. A tobacco pipe for my brother
8. Toys for my daughter
9. A crazy contraption for sucking smoke up and blowing it down a tube and out of a window
10. A retractable motorized snowboard attachment
11. GoPro mounts
12. Parts for a custom CNC I designed
13. A super cool catapult
14. Surfboard leash mounts
15. A surfboard fin
16. Desk toys
17. Cups
18. Parts for various machines I have designed

I usually set up something to print before I go to bed and when I wake up it's finished, so printing seems virtually instantaneous.

In the future, I'm planning to use it more often as an attractive alternative to injection molding until I hit higher quantity sales in my part-time business. This is also useful because I'm planning on changing my design over time and don't want to have to deal with the large upfront costs of creating new plastic molds every time I change my mind, which is quite often. If you have the skills or the resources, it can save a lot of time and money to print rather than buy.

3

Getting the Best Out of Your Machine

Much has changed since 1988, when 3D printing pioneer Scott Crump was burning plastic pans in his kitchen, as he used a glue gun to squeeze out a mixture of polyethylene and candle wax in his experiments to make a toy frog for his young daughter. Even so, operating a 3D printer is still a constant learning experience. Most users learn something new every time they print a new model. Doing this by yourself can be frustrating at first, and even a little intimidating, but fortunately, there are many wikis and user guides out there, meaning that no user has to suffer in silence. My favorite of these is the Makerbot wiki put together by the Noise Bridge Hackerspace in San Francisco.

https://www.noisebridge.net/wiki/MakerbotMakerbot

This page is full of useful tips and tweaks that will make any printer run faster and smoother. I found it quite ironic that the biggest help in getting my own Makerbot up and running was a hackerspace located thousands of miles away, on the other side of the Pacific. Such is the world that we live in today.

Here are a few tips of my own that you might find useful for whatever kind of 3D printer you are operating.

With the arrival of spring, I was worried about The General overheating and so I stuck it right next to an open window to make sure it had a breeze running across it. In the upper floors of Chinese high rises, there is always a good draft to cool things down. I soon realized that this was a mistake and was causing more problems than benefits. These days he runs quietly in a closed room and I have even added paper sides to the open enclosures so as to keep drafts down to an absolute minimum.

Ironically, my supplier takes a completely opposite approach and constantly has a fan blowing through his machine as it prints. I can only assume that this is because my printer is up on the twenty-third floor of an apartment block overlooking the Pearl River, while his is much closer to the ground in a more heavily industrialised area.

Pay close attention to your immediate surroundings and also the climate. In my case, the atmosphere is very humid and heavily polluted (this is after all the Workshop of the World). One tip that I learned from a rostock developer was to always clean my filament before it is fed into the extruder. To do this, simply cable tie a small sponge to the filament after it comes off the reel. Figures 23 and 24 show the filth that was collected from about 750g (~400M) of loose 1.75mm filament. It is amazing how much gunk and fluff is attracted to an open spool that is sitting around for a few weeks. I am guessing that it must have something to do with electrostatic charge, but I certainly do not want all that dirt clogging up my extruder and hot-end. Fortunately, I have not had any more blockages since and so many thanks to Richard Horne aka Richrap for this very useful tip.

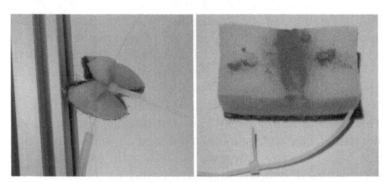

Figures 23. obsessed by cleanliness

And before you ask, yes you can print your own individual cable ties rather than having to buy a huge bag of one hundred. Take a look at http://www.thingiverse.com/thing:58776/variations for a least a dozen different remixes.

I used to print of a lot of excessive raft material, but now I have

graduated through tape, hairspray, and onto blu tack. For a detailed explanation of how to use hairspray as an anti-curling solution, take a long look at this page.
http://www.protoparadigm.com/blog/2013/03/testing-aqua-net-hair-spray-for-3d-printer-bed-adhesion/

I personally did not have any success using hairspray on top of Kapton tape, but found blu tack to do the job perfectly. By sticking down the outer edges (the box of a Makerbot makes access a bit difficult, but I found that it would flatten out quite nicely with a chopstick) bed adhesion was much improved. At the same time, I learned that blu tack can be cleanly and easily removed by using a deft dabbing motion, almost like a hen pecking seeds. Wipe down your print bed when cool with acetone (only when cool) to remove any fingerprints since any curling at an edge will ruin the print. Level your platform with extreme precision.

There are a number of accessories/tools that will make your 3D printing experience better and easier. At first, I thought that all I would need was a big old hammer and plenty of beer, but things are unfortunately never that simple. Here are a few suggestions to get you started that I personally found useful.

Beginners

You will need tweezers or, even better, a pair of long needle-nose pliers for clearing the hanging threads of filament from the nozzle. (There are at least a half dozen tweezer design available for download on Thingiverse,)

Also you'll need a pair of long scissors in case you need to cut away any filament that goes astray while you are printing.

Advanced Users

Calipers can be useful if you need to measure the accuracy of your parts or if you need to measure your filament in several places to get an average.

A good craft knife is useful in cleaning away rafting and support material from your prints. Some people also recommend jeweller's files and a pin vice to dress finished parts.

A ceramic screwdriver can be useful if you need to calibrate the machine and want to avoid shorting out the stepper drivers.

A cheap rotary tool (such as a Dremel (www.dremel.com) with a few dozen attachments will make part finishing and support removal much easier, as long as you are not too aggressive and keep the speed low.

As a humorous aside, an artistic friend of mine who was helping me out in the early stages, offered to zip down to the model store and pick up a Dremel, while I stayed at home and babysat The General. I gave him some money and got back to printing, only for him to return three hours later with an inflatable dinghy. I asked him what had happened to the Dremel and he said that he had to take a taxi back to the apartment, and therefore did not have enough money to buy the Dremel. When I asked him about the dinghy, he explained that it was an ex-display item, and that he had picked it up for the knock down price of $30 There is a small creek that runs nearby the apartment, but considering the entire estate is built on the site of the old sulphuric acid factory, I could not see him wanting to paddle up and down there. He explained that he was planning to use it to paddle around Repulse Bay in Hong Kong, a good four hours away by hi-speed train, and that it would be good upper body exercise. Needless to say, he has only been to Hong Kong once in the past seven years. Talk about sending Jack out to the market and coming back with a bag full of magic beans. Bless him, he is a real whizz when it comes to art and design, but I honestly think that he spent far too much time on planet weed as a youngster. I wonder if Andrea del Verrocchio had the same problems with Leonardo.

Even more embarrassing was the time when we arranged to meet up in a local expat hangout, as I was passing through town on my way to Hong Kong. He was looking after The General at his apartment and I kept sending him new STL files to play with while I was away traveling. As soon as got to the bar, he asked me in a very loud voice, "So Chris, have you got any new STDs for me? Every single customer in the bar turned around and looked at me as if I was wearing a blonde wig, a shell suit, and a Jim'll Fix It Badge.

One useful item that any printer can produce immediately is a desk tidy type tool holder. There is a selection on Thingiverse, but I especially like the YATH (Yet Another Tool Holder) Tool Holder for Replicator 2. It has room for digital callipers, the hex wrench set, a pair of scissors (for trimming filament), a 0.1 mm feeler gauge and/or a points file, super lube, and a toothbrush (for cleaning the extruder head). There is even a blank version, including STEP files so that users can add their own custom slots for their own tools. http://www.thingiverse.com/thing:38949

Finishing

When printing with ABS, acetone vapor will smooth 3D printed parts. The method can cause the object to lose some definition, but the result is a smooth and shiny finish which fixes the problem of a poor surface finish that is sometimes associated with 3D printing. This technique is still in the experimental stages at the time of writing, but be warned that acetone vapor is highly flammable and should be used in the same room as a printer or in a kitchen. In addition, acetone is heavier than air, so the fumes tend to sink and slowly fill up a space, which means that good ventilation is a must. Acetone is a skin irritant and the fumes are toxic, so containers must be tightly sealed.

Finishing can also be done using a brush, so save any thin misprints and piles of extruded threads to make acetone "glue". Extruded threads dissolve much more easily than solid filament.

Start with a ratio of two parts acetone to one part filament. Simply pour in the acetone first to about half way, and then put in filament until another quarter of the container is full. That way there is still a quarter left to experiment with to establish the correct consistency. Use some cheap brushes for this as melted acetone will accumulate between the strands. Use gloves or a clamp to hold the piece while working. Be aware that acetone may eat away at a plastic or rubber-coated clamp. As always, ensure that your work area is in a well-ventilated area away from heat sources, and cover all work surfaces, floors, and clothes, as acetone tends to splatter at the end of every brush stroke. Temporarily transferring acetone into a small working container reduces the potential splash zone. This will also minimize evaporation and reduce contamination as the brush picks up plastic. Be aware acetone may melt straight through any very thin or loosely filled areas. Keep all brush strokes in the same direction, preferably in the direction of the layers; brushing against the grain is likely to leave grey streaks. This works most effectively for thin coats of glue or small holes/gaps that need filling. It is not so useful in filling large areas or physically joining filaments, as the glue shrinks and/or leaves voids when the acetone evaporates. Filaments joined this way may be weak.

When cleaning up, never put acetone down the drain. Clean your brushes with gloved fingers, squeezing out excess plastic from between the hairs and then swishing in acetone.

Until you get a recycler, rather than throwing any excess material away, it can be mixed with acetone to produce a very useful welding glue. Although it is possible to buy clear or black ABS cement in the plumbing department of most hardware stores, it is sometimes useful to know that the grade of ABS you are using as glue matches the items that being printed. At the same time, having control over the color and consistency can be a real benefit. In addition, a light coat can be applied to the heated build platform to obtain an excellent stick that is still easy to peel off, eliminating the need for rafts. An ABS in Acetone mix can also help other materials stick such as polycarbonate being printed on an Ultimaker without a heated bed.

Acetone tends to degrade the surface layer of Kapton tape at a microscopic level, making it susceptible to tearing. This can be overcome by using a 90 percent acetone 10 percent mix and applying to a moderate heat bed at around sixty degrees, allowing the acetone to evaporate prior penetration. Other users have reported that a thinned PVA wood glue works well for PLA on a non-heated bed.

Acetone effects PLA in a different manner. It makes it hard and crumbly and it will develop a white surface. Instead, PLA will dissolve in chloroform or a sodium hydroxide solution.

For a very good write up on this technique, again I recommend the protoparadigm blog:

http://www.protoparadigm.com/blog/2011/12/abs-glue-weld-cast-texture-and-more/

3D printers are notoriously difficult to configure. So before printing off a complete MkII War Machine suit, it is a good idea to spend a little time tweaking and playing with settings to ensure the machine is printing at its very best. Like a DSLR camera or a computer, it takes a great deal of patience to learn how to operate them properly. But once you learn, the sky is the limit. Some new users become very frustrated at this point and are even tempted to give up and send the infernal contraption back for a refund. Spend some time on proper calibration and you'll be so glad that you did. Thingiverse has a whole stack of calibration tests ranging from simple overhang angle assessments to breaking point torture tests that could have been submitted by Torquemada himself. There are objects designed to test accuracy, resolution, bridging, alignment, and warping among other things. I especially like Brainycheddar's collection, but there are plenty of others to choose from too.

http://www.thingiverse.com/brainycheddar/collections/torture/page:1

It is refreshing to see that most of these tests have been

submitted by users. I have heard stories of how some companies have created their own tests so that their machines performance can be viewed as optimal. So far I have only heard about this from a CNC router manufacturer who quotes their accuracy as the resolution of the motion system when the sum of the mechanical errors is thousands of times larger. Fortunately, 3D printer maintenance is much less of an issue than calibration. Most users who I have spoken to agree that the only requirements are the occasional lubrication of the linear bearings or the rare tensioning of a belt. If your machine does not have them, it is also worth investing in a set of rubber feet, to stop it from dancing around on a hard-topped surface.

Most new users quickly develop a love/hate relationship with their printer. Fortunately, the most useful resource when experiencing these problems is the worldwide community of "makers" on websites such as Thingiverse. This on-line network of "makers" is one of the most valuable assets for the current home printing enthusiast. The sheer amount of support topics in on-line forums can attest to the fact that none of us are alone in our frustrations with home printing. Despite all of the obstacles, I am still excited about the prospect of printing my own designs and I'm confident future generations of home printers will continue to fine tune this experience.

I have learned that just like a boat or a car, each 3D printer has its own set of idiosyncrasies. I've learned from working with my own machine, for example, that it runs better at a temperature about 20 degrees Celsius cooler than the default setting. I also know that the nozzle does not like printing at the rear right hand of the bed, and so I usually set it up to print on the front left-hand quadrant.

Try experimenting with fill levels, whereby you can select how solid you want your object to be. At 100 percent, the object comes out a solid mass of plastic. At a lower percentage, the printer builds a honeycomb of ridges inside the object for support, plus a solid outside. We usually opt for 5 or 10 percent and set it to the lowest print resolution to save some time.

One of the first things that we printed was a couple of gunk guards for the sink. The whole process took about three hours including misprints. If we had attempted it a second time, it would have taken half that. There is definitely a steep learning curve that would have been much steeper if I had not had a close friend to share the frustration with. I have no doubt I could have figured it out on my own with the resources available on the Internet, but lessons like running the printer at a lower temperature would have had to come with time.

While many users talk about letting their printers run overnight, this is not something that I would recommend at this stage. If we look at Makerbot's marketing, they never explicitly state that users can just walk away from the machine while it is printing, even though they often use printed examples that have taken twenty or more hours to produce. I am not saying that the Makerbot design is not safe to leave to print on its own or calling it a fire hazard. After all, because of the recent investment in the company, they now have far too many lawyers for me to go out on a limb like that. Even so, I have read that all the safety precautions are firmware based on a discount microcontroller, that is also running the bot. If this fails, there do not seem to be any heat fuses. Other users claim that limit switches have been skimped on. Needless to say, I have an extinguisher next to my machine just in case.

Recent reports state that tiny particles can escape from 3D printers into the air and inhaled by humans, but this news is overblown when ultrafine particles are emitted by laser printers, radiators, cigarettes, and many other household items. Of course. it is not a good idea to sit hunched over a 3D printer in a stuffy room all day, but researchers found that printing with PLA is equivalent to cooking with an electric frying pan. Some people claim that nylon printing is extremely dangerous, but nylon is just another thermoplastic without any special processing requirements. If you have fumes printing nylon then you are probably using the wrong temperature settings. Laser printers which use polystyrene-based toner powder are potentially much worse. I think that there is much more chance of injury from burning your fingers on the extruder, tripping on the power cord, or dropping the printer on your big toe. The only way for a 3D printer to emit really dangerous particles is if you use it to print off a plastic firearm.

4

What to Print

There are so many articles appearing in the press where the writers suggest that 3D printers are only good for making iPhone cases or some useless doodad that will simply gather dust on a shelf. Fortunately, their sad lack of imagination presents a huge opportunity for the rest of us. If you spend any amount of time on eBay, you will know that one person's useless doodad is another quirky collector's hidden treasure.

Of course, any machine is simply a pile of useless components, unless the operator has a clear vision of its practical use and original product ideas. When Charles Babbage developed some of the very first computing devices, he faced stiff opposition from many sides. One of his most vigorous detractors was George Biddell Airy, Astronomer Royal, an influential science advisor to the British government. In 1842, Airy advised the Treasury that the engines were "useless" and that Babbage's project should be abandoned. The government axed the project shortly after. Biddel was a dull and unimaginative bureaucrat, unable to recognize the broader mathematical potential of the engines, despite his mathematical brilliance in an academic university setting. Thanks to Airy, we had to wait another century before computing finally came into its stride. This kind of academic luddism has often been repeated in the realm of technology, and it should come as no surprise that we are hearing its familiar refrain yet again.

The good news is that many successful commercial products already have their origins in the Maker/DIY/Instructables community. And I am not just talking about the Homebrew Computer Club turning personal computers into a mainstream technology. For many years TI Raleigh, the world's largest bicycle manufacturer, ignored the suggestions of its brightest engineers, that mountain bikes were going to be the next big thing, and it took garage-based enthusiasts to ensure that the shape of the bicycle would be changed forever. Such is the oh-so-conservative mentality of large corporations. Another excellent example of the maker community's success was the skateboard, whose history is dotted with random people creating boards for fun in their garages. The sport started as side-walk surfing, for the days when surfers could not ride the ocean waves, and it grew very quickly between 1963 and 1965, with $10 million worth of board sales during that period. Later, with the rise of Powell Peralta's Bones Brigade, skaters such as Tony Hawk, Rodney Mullen, and Steve Caballero went onto to become international stars and even household names.

Rather than give any more credence to the derogators and deprecators, I would instead like to present you with a selection of artists and designers who are paying scant, if any, attention to the cynics and critics, who are forging ahead with their own 3D printing projects and businesses. I will then detail my own discoveries and successes in the field, in the hope that I can inspire you to embark on your own experiments. But to begin with, I should like to showcase the following pioneers, each of whom is finding new ways to monetize their machines and profit from the 3D printer revolution.

Athey Moravetz

Over on Etsy, eBay's handmade equivalent, Athey Moravetz, under the business name of Warpzone, uses her 3D design skills to create a huge range of custom cookie cutters. She prints solely to order, with her two home-based Makerbot Replicators and a Macbook Air. Her range is huge and Warpzone designs include a five piece *Dr. Who* set of her own design, as well as sets for *Game of Thrones*, *Sailor Moon*, and *My Little Pony*. With over eleven-thousand sales on Etsy alone, and with nearly seven-thousand admirers, Athey is certainly putting her 3D printer to the best possible use.

Figure 25. Cookie cutters for all tastes

Once a professional 3D artist in the video game industry, she now stays home with her kids and makes cookie cutters for a side-income. This little venture started because she wanted to make cookies of her and her kids' favorite game characters. Then some friends wanted them. Then more people wanted them. Now she has somehow turned what started as a hobby into a full-time job. http://www.etsy.com/people/WarpZone

Arian Croft

Arian Croft, co-founder and lead designer for Ill Gotten Games in Bellingham, Washington, goes under the moniker of "Dutchmogul" on Thingiverse, where he already has over one hundred impressive uploads to his name. I first stumbled across Arian on eBay, where he was very successfully selling some of his earlier designs such as hover cars and teleporter stations to the Warhammer and RPG crowd. Like myself, Arian was heavily influenced by game designers such as Gary Gygax and Steve Jackson.

Figure 26. Two of Arian's favorite miniature designs

More recently he has created the first open source board game specifically for people with 3D printers. It's called "Pocket Tactics" and can be thought of as a sort of mini version of Risk. It is a fast-paced, modular strategy board game that all fits in a tiny bag! For the full rules sheet, visit either of the starter sets here: www.thingiverse.com/thing:41740 or here: www.thingiverse.com /thing:45269.

Arian spent seven years developing and testing the game that would become Pocket Tactics, before discovering 3D printing. Nearly overnight, the concept became reality in the form of 3D printed parts for the game, including even the dice.

One excellent (and common) alternate use for Pocket-Tactics figures is as miniatures for RPG encounters in games such as Dungeon and Dragons. Recognizing this, Arian has started designing modular map tiles fitted to their scale. He has also designed some very cool "Modular Futuristic Tiles" which are excellent for space-faring games such as Traveller. Arian did much of his design work on Tinkercad and was surprised to see how easily sculpting skills are transferred to 3D modeling.

At the moment his models are printed via Shapeways, but he is seriously looking at purchasing a Makerbot very shortly. His major concern is that of overhangs and assumes that some of his designs will have to be modified, perhaps printing in components to be assembled. This just goes to show that technical limitations are no match for a well-developed imagination.

https://www.thingiverse.com/dutchmogul/designs

Jim Rodda

Another successful pioneer who does all his printing on a Makerbot is Jim Rodda, based in Wisconsin. http://zheng3.com/

He has owned a 3D printer for about a year now, and soon found that his background in broadcast animation and video games (by day he is the creative director for an indie game studio that does coin-op) translated very nicely into 3D printing. He does most of his design work in Maya, occasionally using Meshlab, but is always interested in investigating new tools and anything that speeds up his workflow.

Figure 27. Magic miniatures

Jim has a large assortment of designs on Thingiverse, but focuses largely on tokens for the fantasy card game, Magic: The Gathering. Everything he posts is distributed under a Creative Commons Share-Alike license, so other designers are free to share them, remix them, and even use them for commercial purposes, as long as the original designer is credited. He sells his tokens on Etsy, but has so far shied away from eBay, leaving an interesting opportunity for some enterprising soul.

Robert Bos

Rob's Model Workshop (www.robs-mw.com) provides innovative and unique accessories at the H0/1:87 scale that simply cannot be found anywhere else. Robert models in Sketchup, and production is then outsourced to Shapeways, allowing collectors to paint and assemble the models themselves. He has chosen "White Strong & Flexible" an SLS (selective laser sintered) material for his construction parts, which has the same feel as a molded plastic part, although it does require multiple paint layers due to its high level of absorbency. He chose FUD (Frosted Ultra Detail) for the more detailed/movable kits such as his impressive working scissor lift with forty-four individual parts. This complex model is printed out on a sprue and Robert's site has a fully illustrated, twenty-eight-page PDF for download that details every aspect of assembly. He is currently looking at in-sourcing some of his simpler models with a Makerbot.

Figure 28. A fully assembled scissor lift

I was especially impressed by his Jersey barrier/road divider which is a great example of what can be done with a 3D printer. Here he has created an item that many modelers would appreciate, and one that they would probably order in multiple quantities. The same goes for his scaled down 9t/2.98 meter Accropode. An Accropode is a concrete armor unit for breakwaters and shore protection works. Although I have seen these items many times, this is the first time that I learned that a specific technical term could be applied to the structure.

Figure 29. An Accropode in a logistics diorama

Robert warns that it is not possible to just scale up and down at whim. Most pieces actually require a great deal of modification before they appear properly balanced. Another point that he raises is that of wall thicknesses on scale models. This is very easy to overlook and many of us have found this out the hard way when our first scaled down print came out only as support material. For moving models, clearance between the parts is another important aspect.

Robert has displayed his materials expertise by recently releasing a range of decontamination tents that are also 3D printed. In contrast to the bulky form of the Accropodes, the tent walls are extremely thin and display very clearly the flexibility of the 3D printing technique.

Figure 30. Decontamination tents

As a confirmed miniatures fan, I find Robert's highway creations particularly inspirational. His Jersey Barrier (or K-rail as some people know it) alone has helped me to think about a range of other possibilities that would appeal to hobbyists and collectors. Expounding on the barrier idea, there are many versions of the traffic barrier alone that I could experiment with. Apart from crash barriers, there are concrete step barriers, constant slope barriers, F-shape barriers, and Fitch barriers, those plastic barrels filled with sand or water, used on highways as an impact attenuator. In addition, there are road blocks and automatic barriers (such as those used at railway crossings) not to mention guard rails, crowd control barricades, and all those barriers that are designed for pedestrians rather than traffic. Even the forgiving textures of simple breeze blocks (also known as cinder blocks) come out well on a basic 3D printer. There are so many interesting ideas to play with here.

Figure 31. Scale model cinder blocks

Kacie Hultgren

One of the leading lights in this field is Kacie Hultgren, a scenic designer in New York City who uses her MakerBot 3D printer to create scale models of theatre sets, among other things. Her Thingiverse name is PrettySmallThings.

Figure 32. A miniature stage set

As one of the first artists to be selling the carefully crafted output of her Makerbot, I fastidiously watch out for blog postings on the subject, as she frequently shares extremely useful information about the intricacies involved in operating a 3D printer.

One very useful tip given by Kacie that I would like to reproduce here is as follows: When designing, start at a 1/1 scale. The resulting .STL files will also be at an authentic 1/1 scale. This means that others will be able to modify, mash up, and remix your designs without having to worry about scaling procedures.

Figure 33. A highly detailed scale model
of a colonial lounger

Kacie has written a number of useful articles on printing models to scale in the Makerbot blog. I have found her graphic illustrations to be especially helpful. She also covers the key elements of thread width and towering. Thread width refers to single extrusion of plastic, and towering refers to free-standing vertical columns. Here, for example, are some very important words of wisdom for fellow Makerbot users, such as myself:

> *"...A printer's ability to reproduce without failing will vary based on make, model and the operator's technical prowess. With my Replicator, I can easily reproduce details between 1-2 mm with minimal deviation from the stock setup. Older or less precisely calibrated models may only be able to tower 4 mm details.*
>
> *I use 0.9 mm as my minimum when I design for my Replicator. I do very little calibration of any kind. I run*

sailfish firmware on my rep1 these days. I took the deprive values from the webpage, and that was the only change I made to the stock profile. Small details are a little bit of a moving target for each software and firmware update - when I do update - which I don't do often - if I need help getting back to the my 0.9 mm, I usually ask on the Google group and someone has a simple answer. My Windsor chairs are an example of using 0.9 mm as a minimum. I run most prints at 80/150 for speed, but sometimes will slow it down to 45/65 on fragile prints to give everything time to cool.

Rather than make her ¼ scale Queen Anne replicas and colonial furniture available on eBay, Kacie has decided to cut out the middleman and make her products available on her own very nicely crafted sales page.

http://www.prettysmallthings.com/

This page gives a very good idea of the level of quality that can be achieved by a well maintained Makerbot. I personally would have added significantly more value by offering these items painted with a high quality finish, but for our purposes, it makes the detail of the extrusion process very clear.

The Banned Throne of Swords

Fernando Sosa of nuPROTO (http://nuproto.com/iThrone.html) spent many long hours digitally modeling a highly detailed "Iron Throne" iPhone/Android dock that could be turned out on a 3D printer. When he released details of the project on the Instructables site, litigators at HBO quickly swooped in with a take-down notice for IP infringement.

Fernando is one of my favorite designers at the Instructables site, with a selection of highly imaginative projects from Death Star Christmas tree ornaments to a low budget vertical hydroponic farm design, suitable for even the most cramped of Hong Kong micro-apartments. Considering that two of my greatest passions are science fiction and permaculture, he could have hardly chosen more fitting subjects to grab my attention.

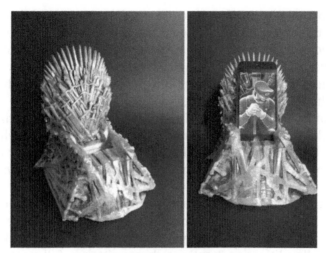

Figure 34. The Iron Throne

I have to admit that I am definitely not a *Game of Thrones* fan. Having grown up on a rich diet of high fantasy and classic swords and sorcery from the masters of the genre, such as Robert E. Howard, Fritz Lieber, and L. Sprague De Camp, the soft-porn ultra-violence of *Thrones* along with the pathetic perils of that pillock Potter, do precious little for me.

Anyway, HBO is claiming ownership of "the copyright in the Iron Throne design," even though a throne is an obvious derivative of chair, making it unprotected under IP law. In a justice system where "might is right," they will probably have their evil way. This is especially ironic, as the producer of the show publicly admitted that file sharing was responsible for the show's enormous success. At the time of writing, the product still appears on the web page, but it is not for sale, and any pre-orders have since been fully refunded.

Of course, this is not the first time that big corporations have pursued 3D printed items for copyright infringement. In my last book, I wrote extensively about the case of Thomas Valenty, who designed two Warhammer-style figurines—a war mecha and a tank—and posted them on Thingiverse. After finding Valenty's 3D model tanks on Thingiverse, Games Workshop, creator of Warhammer, immediately sent a take-down notice to Thingiverse, citing the Digital Millennium Copyright Act, and immediately lost a large number of loyal customers in the process.

It will be interesting to see what happens with the Thrones dock, especially if a copy of the .STL files somehow manages to leak out onto a torrent site, or if some overseas entrepreneurial type decides to print the object in another country, where they cannot effectively be ceased and desisted. In the meantime, it is a good example for the rest of us, and a clear warning that we should steer clear of those enormously popular, but incredibly shallow brands. My advice is to avoid the Hogwarts empire, for example, unless you want a Bloomsbury-Schillings SWAT team unleashing infringement Armageddon upon you in the middle of the night. J. K. Rowling is no longer a billionaire, and now that the last instalment of her Postman Potter epic is over, she is bound to be looking for new ways to fund her fourteenth and fifteenth country estates.

What is even more worrying is that there are lawyers out there that are basing their professional decisions on shows like *Game of Thrones*. Tom Wallerstein, a partner with Colt Wallerstein LLP, a Silicon Valley litigation boutique, has written a full page on legal lessons that he has learned from the "deep, epic themes" of the show. I am not exactly sure when endless tits and bums, and gratuitous violence became epic themes, but I would not be surprised if this is picked up by future historians as a major event in the decline and fall of Western civilization.

http://abovethelaw.com/2012/06/from-biglaw-to-boutique-game-of-thrones/#more-164951

With litigators like this on the loose, is it any wonder so many businesses are upping sticks completely and moving their entire operations out to the Far East?

Eileen Bowen, aka Silverbeam at www.Deviantart.com, has been printing with Shapeways for nearly three years, and is also the administrator of the site's 3D Printing group. With an eclectic range of dolls and geekery accessories from anime, video games, and fantasy and sci-fi fandoms, she has quickly developed a strong following. Her best sellers are ball-jointed ponies, which are very popular among the *My Little Pony* fandom community, a line that nobody else is replicating at the moment. She has taken the cute, loveable pony one step further than anybody else, by creating a poseable model that can be easily customized. This is yet another example of where fans and 3D tinkerers are way ahead of the big toy manufacturers. Other creations include the Kingdom Hearts and Zelda charm bracelets. Keeping items small and unique gives her an important edge in a market that is becoming more competitive all the time. Consistency and product quality is also a very important factor.

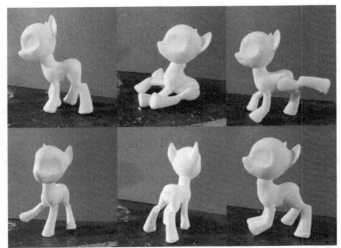

Figure 35. A poseable pony

"I hope soon that I can get my own machine. While getting better, the at home printers are not quite up to the standards that I need for my business. I love that I keep seeing different people doing Kickstarters and other Internet group funding sites, to come up with new machines and printing capabilities."

"My business is still pretty small and fluctuates every month. I earn anywhere from $50-300 minus printing costs etc. More during Christmas holidays."

Turning Inspiration into Profitability

Looking at the above examples, it should now be clear that there are a number of factors to consider when deciding what kinds of product to print. While the aerospace industry and the medical sector are driving tremendous amounts of growth and show enormous profit potential, they are not the suitable areas for those of us with entry-level ABS printers. Here are a few of the more salient points worth considering.

Avoid the temptation of thinking about replacing things that people can already buy, but try to find items that are simply not yet available on the market. These might be as simple as custom cases for projects, small stands and holsters for existing items, or completely new inventions that spring from the subconscious depths of your incredibly fertile imagination.

Popularity

It is important to think about the desirability of your new product in the general market place in order to ensure its financial viability. You might well be able to produce incredibly complex works of art, but are there people out there who want to buy such pieces? Ideally, an item should eventually be able to generate repeat sales in the order of hundreds, although if you are lucky enough to stumble across an item that will sell in the thousands, then it is probably more economical to look into small scale resin molding. When Dicecasters discovered that their Dice Domes were suddenly hot items, they realized that it would be faster to cast copies by using the 3D printed model to make a mold. They were soon casting a copy every ten to twelve minutes using a simple technique that is described in detail on their blog site.
http://dicecasters.tumblr.com/post/33769633770/from-3d-drawing-to-small-scale-production

Their related experiences are full of interesting little nuggets such as the fact that adding powdered bronze to the liquid resin gives the look and feel of a metal part, but is a technique that can still be achieved at room temperature.

When trying to establish whether an item is popular or not, I always start with a search of completed items on eBay. This quickly gives me an idea of how many people out there are willing to pay good money for my product. An extremely useful website that helps to automate this process is http://www.watchcount.com/. The site allows searches by most watchers and, more importantly, most bids. I change the default setting to the maximum number of results (one hundred) and the location where I am planning to sell, which in my case is usually the US. If I find that there are many similar auctions with multiple bids (the more the better) then I know that I am onto a potential winner. The only exception to this rule is if the searches that come up are identical to the item I am researching. This means that the market for that particular item is probably already saturated, and I am better off trying a more unusual alternative, or perhaps some kind of imaginative remix.

Even better than popularity is long term collectability. Some trends turn out to fads or flash in the pan successes while others go on to gain cult followings, or even become classics of the genre. The sooner you can spot these items and designs, the better. After a while, I see no reason why you should not even start predicting what is going to become popular and collectible in the future. In the meantime, start to familiarize yourself with the icons of particular genres and subjects. Some of these I have listed in the cookie cutter section below, but there are many, many more. Try at the same time to identify markets where the volumes are relatively low and the value and complexity of products are high.

Size

Bearing in mind that my Makerbot can take a long time to print larger items, and that they obviously require more filament, I endeavour to keep my items as small as possible. This is why I like the miniatures market so much. I can scale down an ordinary item and yet still be able to sell it to collectors at a good mark up. They receive an item that they would not otherwise be able to find and I make a good profit, a win-win situation for everybody.

There are some beautiful works of art on Thingiverse, but do I really want one print to take twelve or fifteen hours to complete? Surely it would be much better to print a dozen much smaller items that take, say, forty minutes apiece. In addition, my Makerbot is far from infallible and the frustration of having a twelve-hour print go awry at 95 percent completion is infinitely more frustrating that having a forty-minute print go pear-shaped half way through. We are in business, after all, and everybody knows that time is money.

Asher Nahmias, also known as Dizingof, is an Israeli designer who has uploaded a whole raft of complex geometric designs to Thingiverse that would have M. C. Escher in absolute raptures. Even though 3D printing is the only way to produce such works of art, they are notoriously difficult to execute, especially on a basic machine such as a Makerbot, being operated by a self-confessed beginner, which I still consider myself to be. Dizingof's work is an absolute inspiration, but for anybody who wants to make their printer pay for itself, I would seriously suggest sticking to cookie cutters and miniature collectibles.

Figure 36. A deluge of Dizingofs

Shortly after the release of my first book on 3D printing, among all the positive reviews on Amazon, one person left a very brief negative response complaining that I had included far too much information about miniatures. I remain staunchly unapologetic for this focus, and repeat the fact that miniatures are going to be a key market for anyone who wants to make money with a 3D printer. For anybody that still harbors doubts, then I would like to point them to a recent Kickstarter project entitled "Raging Heroes—The Toughest Girls of the Galaxy."

http://www.kickstarter.com/projects/loudnraging/raging-heroes-the-toughest-girls-of-the-galaxy?ref=live

Raging Heroes is a small French studio in Montpelier that is producing three armies of highly detailed space punk heroines. Despite the apparent niche market approach, the project reached its funding goal of $12,000 in just thirty seconds. Within the first hour, they had raised $100,000, and as I write this they have nearly three thousand backers who have pledged nearly $700,000. Even the feedback has been impressive with over nine thousand individual comments.

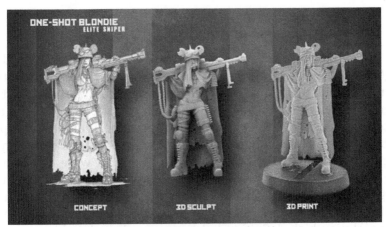

Figure 37. From concept to print

When I see projects like this, it baffles me that many countries are still investing in high tech industrial parks and free trade zones. For a fraction of the cost, a government could set up and promote its own national Kickstarter clone, but it seems that most administrations are still stuck in the 1960s when it comes to encouraging and assisting new businesses.

This particular Kickstarter, as well as having visually stunning figures, was very professionally organized. The organizers clearly had an in-depth understanding of the Kickstarter community and miniature collectors. Not only did they have a very appealing set of bonuses, but they even enabled a Paypal pledge option, opening up the project to customers outside the United States.

Many of the sample display figures have been 3D printed, but the company has chosen to go with cast metal and spin cast resin for production pieces, which is completely understandable seeing the level of demand. The figures themselves are customizable with multi-part ball-joint systems, and are wonderful examples of what can be achieved with 3D printing.

In the meantime, the miniatures company that I mentioned in my last book, Reaper Miniatures, has organized a second Kickstarter project. Rather than go through all of the details, I will let the figures speak for themselves. The amount requested for the new project was $30,000, and a total of 12,332 backers pledged an enormous $1,760,743. If these figures still do not convince you that miniatures can be a lucrative market for the creative 3D printer, then I am afraid that nothing will.

Simplicity versus Complexity

One of the main advantages of a 3D printer is that it can produce highly complex items that are inconceivable with other manufacturing techniques. Or at least that is the theory. In practice, there are a large number of variables that can affect the quality and success of a print. If using a sub-$1,000 machine, then do not expect to be creating museum quality works of art for the time being. Think back to the chunky eight-bit representations that were common on the early desktop computers with their, at the time, enormous ten-megabyte hard drives, and remember that we are still at this stage with 3D printers today. There will be a time when the equivalent of 4K resolution high-definition holograms can be printed in your very own home, but for the time being, that day is not here just yet. Know the limits of your machine and you will be far less disappointed with incomplete or unsuccessful prints. It is true that 3D printers can produce complex internal parts such as ball bearings and clockwork mechanisms, but we did not expect our early computers to run the kind of high-definition video that is commonplace today, and we should not expect these early generations of 3D printers to achieve those kinds of standards either.

Of course, that does not mean that you should not push your machine to do all that it can. In traditional injection molding, there are many shapes and designs that are extremely difficult or expensive to produce, and this is where the 3D printers are at a distinct advantage. Look at items with a number of undercuts, or receding spiral helices, as these are all but impossible for factory production. With a 3D printer, they suddenly become fairly easy. Think about multitudes of very sharp corners. Industrial polymers tend to get stuck in these corners, and result in excessive tearing and ripping, which is why factories prefer to produce smooth curves and designs. This is not a problem for a 3D printer, so look for items that incorporate these kinds of shapes and patterns and you will suddenly be huge leaps ahead of 99 percent of all the plastic factories in Taiwan and Guangdong.

One thing that the Dizingof creations do demonstrate is that even simple 3D printers are very good at handling organic complexity.

Figure 38. Plastic vase or alien seed pod?

Try and use this strength when you are thinking about new designs. Now that I have seen the runaway success of Raging Hero miniatures, I am seriously thinking about a complete line of 28 mm figures that I can design and print in the future. Knowing that organic is relatively easy, I am considering a set of alien carnivorous plant-life. Venus man traps and aggressive, oversized pitcher plants are very forgiving in terms of resolution, and are therefore well-suited to FDM printer capabilities. Try and takes similar design constraints into consideration when thinking about possible products.

Support

While a 3D printer has its advantages, it has plenty of weaknesses too. One of these is the problem of excessive overhangs. Because the item is built up in layers, support material is necessary for constructing overhanging edges of any kind. A prime example of this is a mushroom, where the cap far exceeds the stem, creating a number of difficulties for a 3D printer.
http://www.protoparadigm.com/blog/2012/01/printing-with-support-extreme-overhangs/

Fill

One of the most interesting aspects of a 3D printer is that it can print hollow items. In fact, users can specify exactly what percentage of infill can be built into the product. In real terms, this means that a ¼ scale model of a human head with 10% fill will cost just a few cents when printed in ABS or PLA. Even this cost could be reduced by lowering the fill percentage or tweaking the digital design. At the moment, most printers are limited to either ABS or PLA, but that situation will not likely last for long. A team of pioneers recently printed a small boat using #2 HDPE recycled milk jug plastic. They estimated that if they had printed their boat from commercial plastic filament it would have cost them $800. Instead, 250 clean, empty milk bottles cost them them back just $3.20. This means that the 1/4 scale human head model that I spoke about earlier would cost only micro cents, probably Hong Kong micro cents.

An entry-level machine needs to be tweaked close to perfection when printing large flat faces, as the fill process of laying down filament in a lattice pattern creates a semisolid mesh rather than a solid wall. This can be seen most clearly by holding a finished piece up the light, and I am sure you will be surprised at how obvious the lattice pattern becomes. Unless you are willing to do a fair amount of finishing work in the way of undercoating, then items of this nature are probably left to the commercial printers to undertake.

Just because the raw material costs are so low, do not be tempted to tweak and reprint a design ad infinitum. It takes time to learn when good is good enough, and then discipline to stop at that point.

Adding Price Points

If possible, try to find midpoints in the market that are not yet being addressed. An interesting example of this was where the only 3D products in the baby bonding industry were laser-etched 3D images in crystal glass. There is now a company offering 3D prints of babies that are still in the womb, using advanced ultrasound scanning. As new technology becomes available, so do new market segments.

Finding More Inspiration

Sometimes, all that is needed is a little inspiration, which is why I continuously check the web for innovative new products that have caught the public's attention, so that I can replicate them on my Makerbot.

Here are just four methods that I personally find useful. Give them a try and you might be surprised at what comes up.

1. I spend a lot of time on Quora.com looking for the answers to questions like "What are the best new products that people don't know about?" With more than eighty individual answers, this is just the kind of inspiration that I am seeking. I follow a number of

different categories including "product design," "innovation," and "new products" and suggest that you do likewise.

2. I personally enjoy the very popular image board sites where Internet memes and new ideas evolve and mutate. The granddaddy of all these is the 4chan community, a site that the *Guardian* once summarized as "lunatic, juvenile . . . brilliant, ridiculous and alarming." There are now numerous copycat sites including, but certainly not limited to, the Chive, Joy Reactor, and 9gag. My own favorite waste of time is wawawia.com. Admittedly, it is a long way from being a productive use of my time and, on occasion, it is downright infantile, but I am surprised how many new product ideas I pick up from this one site alone. If nothing else, I can feel the pulse of the net, what is popular, and what makes up the cultural zeitgeist of the moment. This way, I can discover out which TV shows are popular without having to sit through any of them. *Twilight* and *Game of Thrones*, for example, are great inspiration for products that sell well, but I would not want to have to actually watch any of the individual episodes.

3. A slightly more time effective method is to do a search on Google for images associated with "shut up and take my money" + new product. "Shut up and take my money!" is a catchphrase used to express enthusiastic approval toward a product or idea, usually associated with an image macro featuring the character Fry from the animated television series Futurama. There is now even a http://shutuptakemymoney.com/ website, retailing "The Coolest Gadgets and Novelty Items on the Internet" although by the time they have made it all the way to this site, they are probably not that original any more.

Figure 39. Shut up and take my money!

I am a huge fan of Kevin Kelly's Cool Tools site and newsletter.

One of the most prescient visionaries of the internet age, Kelly has a true gift for being way ahead of the curve. According to his site, a cool tool can be any book, gadget, software, video, map, hardware, material, or website that is tried and true. All reviews on his site are written by readers who have actually used the tool and others like it, and items can be either old or new, just as long as they are genuinely wonderful. I was a huge early fan of Wired's first incarnation, Mondo 2000 and, for me, Kelly's site is the natural progression, now that the magazine has become so boringly mainstream.

Slightly more organized than most of the other meme sites is the Odee collection. There are numerous categories relating to new products, but the cool gift ideas is probably as good as any place to start. http://www.oddee.com/cool-gift-ideas/

My Own Adventures in 3D Printing

Here are some projects on which I am currently working. Of course, I am always looking for those items I can charge $50–$75 a pop, but at the same time, I am also interested in trying a wide variety of products that I know are in demand. The ideal situation is to find a product where the perceived value is high, for a material cost that is low. A good example of this would be the eleven pages of custom cufflinks by GothamSmith on Shapeways.

Even if projects are not huge money makers, I am learning more and more about digital modeling and 3D printing all the time. One thing of which I am convinced is the fact that 3D printing is the hobbyist's dream too, allowing people to build almost anything simply and cheaply.

With so much fantastic inspiration all around, it was not long before I had to put my own predictions to the test. Eager to see if my claims were mainly mouth or mostly trousers, I quickly set about trying some imaginative designs for myself. Here are ten separate small scale projects that I am currently working upon. Each one is still a work in progress, but with my own Makerbot now relocated at the Provincial Library I will not be surprised or annoyed if you beat me to the punch on some of these projects.

1. Exotic furniture
2. Halfling abodes
3. Bird houses
4. Hamster agility equipment

5. Cookie cutters
6. Skulls and bones
7. 1/6 Civil War accessories
8. Shafted items
9. 28 mm gaming accessories
10. Luxury car parts

Exotic Furniture

Despite detractors, I am still convinced that miniature pieces are a great entry point for those wanting to learn more about 3D printing. Even though one reviewer of my last book complained that there was far too much coverage given to the production of miniatures, I remain unapologetic. In fact, if anything, I am more assured than ever that this is a superb niche market for 3D printing entrepreneurs to explore. Apart from the examples that I have written about above, I am even more pleased to see that Ikea has now jumped on the bandwagon, introducing their own range of doll house furniture designed especially for Swedish Barbie's Drëamhøuse.

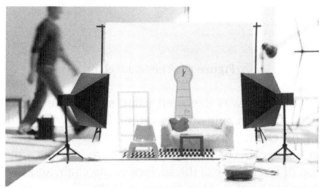

Figure 40. Ikea in miniature

Understanding that youngsters who grow up playing with Ikea furniture will probably become loyal lifelong customers, the company has decided to start producing doll house-sized versions of its iconic pieces, including the Lack table and the Expedit shelving. Debuting in the 2013 August catalog, the $15 set also included cut-out paper accessories like clocks and picture frames to further adorn a doll house. Fortunately, these 1/15 scale pieces come fully assembled so there will be no need to include a minuscule hex wrench and instruction manual. Whatever your opinion of Ikea, they certainly have a knack for identifying highly profitable markets, and if miniatures are good enough for the Swedes, then it should be a clear signal to the rest of us.

Of course, Ikea and I are not the only people experimenting in this particular arena. One example that especially fired my imagination was this one that I stumbled across on Shapeways.
http://www.shapeways.com/model/172358/gaudi-chair-scale-model-1-6.html

Figure 41. The Gaudi chair

The Gaudi Chair was designed using similar methods to that of the Spanish architect and artist Antoni Gaudi, who made models using hanging chains, that upside-down showed him the strongest shape for his churches. Special software scripts analyse the distribution of forces across the surface of the chair, and the direction of these forces has defined the direction of the ribs and the amount of force specified the height of a rib. Despite all this high-tech blurb, we are still talking about a 1/6 scale model that is just 10 cm high. Outsourcing to Shapeways is always a rather expensive proposition, especially if, like myself, you are not in a Western location, but even I was shocked to see that the price for this model starts at $53.91.
http://www.shapeways.com/model/172358/gaudi-chair-scale-model-1-6.html

The Gaudi chair is a nice design, but I can think of hundreds of pieces that are more impressive than this. Of course, the only way to prove this was too actually print a few physical examples.

I am still experimenting, but taking Kacie Hultgren projects as my lead, I decided to start with more obscure styles, as she has done with "bombe" style pieces. My first attempt in this field was a small but charming chinoiserie coffee table.

Obtaining the correct scale was a struggle at first, especially when it came to the size of the walls and making sure that the drawers were working correctly, but overall I am very pleased with the results so far. Of course, the piece has to be printed in five separate parts and then finished and painted, but the final appearance makes it all very much worthwhile. The piece looks even better with a selection of custom paint jobs, my favorite being based on a very nice Uma Thurman Pulp Fiction design that I have spotted.

Figure 42. Chinese coffee table concept

Pleased with the oriental style, I am also working on a miniature reproduction of a traditional wooden "kaidan-dansu" chest, a beautifully geometric piece of furniture, that was originally designed to provide valuable under-the-stairs storage space in Japanese homes.

Figure 43. Kaidan-dansu

While many people think of plastics as being cheesy, déclassé, and disposable, there was a time in the 1960s and 1970s when plastics were the cutting edge of interior design. I personally see acrylics as a material that has integrity, honesty, and lifetime that far outstrips anything organic. Plastics invite designers to do some of their most innovative work, and few other materials can make colors so bold, radiant, and exciting. At last, plastics are finally gaining some recognition for the important role that they have played in twentieth-century industrial design, and I am not the only one who is beginning to see their relevance. Joe Colombo's plastic tube chair recently fetched $10,000 at auction, and I am determined to print a miniature at some time in the future.

Figure 44. Austin Powers style recliners

Cesare Leonardi, Franco Stagi, and Verner Panton are all becoming sought after names for a new generation of furniture collectors, and I hope to reflect this trend in my future prints. Even in popular culture, there are opportunities here that are well worth considering. Coming back to the ever popular science fiction theme, I can see the low chairs and tables from the Star Wars Cantina scene being an easy, uncomplicated print.

A 1/6 scale set of two chairs and an LED-lit table where Greedo was killed, is available from Sideshow toys for $89.99 although over on Shapways, a user by the name of Kodiak3d has the rather innocuously titled Space Tavern Chair in his store at $9.00.

Figure 45. "You will never find a more wretched hive of scum and villainy."

Giger's Harkonnen Biomechanid chairs, on the other hand, I will probably leave to a more capable designer, despite being a huge fan of his work.

Figure 46. Harkonnen Biomechanid chairs

Chairs that use recycled plastic tubing are suitably futuristic and should print quite well even on a simple Makerbot. Going back in history for a moment, there are still plenty of great examples of inspiration. These can range from historical to outright fantasy pieces. Apart from the fabulous medieval gothic toilet, I am keen to make a few more items for other swords and sorcery fans. It is clear that I am not the first person to consider this, even GI Joe at one stage made a fabulous cobra throne, and I am looking forward to designing something similar that would have suited Conan the Barbarian or the evil priests of Stygia.

Figure 47. Chair designs to consider

I have a specific fascination for classic French and Italian furniture that epitomises the baroque and rococo styles, pieces that would have appealed to Bavaria's Ludwig II. I am especially drawn to pieces that are highlighted by imaginative paint jobs.

Figure 48. Straight from Moliere's Boudoir

Painting can change the appearance of a printed item immensely. Below is a very non-descript STL file for an antique luggage trunk, designed as a scale model piece for model railway enthusiasts. The painted pieces by comparison are almost unrecognizable.

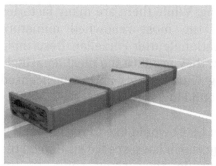

Figure 49. Before and after

In the longer term, I am starting to look at the possibility of doing a few miniature spiral staircases. These would be almost impossible to mold, but might do well on a 3D printer. I have not shown these to my designer yet, for fear of giving him a heart attack, but am really looking forward to seeing what he and The General have to say about their actual practicality.

Figure 50. Spiral staircase

If you are seriously looking at producing miniatures, then take a look at some of the industry leaders to see what kind of quality the competition is capable of producing. While there are many factories based in the Far East, one of the most renowned miniature manufacturers is the German operation Reutter Porzellan. Describing their products as heirloom quality, they produce the most amazingly detailed miniature displays, along with tea sets and even licensed products related to Beatrix Potter and Flower Faeries http://www.reutterporcelain.com/

One more source of inspiration that I would like to recommend is the NHK TV show *Begin Japanology* which has a special edition on the art of miniaturization. Not only do they show some of the contemporary artists and trends, but they also feature miniature styles from Japanese history such as the charming and highly collectible netsuke. The show is a valuable insight into the country's fascination with miniatures and how it has become a multi-million dollar industry.

Halfling Abodes

The location in which I spend much of the spring and summer is the ancestral home of bonsai, and so I was particularly enthused when I discovered these amazing bonsai combo hobbit houses on the net. I am wary of using the term "hobbit house" after the Tolkien heirs went on a litigation rampage and forced the closure of any and all pubs with hobbit-related names. I had already tried a couple of spiral staircase plant pots and was definitely on the lookout for something more complex.

Figure 51. Inspiring ideas

Inspired by the "Bag End landscape" created by Chris Guise of Maidenhead, England, I was keen to have a go at something so beautiful myself.

Figure 52. "Bag End landscape" by Chris Guise

With so many miniature trees available to me locally, and realizing that building the grass roof would be the easiest part, I set about seeing whether I could print the wood and brick constructed facade on my 3D printer. This is still a work in progress, but I am well on the way to producing designs that will be highly desirable in almost any location, among a legion of Tolkien fans that are almost worldwide at this point in time.

I quickly realized that I could let my imagination go when it came to the design, and rather than just a door, I decided to go for windows, chimneys, and protruding beams.

Figure 53. More inspiration

Pictured below is the prototype front door complete with frame, reinforcements, and door handles. It took a few experimental prints to ensure that the scale was correct, and I soon realized that by printing in ABS plastic, it was going to be tough to obtain a convincing wood finish.

Figure 54. Door and frame prototype

The surrounding bricks in their charming circular form were ideal for the printer though. With a quick coat of paint, it gave it an authentic feel I was much happier with.

Figure 55. Prototype wall

Originally, Chris hand-fashioned tiny brickettes, that were cut from a roofing tile, tumbled to knock the sharp edges off, and cemented around a round plastic former. After the window and door were finished the space in between was bricked up. The result was amazing, but too much work for me and so I decided to crank up my Makerbot and put it through its paces.

For the door and frame, I decided to turn to a CNC router, a machine that is not all that different from a 3D printer, and one that has opened up a completely new world of fabrication that I hardly knew existed. Converting from a .STL file format to a .dxf file that can be read by a CNC machine was much more of a challenge than I expected, but the micro-tasking sites came to the rescue once again, and I soon had a promising 2D file that I could begin playing with.

Back in Maidenhead, Chris had cut miniature planks, and then bevelled and sanded the edges before the door itself was cut to shape and sanded smooth. For the window, he used a disk of black reflective plastic. Being reflective, it looks like glass, and being black it gives the impression of a dark interior. I knew that with a bit of careful thinking, I could squeeze all of this time and effort into a small CNC file and save myself many hours of work. Chris used a metalworking lathe to mill a brass doorknob, but my Makerbot faithfully came to the rescue again with its seeming endless versatility.

The website Bonsai Empire gives a full and clear pictorial account of the original building process, and Chris has written an accompanying article that is crammed full of useful tips and tricks to make the process as easy as an art school project.
http://www.bonsaiempire.com/blog/bag-end

While it took the original artist over eighty hours to create this magnificent piece, I was convinced that with a 3D printer I could seriously cut down on all that effort. Of course, if it works out well, I am keen to try out similar miniature dioramas in different vernacular styles. For my local domestic market, I hope to recreate a few elements of the Humble Administrator's Garden (拙政园) in Suzhou, combining bonsai with pagodas, temples, and round moon door entrances.

Figure 56. A typically Chinese egress

And not only real places, but the oriental fantasy that is so epitomised in the artwork of William Li.

Figure 57. A Chinese fantasy landscape

Even so, I intend to stick with relatively simple designs and actively avoid some of the outrageously complex bonsai creations that have been in the news recently.

Figure 58. Bonsai beyond the imagination

For the overseas market, I am looking at the early work of fantasy artist Roger Dean. His organic architecture is quite similar to the hobbit house concept, although his ongoing law suit against Avatar director David Cameron is making me a little nervous about how much influence I should actually display. Fortunately, I have found an artist on the Deviantart website that is producing similarly-themed designs that are very reminiscent of the work that Dean did on the Greenslade and Yes album covers back in the seventies.

Figure 59. Roger Dean examples

Bird Houses

I talked briefly about the infinite possibilities for birdhouses in my first book on 3D printing, but since then there has been a very impressive Birdhouse Challenge on the Thingiverse site, with some really imaginative entries. I am especially happy to see some of the designer animal habitats that I wrote about in my last book being designed and uploaded. I am so pleased to see so many people printing off interesting and innovative items for their pets. From tiny prosthetics for disabled ducklings to a whole range of bird houses in a special collection on the Thingiverse website, for those who would rather print something that encourages life than semi-automatic rifles.

http://www.thingiverse.com/jetpad/collections/birdhouses

For more of the same, check out Bumblecat's full listing of challenge entries.

http://www.thingiverse.com/Bumblecat/collections/birdhouse-challenge/

Here are a few of my favorite entries, to give you a taste of what is yet to come.

Figure 60. Avian fortresses

The Birdhouse Castle Tower (which would also make a great rookery if printed at a slightly larger scale) adds a little bit of medieval splendor to any suburban garden. Complete with crenellated bird bath, look out perches, boiling oil channels, and a simple three piece snap assembly, it requires no support material or fasteners.
http://www.thingiverse.com/thing:117080

For those of us that grew up with He Man and She Ra, the Castle Grayskull Birdhouse is a real blast from the past. But the picture here really does not do the piece justice. I am looking forward to printing this one, just so that I can enjoy giving it a highly detailed and menacing paint job. It is perfect if you live near a cemetery and have some skeletal sparrows or undead jays in the neighborhood.
http://www.thingiverse.com/thing:116297

The American Craftsman Bungalow Birdhouse features two entrances, upper ventilation, carefully sloped drains and multiple interior platforms, making this really a classy avian casa. Tenants can hide out in the wind protected interior or promenade along with the veranda and three individual perches. For human caretakers, the design includes two sturdy center-aligned screw slots for mounting, and two support trusses for extra stability. The whole thing prints in one piece without the need for any support material, but you will need a build platform at least 220 mm long and 150 mm wide.
http://www.thingiverse.com/thing:117808

Some other favorites include the bird house disguised as a surveillance camera (http://www.thingiverse.com/thing:117539) and the classy designer Birdhaus, (high end accommodation for the discerning avian) http://www.thingiverse.com/thing:111522.

Figure 61. The Birdhaus and the Big Brother Birdhouse

And as if these designs were not inspirational enough, I have since been scouring the net looking for similarly imaginative designs that I can reproduce, once I have the original designer's permission, of course. Here are a few birdfeeder designs that I am really looking forward to recreating.

Figure 62. Three wonderful birdfeeder designs

Hamster Agility Equipment

For the time being, I decided to go in another direction and started work on a hamster agility set in kit form. I was inspired by Marna Kazmaier, who keeps a whole menagerie of assorted animals up in the high plains of South Dakota. Marna has been a professional sled dog harness maker since 1986, but has made all kinds of animal equipment for most of her life. She hosts many websites and Yahoo Groups relating to pet care, but it was this one that really got me excited.

http://www.hamsteragility.com/?id=175

Thanks to her inspiration, I have started out with a basic kit of five obstacles, each one being printed in flat parts, and then slotted together for actual use.

Mice are relatively easy to train because they naturally run along the same path every time, but being rather nervous creatures, they do not share well with other small animals, due to the strange scents. When scaling, remember that mice need smaller equipment than gerbils or hamsters, while rats need something slightly larger. The equipment needs to be sturdy enough support the little fella's weight, as most will climb the obstacle rather than jump it. Painting the pieces is also important so that they can be wiped clean should any of your little friends forget their toilet training in all the excitement.

Figure 63. Gerbils, on your marks . . .

So far I have a bar jump, an A-frame, and a teeter totter, but future plans include a tire jump, some hoop jumps, an open and closed tunnel, and some weave poles. Most pets really enjoy this kind of interaction and friends and relatives will love the entertainment value that your small pets provide.

This basic set was relatively easy, and so now I am thinking about customizing them for particular niche audiences. I already seem to have accumulated a fair amount of skull and dragon designs, so I can see a Gothic set being quite simple to create. If there is a market for a Castle Greyskull birdhouses, I see no reason why a hamster assault course graveyard would not go down well in the right circles. I am also thinking about changing the fences into iron pipes with grills and lattices to give them that quirky steampunk feel. I realize that these are tiny niche markets, but that is what makes 3D printing so much fun, having the ability to design and produce for an audience of one.

Of course, it is not just our tiny furry and feathered friends that will benefit from this explosion of consumer creativity. Animal architecture is a fast growing field and there is already a huge range of exotic animal habitats coming onto the market, from unbelievably pricey luxury pooch palaces to simple Ikea hacks that make modern pet furniture accessible to all, and anything but ordinary. My current favorites include the Egg-Shaped Nogg Chicken Coop and the Cat Capsule by Christian Ghion.

Figure 64. Imaginative animal abodes

Chicken coops no longer have to look like farmyard slums knocked together from scrap plywood and left over corrugated tin. Now even the most stylish eco-lover's abode can house a handful of fully organic soil biologists to assist with the recycling, fertilization, and pest control of a well-designed, self-sufficiency plot, rather than the usual ugly wire-and-wood contraption that looks so out of place in most modern homes. "The Nogg" is a modern egg-shaped chicken coop for 2–4 chickens, made from cedar wood, stainless steel, and glass, but could easily be printed out in sections on a larger home printer. This one has a little round window at the top so you can peer in and check the progress of your eggs but there are plenty of other refinements that could be made to this design starting point.

Framebow also makes a very distinctive line of chicken coops. I just wish that Dzingof would convert a few of his amazing designs into chicken coops that would turn the average farmyard into a museum of modern art.

Winter is Coming Cookie Cutters

It was strange that it was cookie cutters that convinced me that 3D printing is already a viable home business. I paid just $800 for my Makerbot and am already churning out saleable products. And I am not the only one doing this. One of the earliest sellers that I saw on eBay was "Longboypeter." Even though he has only recently moved into 3D printed products, I see that he already has almost a hundred completed sales in just the last two months. At the moment he is focusing on just two main products, cookie cutters in the shape of a Dr. Who Tardis and a Dalek, both of which can be freely downloaded from Thingiverse.com. Both are selling in the $5–30 range, which is great because his raw material costs are just a few cents per item. I see that he is also branching out in Dalek salt and pepper pots.

Figure 65. Dr. Who designs

My own foray into the field is far more tentative. I have already uploaded my own "Winter is Coming" Stark House *Game of Thrones* two-piece cookie cutter to Thingiverse, and although it comes out reasonably OK on my Makerbot, I am now in the process of optimizing the design, to have it printed off on a much more advanced machine, courtesy of Shapeways.

Figure 66. Cookies are coming!

In the meantime, I am working on a slew of other pop culture inspired cookie cutter designs. With so many projects on the go, I am happy to share my current list of possibilities here with you, so that you can crank up your 3D printer and start making some money. All of the following have a following:

2000 AD
Alfred E. Neumann
Babylon 5
Battlestar Galactica
Blade Runner
Clockwork Orange
Firefly
Hawkwind
Kiss
Led Zepplin
Masters of the Universe
Mortal Combat
Pulp Fiction
Spawn
Starcraft
Superman
Tarantino
X-Men

Simply do an image search and pick out a couple of iconic images for the category that appeals to you. I have found that solids and silhouettes make the best basis for a good cutter.

Figure 67. Sample icons

It is important to realize here that you are not just printing a cookie cutter for bakers, cake makers, and others interested in home economics. By basing your design on popular icons, you are creating an instant collectible. Just take a quick look at eBay completed sales and you will immediately see, for example, that just about anything related to *Blade Runner* sells to collectors and enthusiasts. With that in mind, go ahead and start designing your own sets.

While cookie cutters are a good way to hone your design skills and calibrate your printer, they may not make you a millionaire. Even if you are able to find a popular design that sells, say, twenty copies per week, taking into account print failures and other aspects such as finishing and delivery, this is quite likely to become a forty hour per week gig. Such an income would be great for paying off the capital cost of your new printer, but it is unlikely enough to pay off the mortgage. Anyway, with experts like Athey Moravetz out there doing so well in this niche, it is probably better to continue looking for something that commands a significantly higher price on the retail market. One suggestion might be icing stencils to take advantage of the latest cup cake craze. These are immensely popular at the moment and even easier to print than cookie cutters.

Figure 68. May the frosting be with you.

For many years now I have been involved in the export of 1/6 collectibles from the very centre of this fast growing industry in Hong Kong and the Pearl River Delta. I supply hard to find items to collectors and kit-bashers all over the planet, but obviously I am always looking for ways to reduce my costs.

One of the most popular items for diorama builders are loose human skulls. We are all familiar with that memorable initial scene in *Terminator*, where the The Cyberdyne T-800 endo-skeletons prowl a nightmarish future battlefield, crushing human skulls under foot. Human skulls can be used in almost any scenario, from vampire crypts and medieval dungeons through to alien planets and castaway astronauts. I have never had any problem selling skulls, but the real problem came in getting them at a decent wholesale price. Even when I eventually tracked down the injection molding facility that makes 1/6 skulls for companies such as Sideshow and Hot Toys, I could not get the price down below $5 per piece. I knew that I could potentially sell hundreds of these, so I quickly decided to start printing my own. Because they are 1/6 scale, each one only took about forty minutes to print on my trusty old Makerbot, and with a 2 percent fill, cost just a few cents in filament costs.

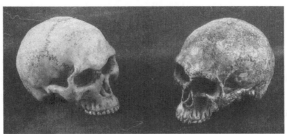

Figure 69. Commercially available 1/6 skulls

Figure 70. Horned skull

Skulls have achieved iconic status in our media culture and

therefore remain a product that can be infinitely customized by the imaginative 3D printing enthusiast. Staring off with human skulls is probably the best bet, but there are so many other directions to go from there. Printing horned skulls gave me a great insight into optimizing designs that require the minimum support material.

It seems obvious now, but simply turning this publicly available horned skull from Thingiverse (http://www.thingiverse.com/thing:65124) upside down, I could reduce the amount of support material down by around 30 percent. By removing the mandible, I was able to reduce the print time even further (as well as making the process less prone to misprints). I soon had a plate of nine skulls that took just under two hours to print, which was a massive improvement on the forty-five minutes it was originally taking me to print each skull individually. Making a plate of multiple items is a great way to reduce printing time, especially if your Makerbot is like mine and likes to spend so much time heating and then cooling its bed before it even starts printing.

Figure 71. A selection of skull designs

One thing that I did learn quite quickly is that bone is quite a forgiving medium for a FDM 3D printer. I have since been messing about with all kinds of different skulls. Dragon skulls are popular and the Hollywood popularisation of Tolkien has meant that orcs, balrogs, and hogoblins all have great potential, as long as I am careful (in legal terms) about how I describe them. As I explained earlier, Tolkien's heirs are notoriously litigious, and having recently seen them force a number of Hobbit-named pubs into closure, I am sure that they would have no qualms about coming after me.

Perhaps my original inspiration was the Predator trophy collection of skulls that are injection molded by Sideshow Collectibles. With individual skulls of various alien races fetching $50 a piece, this was obviously an area that I wanted to explore in more detail. Fortunately, skulls are almost infinitely customizable from the occult carved sigils that Alchemy carves into their skulls, to a huge variety of horns, spikes, and assorted bony protuberances that turn an ordinary homo sapien skull into that of a demon from the seventh circle of hell. Then there are fangs, Cthulhu-type tentacles, and LED-lit gemstones to create to glowing evil eyes that we all associate with the supernatural. The fact that skulls have long been such a popular design among tattoo artists should make it quite clear how much potential this item has to be tinkered with. Thanks to the influence of a few cyberpunk artists in the UK, I am now designing skulls that have gas mask breathers in place of the lower mandible. These look nightmarishly dystopian and yet are relatively easy to print.

One other thing that I learned from printing skulls was that with a machine that has such a high failure rate, it was important to be able to make use of these 60 and 70 percent complete prints. By plunging a miniature sword through three misprinted skulls, I found that I could make impressive looking grave markers and warning signs.

Of course, it is not just skulls that come out well on a 3D printer. I have since started experimenting with all kinds of bone. Imagine my delight when I discovered that dragon bone weapons and armor was one of the most sought after items in the popular computer game Skyrim. I have read on many occasions that Skyrim gamers spend as much time admiring themselves on screen as they do in hacking and slaying. Now, I could combine my knowledge of great axes and skulls to create some very popular items among gamers, collectors, and cosplayers alike. Known in the gaming world as Daedric armor, these items led me full circle back to dragon skulls as totems and focus points of power. They are especially popular in the realms of medieval fantasy interior design, where they regularly adorn gateways, battlements, and parapets.

1/6 Civil War Accessories

Anybody that is considering 1/6 scale collectibles might be interested to learn that even in a hobby that is as specialist as this, there are still some niches that wildly outperform others. One might imagine that it is all special forces or heavily armored SWAT team units that are most popular, and while they do sell very well in some of the more specialist markets such as Singapore and Hong Kong, back in the good ol' US of A, historical campaigns are far more in demand that contemporary conflicts. What is more, there are far less items out there for historical collectors than anybody else. If you do not believe me, simply do a search on completed 1/6 items for the American Civil War, the Revolutionary War, and the Indian Wars and you will clearly see that almost everything that is listed is quickly snaffled by some very serious collectors.

Figure 73. *Blazing Saddles* miniatures, just add beans for extra sound effects

I myself have started small here by designing and printing a couple of batches of cannon balls. I was inspired to print these when I saw another eBay seller sell a set of such balls for an amazing $40. I am now experimenting with some camp cooking utensils and a few other sundries. I hope eventually to move up to flintlocks and muskets, but that might be a while away yet. The main problem for me is that because I am not an American, I am not nearly familiar enough with these events, but I am sure that there are some US-based readers that can pick up the baton where I have left off.

Shafted Items

My knowledge of English history (as gruesome and appalling as most of it remains) is much better, and so I decided to put that to good use. I had come to the conclusion earlier that some printable items can be vastly improved by adding a simple shaft, in most cases a sharpened bamboo chopstick. This understanding had come about when I repeatedly tried to print off a scale version of the enormous long-handled warhammer that is the preferred weapon of the equally huge King Robert Baratheon in *Game of Thrones*.

Figure 74. Robert's Warhammer

After failing to print satisfactorily many times, I realized that the problem was that I was trying to print unnecessary material. Rather than trying to print a long spindly shaft, something that many 3D printers will baulk at, I simply found a common, everyday item to use as a shaft, and printed only the more complicated head. This technique had worked very well for skulls, when I had decided to put them on spikes for added horrific effect, and so I decided to see what else would work in that vein. My first attempts at giant battle axe heads came out really well, and now I am trying a few different designs, including a nasty looking executioner's axe, of which Henry VIII would have been proud. Most axes are not actually flat, but taper to a sharp edge. This can be difficult to print if the shaft is included, because the machine wants to include support material towards the sharpened edge. I overcame this simply by printing the 1/6 scale great axe below, for example, in two separate parts and then gluing them to the shaft. The contact area along the vertical shaft is more than enough to ensure a good affixation that will keep the whole thing secure. The leather banding was added later for extra effect.

The medieval period is not as collectible for 1/6 scale aficionados as it is for 28 mm war gamers, but I was keen to create some mighty twelve-inch field weapons all the same. Now that Tolkien's work has been made into a series of movies, I was hoping that I could still obtain some inspiration from what is quickly becoming a very tired genre.

I decided first to try my hands at wands, not those pathetic little toothpicks that Hogwarts attendees use to poke each other in the eye, but huge dragon skull topped mighty staves, suitable for an arch-mage or grand wizard. Again, I was using the separate shaft method and it worked really well. Unfortunately, there is not such a large market for magical staffs at 1/6 scale and so I am venturing into other related areas. I have since discovered an interesting range of female barbarian armor produced by the wonderful Triadtoys. (http://myworld.ebay.co.uk/triadtoys/)

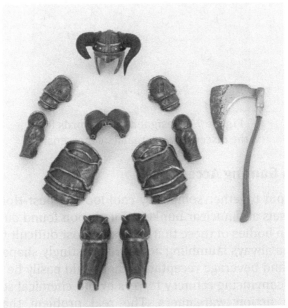

Figure 76. Female barbarian armor

Cast in resin and hand-painted with detailed weathering, the set contains a battle axe, a helmet, breastplate, epaulieres, gauntlets, trusses, and cuisses and sells for $150. Obviously, demand is out there, I just need to design and produce some quality items, and then wait for the collectors to come out of the woodwork. In the mean time, I have found an interesting selection of space marine melee weapons and some very versatile steam punk sword musket combos. Eviscerator chainswords and chattersword katanas are looking decidedly appealing, especially with the current popularity of zombie apocalypse movies. At the moment these are all works in progress, but I have high hopes that they will come out as fearsome looking as the first giant battle axes that I printed.

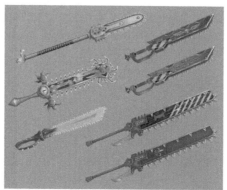

Figure 77. Designer chainswords for
the discerning intergalactic mercenary

28 mm Gaming Accessories

Having put together some very cool looking post-Holocaust-type reactor vessels and nuclear bunkers, I had soon found out that it was not the main bodies of these that were the most difficult to construct. In fact, I was always stumbling across interestingly shaped detergent containers and beverage receptacles that could easily be refashioned into a very convincing refinery towers or bio-chemical storage tanks for science fiction wargamers. The real problem that we were struggling with was the fine details that are added to these pieces to make them look realistic. This realization came to me while I was staying in the Guangxi city of Liuzhou and writing the initial parts of the eBook. A major centre of heavy industrial production, I could find full size wheel-screw pipe valves everywhere, but nothing at the tiny scale that I was looking for. I soon realized that I would have to design my own valves and control boxes.

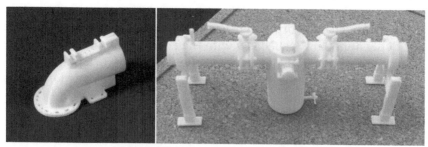

Figure 78. Valves at the 28mm scale

My main inspiration in this area is a small model maker called

Pardulon Models. http://pardulon-models.com/
They very graciously list their top ten bestsellers on their
websites, the ideal reference for 3D printers like ourselves.

1. oil barrels
2. dumpster
3. skull pile
4. lab equipment
5. picket fences
6. wooden barrels
7. ladder
8. steel door
9. generator
10. large crates
11. examination table
12. corrugated roof

I am sure that you have noticed that my oft-mentioned skulls are
up there at number three, and that some of the other items such as
picket fences and wooden barrels would look great outside a hobbit
house. The good news is that many of these items are already
available on Thingiverse. I have already downloaded and printed a
few different types of barrels and crates, but there is plenty more
scope in this vibrant and active marketplace.

Role playing accessories like these can help turn tabletop
skirmishes into legendary adventures. Pencil drawn maps and
pewter figurines certainly get the job done, but there is nothing
better than flagstones and solid walls to really add an extra level of
reality to a session. Over on Kickstarter, The Castle Foundry has
raised nearly $5,000 to produce a set of detailed, easily customizable
set pieces similar to a set of castle-themed Legos, where each 3D-
printed piece fits into every other piece. How about considering the
architecture of other eras for some inspiration?

Figure 79. The Castle Foundry

Exotic and Collectible Car Parts

We are always hearing about how someday people will just print out spare parts for their cars rather than having to order them from the manufacturer. Instructables user "madmorrie" recently had new door trims (interior panels) made for his 1962 Valiant, but he neglected to allow for clearance of the door lock levers on the back door, so that the original levers would no longer work. Rather than have expensive new door trims made, he decided to make new levers. Printed in plastic, the pair cost just under $15 from Shapeways.

With cars being such a major purchase for most people, I was intrigued to learn how I might become involved in this enormous market and as I continued Googling, I kept on reading about Jay Leno and other playboy millionaires who were using 3D printing to replicate all kinds of exotic car components. Potential printing candidates quickly began to emerge, such as the plastic windshield-washer fluid bottle found on the Ferrari GTO. These bottles were originally made without much thought, given that cheap plastic gets brittle with age and exposure to heat, until they collapse into a pile of dust. Plastic parts have long given restorers headaches, as they contemplated the shift from brass-era cars circa World War I, to cars containing plastic that started to appear in the 1930s. Another promising example was the DeSoto grille, a popular hot-rod modification for 1950s Mercury cars. None of the nine die cast zinc teeth on the grille are identical and they are all parts that deteriorate over time. By digitally modelling each of the teeth individually, anybody with a 3D printer can precisely re-create copies of them.

For really exotic cars, even very mundane parts such as rubber boots on wiring connections are good candidates for 3D recreation. In fact, any component that does not suffer excessive heat stress makes a good starting point. These could be cold air intake tubes, brake air ducts or hard to find interior pieces and dashboard parts. Shifter knobs are small enough to be an interesting proposition, (especially if you can squeeze in a thread insert or helicoil for where it screws onto the shift linkage) and I would also consider rare club emblems as items that could potentially fetch very high prices. One thing that did surprise me in the course of my research was the number of differing terms that have arisen in British and American English to describe what are essentially exactly the same car parts. The word auto is the most common example, a word that is second nature for Americans, but relatively uncommon for Brits, but then there are all the component parts from the windshield to the shifter to the trunk. If and when you do start printing car parts, bear this in mind to optimize your sales in a global market place.

As a card-carrying treehugger, I have never been a huge auto enthusiast, although I did have a very stylish MG Roadster called Tallulah during my younger, wilder days, and have always appreciated the sleek lines of a well-designed motor, such as those envisioned by Syd Mead. Now that I am older, I prefer to reside in locations that are well served by convenient public transport rather than go through all the expense and inconvenience of actually owning a car. It was for this reason that I turned to a good friend of mine, who is a rabid Land Rover enthusiast and general auto fanatic, for advice on catering to this market. At first we talked about expensive parts such as Rover V8 breather filters and fancy plastic end caps for oil dip sticks. By far his most interesting idea was as follows:

Figure 81. A standard oil filter

Dear Chris,

So you have just done a filter change, and you now have an old oil filter to dispose of. Rather than just drop it in the bin like you used to, now that the law has changed, you decide to take it to the dump for recycling. How do you get it there? If you had an end cap that screwed in, specific to your car (not as many different threads as you think) all the oil wouldn't leak out. Each oil filter has a threaded hole in it and a ring of holes around that. The filter is supposed to screw on to the car "easily." Trouble is, it contains oil, a small filter holds half a pint, most cars will hold more, a van or lorry would hold up to 2 pints. If it is easy, people will do it. Patent that, print them out, and then retire on a desert island after selling it to Ford, Fiat and all the Japanese manufacturers. A catchy name like "filter buddy" may also help. To trial, buy a filter, fill it with water and a spot of detergent, that's more searching than any oil. If it leaks out then you have a problem. Here are a couple of links to show you exactly what I am talking about.

http://www.ehow.com/list_7458401_oil-filter-specifications.html
http://www.bobistheoilguy.com/forums/ubbthreads.php?ubb=show
flat&Number=1814632

Your old mate, Jim

Professional restorers are perhaps already years ahead of the rest of us in this field, and so the window of opportunity might be a short one. In fact, there is already one company in Wisconsin that can laser scan an entire vehicle as an insurance policy in case of accident. If the priceless antique should ever crash, then the entire thing can be reconstructed using the digital model.

On a wider scale, we can look forward to a time when no classic car will have to die unnecessarily. Recycling for these automotive works of art will be increased dramatically as components can be manufactured new as needed. At the moment, the biggest problem is often parts, either finding one or more likely getting one made specially. Once we see the introduction of metal sintering machines, it is likely that the classic car industry be revolutionized completely. For the rest of us that simply admire these million dollar museum pieces, but commute to work in a Honda, it might not be too long now before we begin to see panel printers and hubcap printers at our local garages, filling stations, and Walmarts.

Many modern cars have plastic intake manifolds and some FDM machines will handle thermoplastics with the needed heat properties. It would also be possible to overprint substrates. This means that if a part with metal threads were required, it would be trivial to start the print, insert a metal nut as required, and finish printing the rest of the part encapsulating the nut. Taking it a step even further, these entry-level printers are great for making wax patterns for casting metals, which means that expensive SLS machines are not really necessary at all.

In a recent development that might be a sign of things to come, the US Department of Justice announced that Panasonic and its subsidiary Sanyo have been fined $56.5 million for their roles in price fixing conspiracies involving battery cells and car parts. The fines are part of a much larger ongoing investigation into the prices of auto parts and have already resulted in twelve individuals at various companies being sentenced to jail time for felony charges, meaning incarcerations of at least twelve months. Criminal fines targeting these companies have totalled over $874 million. "The conduct of Panasonic, SANYO, and LG Chem resulted in inflated production costs for notebook computers and cars purchased by U.S. consumers. These investigations illustrate our efforts to ensure market fairness for U.S. businesses by bringing corporations to justice when their commercial activity violates antitrust laws." Could this be part of a much larger picture where 3D printing will show that vehicles and the components of all kinds can be manufactured at much lower costs that the consumers are customarily forced to pay? It will be very interesting to see where all this leads.

Figure 82. DIY DB4

In the meantime, one eccentric Kiwi is really pushing the envelope by printing his own 1961 series II Aston Martin DB4 replica. Ivan Sentch began the project earlier in the year, when he purchased a 3D drawing of the car from Turbosquid and utilized Autodesk 3DS max software to modify the drawing to better suit his overall building plan. He is using a $499 second generation Solidoodle printer to construct the frame of the vehicle, but the build envelope of 150 x 150 x 150 mm means that he has to divide up the components into sections, and then piece them together. He estimates that at $28 USD for a 1 kg spool of plastic, it will cost an estimated $1,800 for total production. The project is more than a little off the wall, but I salute this gentlemen, because if nothing else it clearly gives the finger to the RIAA who famously used the phrase

"You would not download a car" in their early anti-file sharing witch hunts. Epic fail, again! It really is amazing that one industry can be so incredibly ignorant when it comes to technological advances. My only question is this: Will the 3D printed version of the DB4 come with official MI6 add-ons, such as retractable machine guns and a passenger ejector seat?

Three Bonus Suggestions

With so many ongoing projects, I am loathe to take on any new ideas just at the moment. Even so, every time I surf the web I keep seeing interesting new items that would be suitable for 3D printing. Here are three ideas that you can try out for yourself.

Fellow author Isaac Budmen has a very novel desktop sub on his Thingiverse page http://www.thingiverse.com/thing:49480. This item is a great example of how there are printables on Thingiverse that can be re-purposed for different uses with a little effort and imagination.

Figure 83. Phantoms of the deep

Buried slightly in a shallow layer of gravel, this makes a fantastic ornament in an aquarium. With a few carefully place holes and a paint job it will probably be the best aquarium decoration that you have ever owned. See how well printed skulls look in the same environment?

The only downside to this model is its noncommercial license. Why on earth has he made it impossible to bring this idea to its fullest potential when he is obviously busy doing other things? When I get around to it, I will commission and upload my own sub with a license that others can use properly. Alternatively, have a look at all the other vehicles on Thingiverse for something with a suitable license. There must be a Romulan Warbird or an Exxon Valdez or something else that would look cool with angelfish fluttering around it.

Figure 84. Dr. Who question mark umbrella

I personally did not have any red PLA for this project, but I can see now that I could have used any color really, and then painted it red at a later stage. I would still recommend experimenting, as these iconic brollies are growing in popularity among Whovian costumers, and regularly fetch in the region of $100 on both eBay and Etsy. As can be seen in the picture, it is simply a replacement handle with a lower dot which is then attached to a regular "Ministry of Silly Walks"-type black umbrella, and hey presto, you have increased the value of a $10 umbrella by a factor of ten. Remember that the bottom of the umbrella will also need to be painted to achieve the proper effect. There is no need to make the whole thing solid and I would expect that a fill of just 10 to 20 percent would be fine.

The particular prop was popularized by the actor Sylvester McCoy who played the seventh incarnation of the timelord from 1987 to 1996, appearing in a total of forty-two episodes. The question mark umbrella was especially visible in the episode, "Trial of a Timelord." There is a very detailed set of instructions on how to build one of these using traditional methods on the TardisBuilders website.

http://tardisbuilders.com/index.php?topic=1891

It is certainly worth taking a look at the other props listed on this site to see if you can find something appropriate for your 3D printer, although I would imagine that printing a full-size Tardis or Dalek outfit might be rather expensive in terms of filament at the moment.

Other Movie Memorabilia

Figure 85. "It's a test, designed to provoke an emotional response."

Many of my friends are very much into movie memorabilia and literary-related art. As a huge Syd Mead fan, I have always been fascinated by his movie work, especially the props from *Blade Runner*. Mead's work has been cleverly described in the following sentence: "It reminds you of something that you have never seen before." It was recently announced that his movie classic is soon to be remade, and so I am keen to try a few more Dick-related artifacts. I have already worked on a replica of Deckard's blaster, but its multi-material requirements are rather beyond the abilities of my poor Makerbot, and so, instead, I am looking at a self-assembly Voight Kampft machine. I have seen some nice LED parts on eBay from a seller that specializes in Knight Rider conversion kits, but I am confident that I can get similarly impressive flashing lights in Shenzhen or Guangzhou. I am sure that this will be a great conversation piece and will look great alongside my newly created halfling abode.

Just one last item before I move onto the next chapter. I was not sure exactly how to classify this, but I would really like to print off an example for that Halloween party or punk revival gig. The first picture in the set shows the printed stitches while the following three are much more permanent tattoo versions.

Figure 86. It's alive!!

5

Model Repositories

By far the largest resource for .STL files that can be printed directly is the Thingiverse.com repository. Thingiverse was started by ex-Makerbot founder Zach "Hoeken" Smith in November 2008, allowing members to freely share user-created digital design files for use with routers, laser cutters, milling machines, and, most important to us, 3D printers. By 2011 over fifteen thousand designs had been uploaded and by March of 2013 this number had jumped to nearly forty thousand. At the time of writing (October 2013), the total had risen to over one hundred thousand.

Despite being a useful resource, since the recent Makerbot revamp, I find the search interface a little clunky, and I prefer to use Yeggi.com as a search engine. In addition to Thingiverse, this meta search engine crawls a dozen or so similar repositories including the likes of Shapeking, Ponoko, YouMagine, Physibleexchange, and 3dprintingmodel as well as a few of the many Chinese repositories. New sites are being added all the time.

Thingiverse still has a number of distinct advantages over the other sites and these include the following. The site has a function where users can put together collections of related items. This can be very helpful when you are looking for items based on a specific theme, but which might otherwise be lost in the vast selection of one hundred thousand other objects. The site itself organizes items into categories and then leaves each item room for comments so that users can post their own tips and experiences with printing that particular item. These comments can be extremely useful in deciding whether you really want to spend twelve hours printing an incredibly complex geometric art vase. For this reason alone, I encourage you to add your collections and try to offer some useful comments on items that you print. After all, this is a free service and it is important to try to give back to the community.

Thus far Thingiverse.com has experienced nearly twenty 17 million file downloads and research has shown that compared to the average Internet population, Thingiverse.com's audience tends to be male, childless, and highly educated. In addition, it is estimated to be earning between $30,000 and $100,000 (which shows that I really should be trying a lot harder), and that they view an average of 11.5 unique pages per day. It is clear that marketers are very excited by this demographic, and there is little to no doubt that it was a major contributing factor in MakerBot's $403 million buyout by Stratasys. Thingiverse does not yet claim ownership of the models that are uploaded to the site, but it is painfully obvious that the lawyer drafting the terms and conditions had very little understanding of the open source concept.

Repository Remixes

It is difficult to predict who will be the most successful challenger to Thingiverse, but Cubehero is working on a comments and ranking system. Although options are primitive at the moment, it does look to be one of the better contenders. It is based on the Github site, which means that changes to the file can be tracked, and these changes can even be displayed graphically. PirateBay has a physables section, but it is only really useful if you are looking for very specialist items such as butt plugs and lower receivers. Their ads are not exactly family-friendly and so it might not be a site that is safe to surf at work.

YouMagine, on the other hand, is a repository developed by Ultimaker, described by some as the Luke Skywalker to Makerbot's Darth Vader. So far they have about five hundred designs, but the site software automatically analyzes the printability in the cloud, even indicating how much time and material the prints will cost. It also understands and renders open standards such as AMF, and is planning to add a number of even more useful new features. I would like to see an import feature similar to browsers, so that I can bulk import my models and links from Thingiverse.

Some people have suggested that repositories need to be run separately from any maker of printers, to avoid conflicts of interest. Even open groups such as RepRap, let alone profit oriented companies, will have incentives to make the site work most effectively for their own systems.

One interesting thought is that all the horsepower needed to process all these 3D models may well lead to some much needed breakthroughs in chip and server speeds. Much of the development focus in recent years has been focused on smart phones and miniaturisation. From a PC point of view, it would be nice to see some significant breakthroughs in raw computing power for the desktop, if only to speed up rendering and slicing processes.

There are many other sites out there which host 3D files, but most of them charge for design models, with some of the new incarnations such as Burrito (http://3dburrito.com/) and Cuboyo (http://www.cuboyo.com/), all openly aiming to become the iTunes of printables. It is difficult to predict how long these sites will last when there is such a vast array of free files available. Then again, there are plenty of people still willing to pay for music on iTunes, when anybody with even moderate Internet skills can quickly find half a dozen places to download free music. I sincerely hope that this does not go the way of the music industry, where so many people have been brainwashed into paying for copies. None of us would consider paying a royalty to the plumber every time we flush the toilet, and yet we are forced into coughing up ever larger sums every time we wish to hear our favorite songs on some newly introduced format, even though it is exactly the same music. I am quite happy to pay for a physical object. If a designer's creations are good then surely the quality of their work will guarantee them commissions and an income, in the same way that most independent bands get paid from merchandising and live concerts.

Just recently, I approached a designer on Shapeways to ask him if his designs would work on my Makerbot. His portfolio consisted of custom parts for Transformers models and I was quite interested in some exotic looking sickle swords, even though I thought that they were vastly overpriced at $12.50 a pair. When I messaged the designer, he admitted that he had no idea whether they would work on a Makerbot, but asked me for the outrageous sum of $1,500 for the .STL file, just so that I could try them out. I told him that he was delusional (I suspect that he might have been Lars Ulrich or a director of the RIAA) and had a pair of identical items knocked up from scratch by a Solidworks designer on fiverr.com. When I have the chance, I will upload these myself to Shapeways and offer them at a tenth of the listed price, just to prove a point.

Fortunately, for those who know where to look, there are actually lots of free digital CAD files available on Shapeways. One tip that used to work well was to search for relevant phrases such as "open source" or "creative commons." Interestingly, when I searched for "open source" at the beginning for 2013, I came up with more than 1,200 results, although by October this had dropped to just two hundred. The "creative commons" search, on the other hand, listings had risen from four hundred to 2,166 products.

Some sites are making an effort to stand out from the crowd, but unless they offer something completely new, it is difficult to see how any of them will survive. Singaporean-based Polychemy is operated by the guys behind the very successful Pirate3D printer Kickstarter project. They are clearly aiming at the designer, boutique-end of the market with high end jewellry and mobile phone covers, but it is still unclear how this strategy will pan out.

One repository that I really hope will be able to ride out the storm is the one started up by Blender. This is an excellent resource for blender artists to learn and share with other blender artists by allowing everyone to submit their blends to the wider community.

Unfortunately, there are more printable file repository sites cropping up at the moment than social networking sites. Each one is hoping to be the one object repository to rule them all, but it is unlikely that many will last for long. Most can be divided into two different camps; basically, fee-based and free. It is interesting to try to extrapolate upon how this sector of the Internet might develop in the future.

Let us start by going back to the very first peer to peer-to-peer file sharing site, Napster. Looking at what happened there, it is very likely that the first really successful 3D file sharing site will be gunned down by trigger happy lawyers and other corporate interest mercenaries. Of course, the dark lords of the RIAA should have known that they could not win and by striking Napster down, they only made file sharing more powerful than they could have possibly imagined. Dozens of replacements immediately stepped in to fill the void and a vicious war of attrition began. Despite alienating an entire generation of its very best customers, Hollywood is refusing to stay down and admit that it was wrong.

Shawn Fanning's creation (in true Jedi fashion) was reincarnated in a multitude of new and stronger forms, ranging from Kazaa and Emule to Kim Dotcom and the Pirate Bay. Big media is still using its Storm Trooper tactics to extort and intimidate, even though traffic on the Bit-torrent network now dwarves all of the rest of the Internet put together, and honest content creators are confessing that file sharing is actually benefiting sales. Will the manufacturing industry be smart enough to learn anything from this humiliating defeat? Probably not.

In the 3D file sector, there are currently two breakaways. In the paid arena, Shapeways leads the field, while Thingiverse is way out ahead for fans of open source. There is certainly room for these two separate models, just as iTunes still does very nicely while The Pirate Bay caters to a very different user base. A more important question is how long these two can maintain their positions. Napster was great for mp3s of about 10 MB a piece, but it is doubtful that the software would have scaled up to cope with the explosion of complete TV series, 1 GB DVD movies, and 20 GB blu-ray rips. The amount of printables out there is still a trickle at the moment, and yet the number of files on Thingiverse has increased tenfold over the last year. Just imagine the explosion that will take place when 3D home scanners hit the market. At the moment, they are still $1,000 or more each, but a couple of lasers and a turntable cannot warrant those enormous prices for long. Just as there are printers out there at a tenth of the price of the Makerbot (and arguably better to boot) there will undoubtedly soon be $100 scanners on the market, shortly followed by smart phone apps that will turn every telephone on the planet into a scanning device. If Thingiverse can go from fifteen thousand models to 150,000 in just twelve months, then just think what will happen when scanning a physical object becomes easier than ripping a CD. The torrent network already hosts countless millions of media files, and it will not take long before the number of 3D files easily eclipses that number. After all, there are only so many books, songs, and videos to be digitized. The number of possible 3D objects is infinitely greater. Most people have relatively few books, CDs, and DVDs in their homes, but everybody has a great many more ordinary physical objects, all of which can be scanned and uploaded. Then there are historical artifacts going back thousands of years, items from the countless worlds of myths and fantasy, not to mention all those contraptions that are still hiding deep in our imaginations. I simply cannot comprehend how many remixes there will be. Even a search engine the size of Google is going to be completely overwhelmed.

Add to this the fact that the size of these files is very likely to increase rapidly from simple STL and OBJ files, to formats that can handle far more detail such as color, texture, and material make up. Browsers will undoubted want to view these representations in 3D, and what single organization is going to be able to supply the enormous amounts of processing power required to accomplish such a feat? It is I my prediction that 3D file sharing will inevitably become distributed in nature. The sheer quantity of files available will require a paradigm shift in search capabilities, and it is even likely that we will see a new Google emerge from these changes. My own feeling is that such a successor will be based mainly on its curation skills. Its ability to accurately title and describe individual files will be key.

Much of the maker community would already like to see some healthy competition for Thingiverse and here is a list of some of the improvements that they would like see:

1. More diverse offerings in a wider range of well thought out categories, with a rich set of metadata that is specific to objects. Most new repositories are stocked with designs that already exist elsewhere. Looking again at torrent sites for inspiration, this could take the form of UKNova- or Karagaga-type sites that focus on very specific niches. At the other end of the scale, Demonoid was massively popular because it covered such a broad range with a wide selection of materials that simply were not available elsewhere.

2. A rating system for objects that relies on more than just "likes." Printability, quality, and other design variables could be scale based on the experience, participation, and skills of the user, their number of uploads, and how their own objects are rated by others. In this way, if one user rates an object's quality as low, but his own objects receive low quality ratings, his quality rating would not hold as much weight as someone who has received high quality ratings on their own objects. If multiple people with a good track record report that an object is not printable, it should be flagged as having possible issues and the creator should be notified. News aggregation sites such as Slashdot have implemented effective ratings systems, so it should not be impossible for a user repository

to do something similar.

3. An intelligent system capable of analyzing files and notifying the content creator if the files are duplicates, corrupt, or unprintable. It might also analyze the quality/resolution of the output files, and maybe do some curve analysis of the STL to determine, among other things, how many segments make up the radius and generate a model smoothness factor.

4. An ignore option would be useful to avoid having to mine through content that some users might consider irrelevant. For example, many of the new designs uploaded are printer modifications from users finding improvements to their own machines. It would be good to be able to filter out modifications for machines that differ from our own. I really do not want to see one hundred different Makerbot spool holders, especially if I have Formlab F1.

At first there may be a splintering as has happened with the various private torrent trackers. Each specialist interest will evolve its own group of sites. Just as there are now trackers specializing in everything from anime to wrestling, the same is likely to happen with 3D file repositories. One of the frustrations at the moment with Thingiverse is that users searching for ornamental items are inundated with 3D printer parts. I can imagine some sites will specialize in components and upgrades. Others might focus solely on miniatures, each one catering to a different specific scale.

Of course, not all 3D models are created equal. The range of materials with which they can be printed is increasing all the time. Users will want models that are specifically suited to their machines. Some will want models for FDM printers, others for SLA, others still for metal laser sinterers. Could this lead to further splintering where different repositories concentrate on catering to audiences with certain kinds of machines? It certainly sounds feasible.

It has been suggested that someone start a Kickstarter campaign, we all chip in and buy Thingiverse, and then give it to a site like Hackaday or Instructables. Many users are complaining that an ever-growing number of forbidden objects and topics keeps thousands of designs off its database. It may be the largest site in terms of uploads, but it is certainly not the Wikipedia of home fabrication. I for one have begun deleting many of my own uploads and am looking to support a better qualified competitor.

The Pirate bay has set up Physibles.org mainly as a means of accessing controversial objects that may not find reliable centralized hosting elsewhere, rather than trying to be a serious contender as a general object repository. The Pirate Bay has the necessary distributed infrastructure and the trust of the maker community, but this is a specialized purpose and it requires a specialized interface. Perhaps RepRap.org , Wikipedia, or CNCZone.com could step into this role? Each one has the credibility and the labor force to make it happen. It has been suggested that alternative sites could somehow lure users/authors in by paying authors per download from a pool of money generated by advertisements displayed on the site.

Because Thingiverse has the most users, it is growing the fastest. Once a site like this has gained a certain amount of traction, all of the competitors have the same problem of overcoming social momentum. Just think of the situation with Facebook or iTunes. eBay is another good example. The site's management has gone from bad to worse over the years, with recent price hikes pushing many small businesses off the site altogether. There are many cheaper alternatives, often far superior in form and function, but eBay has a de facto monopoly because of its dominant position. Even if Thingiverse's competitors are able to offer an easier better service, it might now be too late for them to catch up.

3D Scanners

While 3D printing has taken the tech world by storm, in the longer term, we will see that developments in 3D scanning are going to be just as disruptive, if not even more so. The field has changed immensely in the short six months since I last wrote about this subject, but there really was not all that much public need for 3D scanners until 3D printers came along. Fortunately, there is room for more than one interpretation of what a 3D scanner should be at this point. It has been said the gaming miniatures will be the first area to explode with this technology. Suddenly, anybody with a cheap scanner will be able to upload a miniature design for anyone else to use.

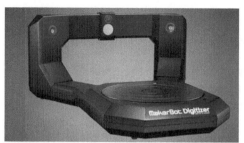

Figure 87. The Makerbot Digitizer

The most heralded machine to arrive on the scene is the Makerbot Digitizer, which can scan objects up to eight inches across and eight inches tall. The turntable can support up to 6.6 pounds, is accurate to within 2.0 mm and takes about twelve minutes to scan an object to a digital file. The lasers are of very low power and, according to the company, totally eye-safe. The Digitizer can then send the scan directly to the Thingiverse repository of 3D object files, or import it into the company's MakerWare software for output on a Replicator. The Digitizer costs $1,400 with an optional $150 service plan, but despite its high price tag, it still looks like a gramophone. An armature attached to the turntable houses two lasers which essentially act as range finders as the object spins around. They track the curves and lines of the entire surface, eventually recording hundreds of thousands of points in three dimensions.

While offering a $2,000 printer for sale, it seemed very unlikely that Makerbot would offer a $200 scanner, but that is what it will take to really set this market on fire. A look at the competitors that are cropping up clearly shows that the downward price trend is already taking place.

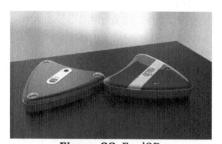

Figure 88. Fuel3D

Fuel3D is a simple point-and-shoot 3D imaging system that captures high resolution mesh and color information, based on medical 3D imaging technology first developed in 2005 at Oxford University. When announced on Kickstarter, the project surpassed its target funding of $75,000 in just two days. Even so, the $1,000 scanner is not fixed-position but a hand-held device that claims to compete favorably with products in the $15,000 range. A further claim is that it is the world's first 3D scanner to combine pre-calibrated stereo cameras with photometric imaging to capture and process files in seconds. The developers say that their device is particularly useful for rendering surfaces like skin, fabric, stone masonry, and organics such as plants or leaves, but we will have to wait until May 2014 for the first production batch to ship so we can check it out for ourselves.

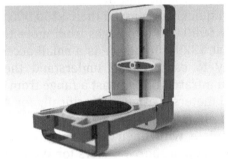

Figure 89. The Matterform Photon Scanner

Matterform, a Toronto company, recently wrapped up a crowd funding campaign on Indiegogo seeking $81,000, but which ended up with nearly $500,000 for their high resolution "Photon" scanner, featuring a high-definition camera and dual lasers. Backers that paid the starter level $599 for a single scanner came from a huge range of backgrounds, from archaeologists and dentists, to a loving father who wanted to scan and save the plasticine creations of his youngest son.

The USB device is able to scan objects up to 190 mm by 190 mm by 250 mm (7.5 inches diameter and 9.75 inches height) with a resolution of 0.43 mm at 0.5 degree scans, with an accuracy of +/-0.2 mm, all in an average time of about three minutes. Dual stepper motors offer full control over the scan bed and the Z-axis to produce .STL, .OBJ, and point cloud .PLY outputs suitable for PC, Mac, or Linux.

Figure 90. The Structure Sensor

The Structure Sensor is a 3D sensor for mobile devices, designed to capture models of rooms and 3D objects. Yet another Kickstarter project, the team quickly surpassed their $100,000 goal and went on to receive nearly $900,000 in pledges from more that two thousand backers. Priced at $329, the device is a small accessory that allows iPads the ability to capture and understand the world in three dimensions. Dual infrared LEDs boast a range from forty centimeters to more than 3.5 meters. Designed specifically for Apple devices, the scanner is easy to mount on almost any platform that supports USB, and comes complete with open CAD models for creating custom brackets, as well as open source drivers for Windows, Android, OS X, and Linux.

The Structure Scanner will give developers the ability to build mobile applications that interact with the three dimensional geometry of the real world. This means that we can look forward to some very interesting augmented reality games where the user's own physical environment becomes the virtual game world. This will mean that Counter Strike players will be able to shoot it out in their very own apartments, although flash mob Quake tourneys down at the local mall might prove a little disconcerting to the non-gaming general public.

Figure 91. The Rubicon

The Rubicon is a low cost Arduino powered 3D scanner created by Robert Mikelson from Riga in Latvia, for just $199. With a 13 megapixel camera (compared to Makerbot's 1.3 megapixel) it is able to capture texture and form as well as reducing scan times considerably. The camera on the Rubicon can be moved to allow for the scanning of larger objects. Crowd sourced again, this time on Indiegogo, delivery is slated for December 2013.

The web cam takes a picture of an object on the turntable with both lasers on and off, then a program written in c# looks for differences in those pictures to detect the shape of the object. The turntable then turns 0.45 degrees and the process repeats with eight hundred steps for a full 360 degree revolution. This looks like the best scanner so far, but like many others, I wish that he had offered a reward level that included just code for the digitizer and the Arduino code. Many of us already have a web cam, an Arduino, and a 3D printer, and this would have allowed us to build our own versions based on his programming work.

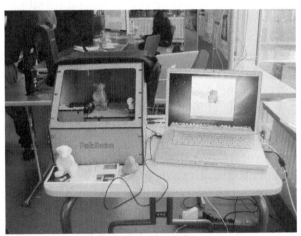

Figure 92. The Fabscan

A much earlier attempt at this idea was the FabScan project, created by Francis Engelmann at RWTH Aachen University. True to maker traditions, the fully open source kit is housed in a nicely designed, laser cut MDF case, and includes Arduino-controlled stepper motors. The object rotates slowly on the turntable so it can be scanned in 360 degrees, and although resolution is limited by the web cam, it can handle a maximum object size of 20 by 20 by 16 cm. The software (Win/Mac/Unix) generates point cloud data from any

3D form with a Logitech Quickcam Pro 9000 web cam (cost €120), a laser line level, and a FabScan-Shield Arduino plug-on module. The shield has the SMD components assembled and the connectors are included. Schematics are available at github.com/watterott/FabScan-Shield. Engelmann has provided all the files for laser cutting, PCB boards, and well-documented assembly instructions including video for anyone interested in building their own in just a couple of hours for a total cost of about €200. The group is now developing a simpler form of the FabScan with only the table rotating and the laser moving by hand. It will be called the FabScan 100, because the cost will be about €100.

MDF laser cutter VisiCut software: http://hci.rwth-aachen.de/visicut
Documentation: http://hci.rwth-aachen.de/fabscan
Google Group: https://groups.google.com/forum/?fromgroups#! Forum /fabscan

A similar project already exists on the Instructables site http://www.instructables.com/id/Lets-cook-3D-scanner-based-on-Arduino-and-Proces/

There are a number of other less well known 3D scanners already on the market, but it remains to be seen how well they can compete with the flurry of new models being released at this time. The Nextengine is a small commercial scanner that runs on windows, has a rotating platform, but still costs about $3,000. Better results have been reported with the DAVID Structured Light Scanner. Structured light is more accurate than laser and does not require a calibrated background, but it is still expensive at €1,993. The cheaper DAVID Laser Scanner requires users to move a hand-held line laser around an object against a calibrated background. It costs €449 and again supports Windows only and is not open source. http://www.david-laserscanner.com

None of the other choices are really up to the task just yet. The Trimensional Iphone app (http://trimensional.org) is still mostly a gimmick, and the Matherix Labs (http://www.matherix.com) Kinect software is rather impractical and takes at least five minutes to scan and another thirty minutes to upload.

The AutoDesk 123D apps family (http://123dcatch.com) now includes 123D, 123D Catch, 123D Sculpt, and 123D Make. Users take twenty to fifty pictures of a model, but the results remain inconsistent and results can sometimes take two hours for construction. Hopefully, the company will open source its research to encourage faster development.

Other software options include ReconstructMe (http://reconstructme.net/) and http://www.blablablab.org/ but both are still clunky and unpredictable. For cleaning up captured point clouds, MeshLab is useful as it can view and edit a variety of file formats and NetFabb is reported to have excellent performance. One more useful tool is MeshMixer for creating 3D mash-ups. It is great fun to use and with a growing number of YouTube tutorials, this is certainly one worth watching for the future.

One future possibility is that scanning may well go the same way as 2D printing and copying. While the current trend is for scanners to become smaller and cheaper, many people are still happy to head to the print shop rather than having a printer at home. My local copy shop has a top-end machine with a skilled operator who can help me optimize my documents and pictures before they are printed. His three industrial-sized machines can easily handle half a dozen complete books in a single afternoon, while the printer I have at home struggles to print out a resume without running out of ink.

Most print and copy shops have a back room studio where they can do passport photos, and so it is easy to imagine them installing a large scale scanner if the demand arises. I am not talking about a tiny Makerbot digitizer, but a full-size, Orcam-type scanner.

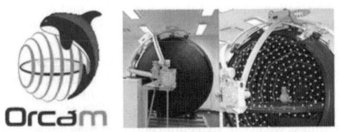

Figure 93. The "OrcaM" Orbital Camera System

The "OrcaM" (Orbital Camera System) is a giant automated 3D scanner on steroids that belongs to scientists at the Germany's Research Center for Artificial Intelligence. In the OrcaM reconstruction sphere, objects as wide as 80 cm and as heavy as 100 kg will fit into the maw and are then scanned in full color with highly detailed textures. The object is photographed simultaneously with seven cameras, and spotlights help to capture an ultra high resolution image.

Camera resolution is improving all the time and so it is not hard to imagine a copy shop's back room studio having just two or three cameras rigged up to a automatic frame doing the same job. They already own cameras, backdrops, and flashes, so the addition of a frame would be the only significant investment required. Users could then hire the room by the hour for their digital scanning needs. I would start by scanning myself, so that I can make the most of all the new 3D printed shoes and custom-tailored fashion items. By that time I am sure that personal body scans will be incorporated in some of the smart phone medical health apps that we are seeing explode at the moment. A full personal body scan may in fact become something that I do regularly, just like jumping on the scales at home. I am especially looking forward to the day when I can have a full facial scan, and then scare the pants my friends by having ten people show up at a party with my identical visage.

At the moment, both companies and individuals regularly pay for high-resolution renders of physical objects that have to be laboriously crafted by highly skilled 3D digital artists. If there was a on-line "wants list" of digital representations, then maybe I could pay for my scanning session with an Orcam type device, simply by capturing a few items on the list that I just happen to have at home. I could make a few bucks by scanning ordinary household items down to the micro millimeter scale, and 3D artists would be freed up to do much more worthwhile projects, like new product concepts or fantasy illustrations. Some of them might even find employ at these new scanning studios, fixing meshes and repairing dodgy scans for customers like myself.

At the same time, I would like to donate more than a few scanning hours to my local museum so they can start scanning some of their artifacts and treasures. Hopefully, this would be done both for insurance purposes, as well as to put the digital files into the public domain. Unless we live in sixteenth-century stately homes or are avid art collectors, the contents of most of our homes are pretty much the same the world over. We all share the same mass produced consumer junk, but museums are very different. They are vast repositories that can enrich the public 3D digital archives in the same way that YouTube and iTunes have built up huge audio and video databases.

6

Designing Digital Models

$\mathbf{F}$reelancer.co.uk, publisher of the world's largest on-line jobs survey, announced in April that the demand for 3D designers is growing faster than almost any sector of industry. Increased interest in 3D printing has resulted in a surge of demand for 3D Modellers, up 21 percent, 3D Renderers, up 13 percent, and 3D Animators, up 6 percent.

This will probably come as no surprise—otherwise you would not be reading this eBook in the first place. Fortunately, it is not too late to become a CAD expert and as long as you have access to a PC, there is nothing stopping you from beginning your education in Computer Aided Design this very afternoon.

Understanding the STL

For the time being, the STL format from the SolidWorks software remains the standard for 3D printing. This acronym stands for Standard Tessellation Language or Stereo Lithography, depending on your source. In technical terms, the model describes a raw unstructured triangulated surface by the unit normal and vertices (ordered by the right-hand rule) of the triangles using a three-dimensional Cartesian coordinate system. Current limitations mean that STL files only describe the surface geometry of a three-dimensional object without any representation of standardized color, texture, or other common CAD model attributes. With proper texturing, for example, scanners would have a much better idea of what color should be printed. This way, that 1/3000 scale model of the Starship Enterprise could emerge from the printer in a much more finished format, with call signs, names, and maybe even solar wind weathering, all printed in place.

Other criticisms leveled at the format have included a lack of resolution-independent rendering, bulky generation, and a "brain dead" vertex format. STL does not specify a relationship between vertices. Sometimes that relationship needs to be put back in, to allow software to better determine the normal for lighting purposes. Sometimes curves are visually smoothed by normals, other times they can be hard. Vertices directly affect watertightness issues, where they need to be essentially identical for facet-to-facet joining a watertight shape.

The STL format specifies both ASCII and binary representations. Binary files are more common, since they are more compact. Even so, with all of its weaknesses, few people imagine that it is here to stay. At least, we hope it is not here to stay. It would be an instant improvement if users could specify splines, NURBS, or some equivalent mathematical structure, enabling machines to print at specific resolutions. Facets would instantly become a thing of the past. Software could, and should, determine the resolution, and thus the resulting file as sent to the printer. Currently it is the author exporting the file to STL that determines the resolution.

One of the main problems with the STL format is that each program parses the file uniquely and translates it into its own proprietary representation of a 3D mesh that has evolved along with the features of that application. Templates and customization could be achieved if the models were parametric, as is the case with OpenSCAD. In theory, OpenSCAD could become a standard "language" for customization as it is free and open source.

As yet, 3D printer manufacturers have not yet agreed upon a universally accepted programming language that accepts templates, while also permitting user-friendly customization. Some enthusiasts favor the X3D format. Shapeways uses this internally, up-converting STLs and other formats to X3D. Its main advantage is that it includes the notion of "profiles." In simple terms, this means an X3D reader does not need to support 100 percent of the specification, but needs to only support enough to handle the "profile."

Despite this, the front runner at the moment seems to be the AMF file format, also known as STL 2, which could become the new industry standard file format. It has yet to be adopted by many CAD and 3D modelling applications though. Even so, it has been designed to be extensible and open for future applications. It allows for multi-materials, colors, textures, and even constellations of models, etc. AMF could be seen as a language, similar in versatility to XML, and could evolve in a way similar to how HTML evolved.

In practical terms, users would be able to define all materials and their locations as well as defining process steps and toolpaths. In the case of a robot design, electrical connections would be recognized by the software as conductive materials, limbs as regular plastic, and energy cells as battery material etc. Even the equipment and material required would be included. This way, customization would be much easier. Changing the color or scale, even adding an extra arm, could be achieved simply by altering XML-type syntax in the same way that we change web pages at the moment. While space here is limited, I would highly recommend the AMF Google Group discussions on this subject, especially the contributions of my fellow author Hod Lipson.

And this is the Google group:

https://groups.google.com/forum/#!forum/stl2
ASTM International Technical Committee F42 ASTM subcommittee that deals with standardization of 3D printing.
This is the wiki that has all the information on the AMF format:
http://amf.wikispaces.com/

In the meantime, apart from standard .STL files, I would advise 3D printer enthusiasts to familiarize themselves with part- and assembly-related files, as these can be very important building blocks for designers wanting to create new products, a little bit like lego for Solidworks.

SolidWorks Files (*.sldprt;*.sldasm;*.slddrw)
Part (*.prt;*.sldprt)
Assembly (*.asm;*sldasm)
Drawing (*.drw;*.slddrw)
Template (*.prtdot;*.asmdot;*.drwdot)
ProE Part (*.prt;*.prt.*;*.xpr)
ProE Assembly (*.asm;*.asm.*;*.xas)
Solid Edge Part (*.par)
Solid Edge Assembly (*.asm)

Training

For average individuals, the training materials of the more established suites can often be as prohibitively expensive as the software itself. Unfortunately for us all, continued corporate greed and government corruption has seen the continued closure of more and more public libraries, some of the most important assets that a developed society can provide. For those who still want to learn, the good news is that there are a growing number of on-line digital libraries, providing "fair use" access to a wide range of educational materials. The majority of these fly low under the radar, as vested interests use misinformation, outdated copyright laws, and blatant intimidation to keep information out of the hands of those who need it most. The myth of piracy is perpetuated by these criminals, while the rest of us understand that, in the field of human creativity, copyright is the real barbed wired fence. Despite constant protestations that file-sharing hurts sales, 2012 was a record year for Hollywood with a massive $10.8 billion in sales, but this inconvenient fact is still being ignored.

The torrent network is one of best resources available on the Internet today, and there are a number of private trackers that are of interest when it comes to education. While one of the very best sites, Demonoid.com (RIP) was killed by the MPAA in 2012, a number of smaller sites have stepped up to the plate, and are now offering quality learning materials to those who would not otherwise have access. I recommend the following.

Thegeeks.bz is an outstanding e-learning site. Crammed full of textbooks, journals, videos, and apps, it is an absolute treasure trove of knowledge both academic and practical, with categories on everything from philosophy and maths, to DIY and 3D computer design.

Bitme.org has more members and has been around longer, but is not as well managed as the Geeks and has quickly lost its lead as the foremost educational tracker. Much of the material available here has quickly become available on Thegeeks, as more and more members defect.

Bitspyder runs a close third in terms of membership numbers, but cannot match the two front runners for sheer selection, although it does continue to grow at a steady pace.

Other useful contenders include biztorrents.com which, as the name suggests, specializes in business-related content, myanonamouse.net for eBooks of all types, and bibliotik which tracks all kinds of textbooks, eBooks, comics, audiobooks, magazines, scholarly articles, and journals, just like a traditional library. Docspedia.org, Elbitz.net, and Learnbits.me are all also worth a look. All of these sites are ratio-based private trackers and therefore invitation only. If you are a seasoned torrenter with good sharing stats, try politely asking around on the forums of other trackers for an invitation. Otherwise, keep checking back for open sign-up days.

For a regularly updated list of all kinds of torrent trackers, not just educational ones, the following site is a very useful resource. https://www.underground-gamer.com/wiki/index.php/List_of_torrent_trackers

Modeling Software

There are so many different modeling software suites available that simply choosing the right on can be a daunting task, let alone mastering all of its intricacies and specialized functions.

Two simple examples to start out with are 3Dtin (http://www.3dtin.com/) and Tinkercad (http://tinkercad.com). 3DTin is so simple that young children can pick it up with ease. It is fine for straightforward objects, but for more complex renderings more powerful tools will be required.

Tinkercad is a cloud-based 3D modeling web application that requires no installation and is far less demanding than heavyweights like 3D Max and Maya. It is a "solid modeler" and allows the adding and carving of material, allowing users to quickly mold shapes and final products. It outputs into STL and connects directly to 3D printing services such as Shapeways. The website closed down last year, but was quickly acquired and revived by Autodesk Inc. iMaterialise.com have some useful tutorials here: http://i.materialise.com/creationcorner/tinkercad

In my previous work on 3D printing I was rather dismissive of the open-source 3D creation suite Blender, but I am pleased to report that that the new 2.67 release has many major improvements, including a new 3D printing toolkit. This a brand new collection of tools including statistical options to calculate mesh volumes and clean up functions, enabling isolated and distorted faces to be removed before the model is exported for 3D printing. Most importantly, there are now built-in checks for all too common errors such as self-intersections, walls that are too thin to be printed, or steeply overhanging faces that exceed 45 degrees.

Dutch artist Dolf Veenvliet has put together a three hour training DVD introducing Blender modeling for new users. Veenvliet owns a MakerBot printer and has many years of experience in 3D printing and sculptural design. The DVD which retails for €27.00, covers all aspects of the subject including color, wall thickness, or overhang problems and there are even some printable models included with which to experiment.

In addition, Blender benefits from a very lively community. There are tutorials, forums, meet ups, and everything you would need to get started or ask for help. Other tools have similar ecosystems sustaining them, but the Blender community is particularly impressive.

SketchUp has been criticized as being unsuited organic modeling and better for mechanical or geometric design, as is 123D Design. SketchUp is also notorious for creating many 3D print errors. Sculptris is a good alternative for organic/clay design, and Modo has been suggested as a useful poly-modeling tool out there for the low complexity, price and powerful features. (http://www.luxology.com).

As always, China insulates itself against the rest of the world by adopting a set of tools completely different from any other country. Critics have noted that for an authoritarian regime, censorship needs are much less when the population neither speaks the same language nor uses the same tools as their peers abroad. The current leader in both 2D and 3D design software is CAXA and despite being the most popular choice in both industry and education, the system is heavily proprietary, and therefore may struggle as open source becomes more and more of a driving force in the rest of the world.

www.caxa.com

One interesting alternative to the usual CAD suspects is the Spore Creature Creator, suggested by Joseph Flaherty. Unlike most games that allow avatars to be modified, Spore provides all the power of a CAD program. Within a week of its release there were a million creatures in their online library, the Sporepedia. In three weeks, there were more creatures in Spore than on earth. The true mark of a tool is when people can use it to create things the tools creators never imagined. The following examples are great illustrations of that principle.

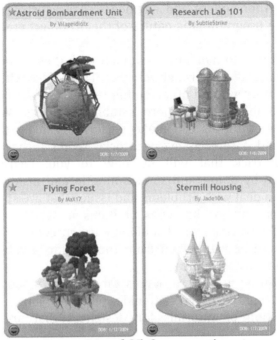

Figure 94 and 95. Spore creations

I personally have not had a chance to either play Spore or use its design tools, but I would urge readers to at least have a closer look before investing large sums in expensive mainstream CAD tools.

OpenSCAD is different from other 3D software in that it is not an interactive modeler. Instead, it is something like a 3D-compiler that reads in a script file that describes the object and renders the 3D model from this script file. It is free software, available for Linux/UNIX, Windows, and Mac OS X, and saves objects in the STL format. The power and weakness of OpenSCAD is its use of a programming language (script file) to build models. This is in contrast to a traditional 3D modeling program digital artists use, such as Blender, in that it does not focus on the artistic aspects or support an interactive mouse-driven style of object creation.

One of the most common complaints regarding traditional 3D programs is the complexity of the user interface, due to the variety and complexity of the operations users are performing interactively. The OpenSCAD interface is quite straight forward in comparison. Once users have an understanding of the scripting language syntax, it is possible to create simple 3D objects fairly quickly. This is often better suited for coders and engineers than artists and designers, who find the programmatic nature of the 3D object creation process appealing.

The best way to familiarize yourself with these programs and to improve your skills is through practice. These days with the likes of YouTube, Bittorrent, and other online resources, there are plenty of examples to follow from more established users. Watching and reading these tutorials can make performing many tasks become almost second nature, as every tutorial seems to have some little shortcut or trick that will be new to you. Learning is best accomplished by doing, and so steaming in and making things will enable you to deal with problems and issues that are specific to your toolchain, as well as the types of items in which you are most interested. Try working on a list of increasingly complex targets, such as, an apple, a house viewed from the outside, a table, a car, the engine of the car, a human face.

One of the very best resources for training videos that I have found so far is http://www.cadjunkie.com. Here you will find a very useful selection of tutorials for designers that are created by designers.

For those wishing to customize preexisting items both i.materialise and Shapeways have their own customization tools.

http://i.materialise.com/creationcorner

http://www.shapeways.com/creator/

For fixing errors due to intersecting facets and other problems that prevent them from being sliced correctly by programs like slic3r, I recommend MESHLAB http://meshlab.sourceforge.net/. This is a freeware, open source software for working with mesh data that can be used to fix STL scan data from 3D scanners. A second option is Netfabb http://www.netfabb.com/basic.php and both are supported by a very useful tutorial on mesh repair at Shapeways. http://www.shapeways.com/tutorials/how_to_use_meshlab_and_net fabb

A useful ACDsee type image viewer and organizer that works with 3D CAD designs is MiniMagics. This free viewer can be used to measure parts, compress STL files, zoom, see volume, see bad triangles, and more.

Despite all of these improvements, traditional CAD and 3D modeling tools are simply too difficult, taking days or weeks to use effectively, and then months or even years to master. We only need look at the state of CAD/CAM industry to see why things have not progressed as much as they could have in the last twenty or thirty years. Any disrupting tech is simply bought and buried.

Fortunately, much more will be possible in the reasonably near future than most people can currently envision, especially if those people are closely involved in manufacturing things and are thus "too close" to be able to see alternate approaches. To quote Bill Gates: "We always overestimate the change that will occur in the next two years and underestimate the change that will occur in the next ten."

The situation at the moment is very similar to the Internet in the 1990s when anybody could publish anything online, but they had to learn HTML first. Blogging software made things slightly easier, but it was only when Napster opened up large-scale interaction, followed quickly by MySpace, Twitter, and Facebook, which suddenly allowed hundreds of millions to publish online.

It is difficult to accurately predict which applications will open up this field, but some experts are already making imaginative suggestions. In the Netherlands, Joris Peels has talked of apps that ask a series of seemingly abstract questions that based on research, determine the types of shapes a person would enjoy. Or apps that scour web histories or personal photos to determine shapes that would be useful to the user. Or apps whereby a series of choices between images of different shapes, paintings, landscapes etc. would determine user preferences and in so doing the type of bracelet someone would want.

In the meantime, it is still possible to farm out your 3D design tasks to freelance experts. My favorite micro-tasking site of this type is fiverr.com. Here, folks offer all kinds of specialist tasks for just $5. I use the site for all kinds of tasks from promotional flyer distributions (how else could I have promoted my book on the campuses of MIT, Princeton, and Harvard?) to custom SolidWorks designs. One particularly reliable designer is based in Sri Lanka and does some of the most fantastic 3D Solidworks that I have ever seen, often much too detailed for the current capabilities of my Makerbot. Find a good designer and build up a good long-term relationship with them. In the very near future these guys are going to be as useful as website designers and apps coders are today.

As demand for 3D design skills continues to increase, the designers on popular sites like Fiverr are quickly becoming inundated with work. My next recommendation is to watch a Chinese micro-tasking site www.darengong.com, which translates as "huge labor force," very carefully. It is significantly cheaper than Fiverr, charging only 10 RMB per task. This is a quickly growing site that holds great promise for leveraging the skills of the world's populous nation. The combination of Google Translate's rather weak abilities with the lack of grammatical complexity in the Chinese language means that there are likely to be initial communication difficulties between clients and providers in the beginning, but at this price, surely those difficulties are worth overcoming. The Chinese Internet dwarfs the rest of the world put together and has been almost impenetrable to outside forces. Behind the Great Firewall, Internet giants such as Google, eBay, and Facebook have been stopped dead in their tracks. Despite its niche domination outside China, Fiverr has made little impact in the Chinese speaking world and so an interesting opportunity awaits providers such as Darengong.

Since designing for 3D printing has a number of pitfalls, it is better to work with 3D modelers and designers that have had previous experience with 3D printing. Be as clear as possible in your brief. Provide details to specify, including size, scale, and the final purpose of the finished object. Each 3D printing material and process has its own constraints. A sketch will make a clear description even more useful, and I find that it often helps to include images of similar items that you feel are relevant, or that include impressive design and style elements. Some clients even include a mood board. If the design has architectural or mechanical components then simple sketches are absolutely essential.

It is also important to get a good feel of what is possible with 3D printing beforehand, and this can be done by studying existing projects. Familiarize yourself with the materials so that you have a better idea of what your finished item will look like. Pay special attention to the types of materials available.

http://i.materialise.com/materials

http://i.materialise.com/gallery

http://www.shapeways.com/materials

One original approach that I would like to share with you I discovered in a group of DLP DIY enthusiasts. The maker in question regularly arranges design competitions at Zbrush Central, a forum of digital sculptors that use Zbrush software. Each artist is requested to submit one model, and the winner's model is then 3D printed and sent to him as a prize.

Figure 96. A classic portrait of Keith Richards by Ralf Stumpf, cartoon artist

Notice the super smooth surfaces even at 100 microns on the XY axes. There are many companies out there leveraging contests in the businesses, ranging from InnoCentive and Xprize to Topcoder and Threadless. This is clearly a successful model and could be useful in finding 3D design talent in the future.

Just think for a minute of the disadvantages that face those who never bothered to learn the basics of word processing or Internet use. A similar situation might arise in the future for those who cannot perform basic manipulations of 3D digital objects. Fortunately, the learning curve is likely to decrease significantly over the next few years as 3D design software becomes more intuitive and input devices become more suited to 3D environments. A haptic pointer for example is really just a mouse that provides force feedback. At the moment they are available on eBay at around $1,000 each, but that should quickly drop to $100 or less, as 3D design becomes more and more common in the work place.

Earlier in the year at the CES 2013 exhibition a Hungarian company introduced the 3D VR Kit Leonar3do, hoping to turn standard 2D screens into real 3D working environments, bringing virtual reality closer to the average consumer. Leonar3do's system includes a 3D mouse called the Bird and custom software that enables interaction with the created objects in real 3D space, adding the dimension long yearned for by designers and other 3D enthusiasts worldwide. Unfortunately, the full professional still costs €1,500, which will put it out of the reach of most hobbyists, but at least it is another of the necessary steps forward.

Figure 98. The Leonar3do in action

Gesture-based controls may quickly take over from haptics and could, in the hands of professionals, become a very powerful design tool, particularly as 3D interfaces become more immersive. In a recent peek at what the future might hold, Elon Musk tested an Oculus Rrift and a leap motion controller to design 3D printed rocket parts, assembling parts in mid-air, using hand gestures to manipulate the rocket components, as well as zooming in and out, before showcasing a 3D CAD model of the engine part. The Oculus Rift is a fully immersive virtual reality headset that can work with free-standing glass projector screens of the type seen in the Iron Man films. In fact, director Jon Favreau has previously said that the movie version of Tony Stark was partially inspired by Elon Musk.

This approach allows designers to interact directly with 3D models, focusing on the fundamentals of the model's structure, as opposed to thinking how to operate the computer in order to manipulate the object. This ensures that designers achieve much more in shorter periods of time, a factor that is critical to commercial space companies. Musk's own company, SpaceX, is pushing the boundaries of the speed of design to trial, bringing down a process that once took years to mere months and even weeks, relentlessly pushing the industry forward.

There is an active race going on at the moment to see who can develop the first practical gesture controller.

Researchers at Purdue University are using a Kinect and some specialized algorithms to produce the Shape-It-Up, although the first generation of devices are not especially sophisticated and certainly could not create the intricate details of facial expression in a modern video game.

Sixense displayed its MakeVR software at the Inside 3D Printing Conference and Expo in San Jose earlier in 2013. Using a joystick control, non-designer civilians are able to create relatively complex models. The process becomes even easier with imported objects, offering natural, intuitive creative control, and will only improve when combined with accessories like the Oculus Rift.

In the future we will likely see more and more bespoke CAD software such as the Cell Cycle webgl design app, created by Jessica Rosenkrantz and Jesse Louis-Rosenberg of Nervous System. Using their backgrounds in architecture, design, math, and biology, they developed a piece of custom software using Processing, an open source programming environment aimed at artists and designers, that could create 3D-printable cellular models.

The code can shape, twist, and subdivide, transforming a simple mesh into a complex patterned structure than can become anything from jewellry to a lamp shade. Interested in the idea of cellular subdivision, they took two 2D conceptual meshes and wrapped them onto a cylinder. One layer relaxes inward and one relaxes outward creating an interstitial space that would be difficult to replicate using conventional manufacturing methods. Because it creates rigid forms that enclose a large amount of space, they use only a very small amount of material. This minimizes the material usage and therefore lowers manufacturing costs.

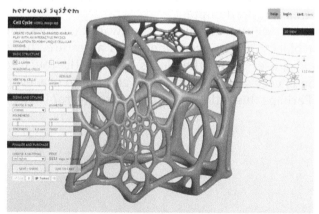

Figure 99. Cell Cycle

It is interesting how architects can apply their background to something as foreign as jewellry manufacturing and create one-of-a-kind, organic-looking, yet algorithmically-created 3D printed nylon and stainless steel rings, necklaces, and earrings. At first look these rings appear to be rubber or silicon, both intricate and simplistic in shape and form.

Another advantage of using computational design is that once the system is in place, there is so much ease and freedom to iterate over many different designs. Using this process, the pair were able to select eight bracelet designs and four ring designs for manufacture from more than a hundred variations, created in just a couple days.

They have now written a more user friendly version of their software that anyone can use. When recently commissioned by Disseny Hub Barcelona to create a unique collection of Cell Cycle pieces for their Laboratori De Fabricacio exhibition, they simply sent them a copy of the software, with which the curators we able to coauthor fourteen one-of-a-kind designs for the exhibit. In a very interesting twist on distributed development, not only is the manufacturing done by a third party, but even the product design is now being outsourced. The rest of us can design and purchase our own designs here:

http://n-e-r-v-o-u-s.com/shop/

Until now, 3D printers have mainly used pre-existing 3D modeling software, but innovators are now developing custom applications especially for this new technology. As well as Cell Cycle, another great example of this trend is Blokify, a simplified iOS application demonstrated at the World Maker Faire exhibition in New York by Jenny Kortina and Brett Cupta.

Blokify is revolutionary piece of software that does not have any tools, just blocks, where every motion is a gesture. To construct a virtual model, users move the blocks by using the touch screen. The application is very simple, interesting, and fun to use, even for small children. Perhaps this is the future of CAD software?

7

Outsourcing

If a home printer is still out of your budget, then there are a number of specialized companies that will take care of all your printing needs for you, and new ones are opening up all the time. This provides individuals with access to manufacturing processes normally reserved for large institutions and people with very deep pockets. Fortunately, the days of having to fly all the way out to Hong Kong to negotiate with some condescending Chinese factory boss that can barely speak Mandarin, let alone English, are long gone. There are a growing number of large scale 3D printers based in the West that are actively putting the "custom" back in customer. Even if you already have your own printer, there are times when ABS or PLA is simply not enough and you have a design that needs a more exotic material or a more professional-looking finish. As Apple has shown, an attractive housing can help your product stand out in a crowded world.

For detailed pricing, go to 3D Printing Price Check, which compares the actual costs of the different companies. http://3dprintingpricecheck.com/

Shapeways was founded in 2007 as a spin-off of Royal Philips Electronics, when it began as a one-off 3D printing service offering basic plastic items for sale on-line. Over the years, they have added a huge range of materials and have now produced more than 1 million

3D printed products with sixty-thousand new designs uploaded each month.

More than 25 million members now design and upload their files to the cloud. Shapeways sets a production cost and prints them on industrial machines in a variety of materials more interesting than simple plastics. Members can then open a "user shop," add as much mark up as they like to set the final sale price, and let Shapeways handle CC processing and fulfillment, crediting members with the profits at the end of the month. Depending on the material, customers are supposed to receive their items within 10-15 business days, but this usually works out to about a month.

For plastic, the most popular choice is FUD that comes in 0.016 mm layers. Desktop 3D printing goes down to about 0.02 mm, but at that resolution printing speed slows right down because there are so many layers to wait on. Some of the other more interesting materials include mock sandstone, ceramics, precious metal clay—a clay filled with gold or silver dust that can be sculpted into jewelry—and a squishy Elasto Plastic material. For a full list of the more than thirty materials options they offer, check out Shapeway's website. https://www.shapeways.com/materials?li=nav

All of these companies have a material sample kit available. The Shapeways kit costs $24.39 and you then receive a $25 coupon you can use on your next purchase.

The following formats are supported: STL, OBJ, X3D, VRML, and Collada, and they provide a full list of supported applications on their website. http://www.shapeways.com/tutorials /supported-applications as well as a tutorial on how to upload a file in the correct format https://www.shapeways.com/support/design_upload_and_3dprint. The site also hosts a number of 3D modeling apps that can be used to create products, all of which connect directly to Shapeways for 3D printing. http://www.shapeways.com/creator/

The company is planning a series of facilities in the US, but their main HQ is a massive, warehouse-like space in Long Island, New York where they have more than thirty acrylic printers as well as a small customer service team. Their eventual goal is to offer 3D print shops close to major US metropolitan areas to reduce wait-times and to spread out the manufacturing process among different factories.

Shapeways is actually much more than just a collection of printers. It is a wonderful community of expertise, comprised of 3D printing engineers, designers, and innovators. Questions posted on the forums usually receive a response within the hour, often from some very helpful people. There is even a full time Shop Owner Coach who can help with professional tips and marketing content. This is where a home printer falls a bit short.

Despite its popularity, there are still a few areas in which Shapeways struggles. One of these is the problem of a low polygon cap. In some areas such as puzzle making (think Rubik's cubes) it is very difficult to create puzzles with a low enough polygon count to meet the requirements of the site. There are plans to augment restrictions in the future, to allow for higher polygon count models, but increasing polygon count does not scale linearly with the amount of server memory used in processing, nor processing time. In addition, some printers have a hard-wired polygon cap for their build tray.

Another weakness is the propensity for models with large flat areas to be ruined by the striations generated when being printed with FUD. In theory, this is easily fixable by allowing you to control the orientation when printing, but the resulting bad prints makes the service almost unusable. Shapeways currently claims that as they do not own all of the printers used and because they have to subcontract, they do not have the ability to control this. This seems to be a bit of a cop-out though. Many people use subcontractors, and they do what they are told or they simply do not get paid.

Although Shapeways is focused on being a vertically integrated printer, owning all of the process and equipment, this may eventually be their downfall as a great deal of their current capital investments are focused around machinery that will essentially be dated very quickly.

One of Shapeways' biggest problems is that the company cannot buy enough advanced 3D printers of the laser-sintering kind to keep up with demand. This is because 3D Systems, the company that makes the models that Shapeways uses, has a twelve- to eighteen-month-long waiting list for its printers.

On the positive side, the company does have a lot of room for process automation for tasks that are currently done manually. In the future these will include 100 percent automated bed layouts, powder removal, and air cleaning, high-speed part sorting and packaging. This is a very new business and there are many areas in which efficiency can be improved. Whether this will result in lower prices for customers or bigger bonuses for directors remains to be seen.

Kraftwurx, based in Houston, Texas, was first launched in 2006 and has a pricing set up similar to Shapeways. The company's two largest advantages are that it has twice as many materials (seventy-four at last count) as its competitors, and is networked to over 120 printing bureaus around the world, helping reduce transportation and shipping costs.

Designers can upload and print their own models using Kraftwurx as a personal factory, as well publishing designs and selling them retail, both on and off site, even inside Facebook shops. The company also runs a crowdsourcing initiative similar to 99designs.com where designers can be hired for modelling tasks.

iMaterialise in Belgium houses more than forty types of 3D printing systems from 3D Systems, EOS, Stratasys, Zcorp, Objet, and even one that they make themselves. The company is pricier, more targeted towards designers, and if your expected volume is five or ten models per day then this kind of outsourcing would make good sense.

Ponoko is a New Zealand startup that is about the same price as Shapeways, that also does laser cutting (where they started out), and offers a look or feel that seems to be more targeted towards makers. They also allow you to sell directly, meaning they will ship to you (and you can post process) then ship to your customers. Ponoko will also help you resell your designs in their galleries and handle payment and fulfillment details. You can even open source your design for others to experiment with. As with Shapeways, there is a vibrant user community and a wide range of materials.

Sculpteo is a French company with facilities in France, America, and Israel. They are working particularly hard on cooperative projects with larger companies to build their brand name. These include customized iPhone cases for the telecom company Orange in Britain and eBay Exact to create a 3D printed-object store.

The company has a fast turnaround time with White Plastic (the equivalent of Shapeway's Strong & Flexible Plastic) being shipped in three days. At Shapeways, it can two to five days for the model to be approved and another week before it is actually printed. Part of the reason for this is superior automated mesh integrity services. While Shapeways still operates manual thinness checks on Sculpteo, this can be done in real-time. With just the toggle of a button, all thin parts will be highlighted in red and can be adjusted according to scale. Shapeways does not even offer scaling services.

This ease of use definitely comes at a cost, being at least twice as expensive as Shapeways and up to eight times as much on some materials. For small objects, like plastic rings, the base price is $8, while in Shapeways, it's priced by the volume. Shipping is also a letdown. For orders that costs less than $10, a budget shipping option is available, but one which takes a month, and which severely negates the speed benefit. Orders between $10 and $50 cost about $20 to ship, while orders above $50 cost about $6 to ship, so it is often worth scaling up or printing a second object just to qualify for the $6 shipping than pay $20 for shipping. Even then the discount is not nearly enough to match Shapeways' prices.

Sculpteo's website is a lot less like a marketplace platform, with lots of time wasting nested menus and an overall interface that just is not as user friendly

Protomold is a low cost, quick turnaround service that specializes in injection molded parts, which is useful if you plan on producing your product in significant quantities, have already prototyped your design, and have some knowledge of mechanical engineering. Protomold is a high quality option and pricing is very competitive for injection molding, but if you plan on making production molds expect to spend tens of thousands of dollars, especially if you have a complex design. This is not something unique to Protomold, manufacturing is just expensive. Molds can take weeks to prepare depending on complexity. You should also be comfortable with the mechanical design of your parts and have an understanding of designing for injection molding. At least their quoting system is relatively simply.

eMachineShop aggregates all the services traditionally found at machine shops and if you need exotic processes such as steel-rule-die blanking, photochemical milling, or rotational molding, this might just be the place to go. They also do standard machining, but their breadth of services is the real value. Costs and lead times are going to vary significantly based on the process you select, but you can get instant quotes using their software. Expect prices to start in the hundreds of dollars for most projects and reach into the thousands for more intensive processes. A thorough understanding of manufacturing processes is required to get the best value using eMachineShop.

Indirect Competitors

While those listed above are the largest names in the business, competition is cropping up all over the place. For example, the Color Company—a successful reprographics franchise—has made the dimensional leap from 2D to 3D by offering a 3D printing service at its central London store, and we can soon expect to see more and more copy shops and photo labs trying to get a piece of the action. Even so, makerspaces and FabLabs are trying to leverage their expertise and experience, looking forward to a time when it will be easier to go around the corner to your neighborhood FabLab than to wait for on-line service bureaus to print and ship.

We should also consider all the privately owned MakerBots, Ultimakers and RepRaps out in the wild could turn out to be the most dangerous competitors in the long term. Currently, I see desktop printers and service bureaus as two separate markets. Once it is possible to buy a printer for a few hundred dollars, with a print comparable quality to Shapeways, then we will start to see some serious competition.

With the rise of 3D printing networks, that day may not be so far off. I have already written about $100,000 Garages in my last book, but now similar start ups are showing up all over the place. The idea behind the distributed manufacturing hub is to leverage the masses of idle personal 3D printers and have them run print jobs for money by routing and dispatching work to them. However, this is a complex business requiring management of perhaps hundreds or thousands of unpredictable participants for very small margins. 3D Hubs (http://www.3dhubs.com/) already connects users to nearly 1,500 local printers and Makexyz is determined to become the Airbnb for 3D printer owners. Actually, I really like their attitude, with one of the founders saying: "Instead of being printed at some Orwellian factory, our objects are printed by real people." They claim that Shapeways takes too much time and are more than twice the cost of something printed on a personal machine that is sourced locally.

Where to Sell Your Prints

Beyond the user stores of the large printers such as Shapeways and Kraftwurx, there are still many more established internet outlets to consider. These obviously include favorites such as Etsy, Craigslist, Amazon, and eBay.

eBay is, at least in name, an auction website, but auctions play a smaller and smaller role in the company's business as insertion rates continue to increase. I find that eBay is more for collectibles than commodities. With eBay, sellers need to take a picture of each item being sold, upload it to the site, and provide a brief description.

Unlike Amazon, there is a fee for listing each item on eBay, whether it sells or not. There is also the commission that eBay takes from each sale, which is based on the cost of the item. Finally, there is the percentage that PayPal takes as well.

Amazon is better suited for items that are closer to "brand new" condition than eBay. The customer base of Amazon is more prone to buying brand new items there, rather than poring through multiple listings and willing to pay for "used" items. Amazon usually institutes at least a two-week hold for your money.

Craigslist is a classifieds site that has been around since the 1990s, but items can sometimes sell well on here despite the rising number of scams.

Most eBay alternatives have not been around long enough to obtain any serious traction, but there are a few on-line marketplaces and auction sites worth considering.

Oodle.com operates a network of marketplaces and has more than 15 million users. Oodle also operates the Marketplace on Facebook app.

eCRATER has been around since 2004. This is a 100 percent free on-line marketplace that is made up of stores which are hosted on Ecrater.com subdomains.

Bonanza.com (originally called Bonanzle) has only been on-line since 2008, but has quickly gained popularity. This is an on-line marketplace that offers easy to set up stores which receive their own vanity URLs.

Ebid.net has been around since 1999 and is amongst the very few general merchandise auction sites left on the web today. Aside from being an auction site, sellers can set "buy it now" and "make an offer" buying options.

There are also many marketplaces sites that have adopted Amazon's business model. These sites really have a lot of potential because they can generate a lot of sales for merchants due to their popularity. Most of them require users to fill out an application, but this can often be well worth the effort.

Newegg Marketplace is an especially popular place to shop for computers and electronics and has been allowing merchants to sell on their site since 2010. There are many categories in which to list: apparel, automotive parts and accessories, jewellery, and toys are just a few.

Sears Marketplace is a very popular retailer that operates many department stores across the US and uses this to promote their on-line store and marketplace.

Buy.com was founded in 1997, while the Buy.com marketplace was created in 2006 and features a large variety of items for sale.

Bear in mind that smaller, more affordable sites also means smaller advertising budgets which usually results in fewer sales. For this reason, you may want to look into setting up your own on-line store, which is now very affordable and easy to do, especially since many e-commerce software solutions are available for free. Although opening an on-line store is relatively painless, it is the marketing that takes time and effort. However, it makes more sense to promote a store that is hosted on a website that you name, you design, and you control. This way you are able to build a stronger brand name and on-line presence, and cross-promote other products and retain visitors with strategies such as newsletters. In addition, you can decide on where to advertise and how much to spend. Shook, for example, is now one of the most social ways to sell on-line because it uses Facebook to connect you with others in your social network.

Setting up a professional web store that looks and functions as well as the leading on-line retailers, e.g. Amazon.com and Newegg.com, can be achieved simply for just the cost of registering a domain name and signing up to a simple web hosting plan. Free solutions are pretty easy to set-up, but they may require a little more work to get your shop set up just the way you like it. Also, if you need technical support, you may have to turn to forums for answers. There are many add-on options from Authorize.net and Paypal payment modules to Checkout by Amazon and Google Checkout. This can be as easy as clicking a button on your mouse or as difficult as having to modify the software's source code depending on the software, and so it important to choose a solution that meets your skill level.

A paid e-commerce software solution does not necessarily guarantee more sales as you are paying for the work that was put into developing it, not for marketing. In order to be successful on-line, you have to build a reputation and this requires a human approach rather than a programmatic approach.

There are many subscription blogs or eBooks about on-line selling and most make their money from selling advice, not selling merchandise. I like the material produced by Skip McGrath (http://www.skipmcgrath.com/) because he really does sell product, experiment with various techniques, and then discuss his results. Initially, he sold antiques and collectibles, but more recently he has settled into commodity merchandise. I have followed his activities for a few years and have come to believe that he is a very successful seller sharing what he has learned.

Do not forget that there will always be opportunities for selling in the physical world. I originally bought my printer in the hope that I would be able to sell small collectibles at the rapidly growing number of cosplay conventions. Others might prefer art fairs or perhaps popular tourist destinations, depending on what you are printing.

8

Printing in Education

"Plastics, my boy, plastics."

This 1960s piece of career advice, given to Dustin Hoffman's character in The Graduate, resonates with a new generation of makers and hackers nearly fifty years later. Talk of 3D printers is everywhere—in print, on the web, on television, and now set to arrive in the classrooms of schools, colleges, and universities.

Schools

Across the globe, schools are finding useful ways to incorporate 3D printing in their curricula. Sometimes it is passionate individual teachers that are introducing printers into the classroom, no small sacrifice on a teacher's salary. One story that really impressed me was that of Wayne Caudle, director of technologies at Boaz schools in Alabama. During the replacement of their computer network, none of the mounts that came with the new switches would fit flush to the walls. Caudle was told by a local machine shop that custom made mounts would be between $5 and $8 a piece. For a total of 364 mounts, this would be in the region of $2,000. Instead, he spent the $2,000 on a Makerbot Replicator 2 and printed them out for less than a nickel a piece, ensuring that the machine paid for itself on its very first job.

Leading the charge among manufacturers is Airwolf, who has already helped put 3D printers in many classrooms around the world, from middle and high schools in the United States to universities in the Middle East and trade schools in China.

Figure 100. The Airwolf AW3D V5

Airwolf clearly understands that what is lacking in schools these days are opportunities to apply maths and science to the practical fields of engineering and industrial design. 3D printing creates ways to reengage students with STEM programs (Science-Technology-Engineering-Maths). Even more importantly, it fires imaginations. During the last few decades, many schools gave up their metalworking and woodworking departments for more intellectual career paths. Lathes, mills, drilling machines, and even CNC equipment were let go and sold on, due to a lack of technical capacity in the teaching staff. Hopefully, the introduction of 3D printers can help to reverse this trend, especially as the manufacturing base of a country is unable to expand unless the leaders make a serious investment in education.

This technology assists a wide variety of disciplines. Medical students can fabricate three-dimensional molecular models, architecture majors can create physical representations of their designs, and fine art students can 3D print real life examples of their designs. Just as art students create a portfolio of their work, I wonder how long it will be before we see engineering students assembling portfolios of 3D printed objects to show prospective employers or universities. Will high school students begin including a custom 3D printed object with their applications to engineering colleges to demonstrate their CAD accomplishments and abilities?

These days, few students have the opportunity to take apart automobile engines and it is unlikely that they can take apart an iPod like they could a radio. Designing and printing engine parts in the shop, on the other hand, shows students what the actual inside of an engine looks like. It is very empowering for a young person to actually build something, and it is even more remarkable how prolific they become once they gain the ability to turn their 3D designs into real physical objects.

We have already seen, in both the US and the UK, what happens when we create an excess of MBAs and so called finance whizzes, and then let them loose on the real estate markets.

It is very easy to see the new doors that are being opened in the young minds that are exposed to 3D printing. I read about one class that printed a miniature working catapult to study the physics of velocity. Students in this particular program even showed increased vocabulary. This kind of study also offers the chance to improve spatial intelligence, something that is often overlooked in public education. A 3D printed object held in the hands of the student-designer can bridge the important gap between simple visual perception and three-dimensional spatial visualization. This ability is key to bolstering the current scientific and technical workforce.

This technology can be utilized to bring a great deal of ingenuity into any classroom. Just imagine, for example, a youngster developing an Arduino platform and a case to go around it using a 3D printer, thereby creating a hand-held device to analyze bacteria in the air. Science projects of the future are going to become a whole lot more interesting, thanks to 3D printing.

One of the most important things that youngsters need to learn is about the limitations of their tools. I have talked extensively about this in the previous chapter, explaining that we can design anything you want on the computer, but we do not always have the machines to create it. Another key lesson is that of nomenclature, all the names of those fiddly engineering parts. Knowing what an item looks like is one thing, but figuring out what to call it, so that it can be ordered from a catalog, can be a real challenge.

A recent announcement by the UK Minister of Education stated that all secondary schools (ages eleven and up) will be required to have a 3D printer and introduce children to laser cutters and robotics in the design and technology course. As yet, there has been no indication from where funding for these developments will come.

3D printing is able to help students understand and learn core STEM principles, but it also allows teachers to bring in cheap, easily made visuals that assist the learning process in almost any subject. 3D printing will revolutionize education, empower invention, enable experimentation, and invigorate our rural economy. The technology is perfect for dreamers, tinkerers, inventors, educators, artists, architects, designers, entrepreneurs, and renovators.

Printables enable teachers and students to answer complex questions and demonstrate their answers in three dimensions. They can solve real-world problems by constructing and experimenting with a variety of possible solutions.

Language teachers can print out physical representations of objects rather than simply handing out vocabulary lists. This allows kinaesthetic learners to use their sense of touch as a valuable aid to memory, something that is ignored by most commercial textbooks. Geography teachers can print out topography, demographic, or population maps, while history teachers can print out facsimiles of historical artifacts for classroom examination and discussion. Instead of just showing a picture of a medieval tool or a King's seal, students will be able to handle copies of the actual objects. In science classes, such as biology and chemistry, students will be able to print 3D models of molecules, DNA, bacteria, cells, viruses, and even organs. Complex excel graphs might be easier for accountacy students to read if they were printed in 3D to look like wireframe buildings using cubes of colored resins. Maths students could work on data visualizations that put simple numbers and formulas into tactile form. Students in cookery classes will be able to create all kinds of original molds, and the list just goes on and on. All we need now is for those of us with 3D printers to get into schools and start showing teachers how to make the best use of this technology.

Another manufacturer, Afinia, has teamed with Pitsco Education to make a start by offering an affordable 3D printer combined with curriculum and activity materials. As well as important back up services such as a one-year warranty and telephone support, the package includes a custom designed "3D Printing: Designing and Prototyping: curriculum that includes three weeks of hands-on lessons and activity materials.

Colleges and Universities

A team at Michigan Technology University has begun work on a library of open source printable optics for study in a laboratory setting. In addition to providing the STL files, the authors point out that such printable equipment could make scientific experimentation much more affordable and efficient. At present the cost of outfitting an undergraduate teaching laboratory with thirty optics set ups including a 1 m optical tracks, optical lens, adjustable lens holder, ray optical kit, and viewing screen, costs about $15,000 for commercially available equipment. In comparison, the total cost using the open-source optics approach is about $500, providing over $14,500 in savings.

The study found cost reductions of more than 97 percent, with some components costing only 1 percent of the market price for products of similar function. In addition, commercial suppliers can take weeks to deliver orders. With open source printables, there is no sales tax, shipping costs, or waiting for parts to come into stock. An experimenter may not know so far in advance exactly what type of equipment will be required. Printables solve that problem by making individual pieces completely on demand.

Figure 102. Open source 3D printable lab jack

Experimental science is still severely underfunded in most of the developing world, despite the fact that these regions possess very talented scientists, many of whom have training and theoretical backgrounds that rival the West. These scientists are unfairly economically handicapped by not having access to experimental equipment. It is hoped that this project will inspire others in the

scientific community to create open libraries of objects for other branches of scientific study so that anyone anywhere can study anything easily and affordable.
http://www.plosone.org/article/info%3Adoi%2F10.1371%2Fjournal.pone.0059840

Examples of 3D-printable optical mounts, along with downloadable designs, can be found at http://www.thingiverse.com /jpearce/collections/open-source-optics.

Projects like this are clearly part of a larger effort to democratize education globally. In an age where, even in the West, a college education plunges students into debt for much of the rest of their lives, this situation desperately needs addressing. Corporations are intent on locking down as much information as possible and severely punishing those who attempt to share, leaving home schoolers, independent scholars, and those without the finances to obtain a formal education, in a very difficult situation. While the sharing of educational materials is something that I have covered in a forthcoming book, here I would like to concentrate upon ongoing projects to reduce the costs of physical equipment.

A number of collections are springing up on Thingiverse and Shapeways that bring together budget priced laboratory equipment. www.thingiverse.com/emilyjanedennis/collections/lab-supplies/

This collection currently includes around two dozen useful items ranging from simple tube racks, tube clamps, and gel boxes to USB powered centrifuges and mobile spectrometers. Cathal Garvey, a genetics post-grad at the Cancer Research Centre in Cork, Ireland, has also put a useful listing together.
http://www.thingiverse.com/cathalgarvey/designs/

Figure 103. The old and the new

One of the most active projects in this field is work being conducted on various printable microscopes. This particular example at Thingiverse (http://www.thingiverse.com/thing:77450) requires just four disposable camera lenses and a light source. In this case the designer used a cheap LED wall light from Walmart. When he visited his local photography shop, they were kind enough to give him an entire bag full with which to experiment. (Kudos to this shop http://www.lensandshutter.com/.) His first version boasts a magnification of nearly seventy-four and is already attracting upgrades from other members, including a focus lock (http://www.thingiverse.com/thing:85698) and a smartphone adapter (http://www.thingiverse.com/thing:92355).

Thingiverse user ZombieCat has published designs for a low-cost teaching microscope designed to be built and used by students learning microscopy. This new and improved version features a snap-together design that does not require any glue and costs between $0.40 and $3.50 per microscope, depending on the choice of lenses.

Figure 104. The Zombiecat snap together microscope

A group of engineers at the University of Cambridge is taking the idea even further by developing a budget priced professional microscope based on open-source technologies. Part of the OpenLabTools initiative, aimed at providing a forum and knowledge centre for the development of low-cost and open-access scientific tools, the prototype will cost around $800, whereas conventional microscopes can cost anywhere from $15,000 to $80,000.

The frame is an open beam modular structure, simple to replicate, and easy to adapt and improve upon. Webcams and digital cameras with high levels of magnification and resolution are now commonplace, but the ability to automate the imaging process remains restricted to the most expensive range of microscopes.

This team is using a $25 Raspberry Pi for imaging and image processing, and Arduino controllers for stepper motors to control zoom and focus. Many of the parts such as the frame joints and lens mounts are being printed on a Makerbot. Project supervisor Alexandre Kabla aims to share results and build a community that will progressively make these instruments better.

Figure 106. An antique and the modern OpenLabTools microscope

During the recent LEGO2NANO, the third in a series of China-UK Summer Schools held at Tsinghua University in Beijing, a group of PhD students developed a new type of low-cost scanning probe microscope in just five days, using LEGO and 3D printed parts. Atomic force microscopes are capable of seeing objects only a millionth of a millimeter in size—far smaller than anything an optical microscope can observe. Commercial AFM typically cost $100,000 or more, but the newly designed low-cost version cost less than $500 to produce.

All kinds of hobbyists are turning to 3D printing to see what this exciting new technology can do for them. Despite the fact that digital cameras are almost ubiquitous, a few photographers are rediscovering the enjoyment of going back to basics. Analog die-hards at Lomography's recently released the Konstruktor, a $35 build-it-yourself plastic camera that gives photographers a crash course on camera design. The company has been at the forefront of keeping the 35 mm alive with unique cameras that always seem to bring a new approach to film photography. This one takes one or two hours to build, and needs to be done carefully to avoid any light leaks inside.

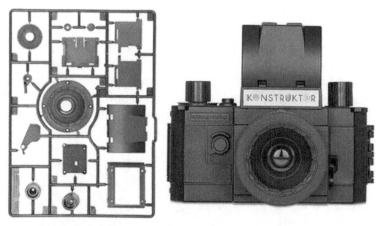

Figure 107. The Konstruktor Do It Yourself SLR camera kit

3D printing technology is also contributing to the development of a new production technique for fully functional photography equipment. The RepRap 3D printer movement has recently fabricated the basic structure of a Canon 5D DSLR, including an attached zoom lens.

Elsewhere, existing 35 mm film devotees have taken up the baton by releasing files for the OpenReflex camera that can be 3D printed with just over $30 worth of parts (minus the film). Saint–Éttiene School of Art and Design graduate, Léo Marius, promises compatibility with any glass lens thanks to a custom lens mount. It has a mirror Viewfinder and a finger activated mechanic shutter (running ~1/60 degrees). All the pieces are easily printable on any recent RepRap-like ABS 3D-printer without using support material. All parts are separate (film receiver, shutter, and viewfinder) to simplify builds and modifications.

Figure 108. The OpenReflex 3D Printed Camera

Visually the 3D printed product bears a striking resemblance to the actual camera.

The current development does not yet incorporate the other needed components and parts such as optics, but many in the 3D printing community believe that the day of homemade, fully-functional cameras is much closer than traditional camera manufacturers would like to believe. Some designers are already 3D printing lenses. To create an "adjustable focus liquid-filled lens" a thin plastic film bladder is stretched between two printed frames and then inflated with water. The water, under pressure, stretches out the plastic and forms a lens shape. Dissolved gas bubbles can be avoided by boiling the water before use and surface imperfections can be removed by using a hair dryer on the plastic film. This is actually rediscovered technology as "inflatable" glasses produced for poorer citizens can still be seen in museums today.

Of course, nobody is claiming that a geeked-out pinhole camera is going to bring the big names to their knees. This is much more about taking a technology and giving back the keys to the users in order for them to understand it again. We all know that it is now possible to pick up a Nikon N90S/F90x, which was a $1,000 camera when it was new for $50, but if there is a satisfaction in taking your own photos, then there must equally be a real sense of achievement in building the camera yourself.

In a separate development, Tekla Labs is an on-line community set up by the University of California which aims to provide DIY guides for making lab equipment as well as linking up researchers, graduate students, and other scientists who already build their own kit.

The team recently carried out a survey of twenty research labs across Latin America. Somewhat surprisingly, only 20 percent said they had a microscope capable of viewing cells, while the remainder said that they needed one and would certainly use one that was built in a local workshop. More than 90 percent said they needed a rotator (used to gently agitate biological samples for long periods of time). Many reported that part of the problem was prohibitively high import costs. Some have benefitted from donations, but this is limited because demand is much greater than supply. In addition, if equipment breaks, repairs are often impossible. Here is an ideal opportunity for 3D printer evangelists to step up to the plate and put their money where their mouth is. I have contacted Tekla and asked them to include details of the most sought after spare parts in their next survey so that we can become involved in this most worthwhile community.

Other equipment that was lacking included incubators, hot plates with a magnetic stirrer, centrifuges, sterilization equipment, and tissue culture hoods, all of which can be built DIY. In Bolivia they found a repurposed record player that now works as a rotator unit used for destaining DNA gels, and a converted kitchen blender working as a tabletop centrifuge. The group is currently working on detailed instructions for constructing a magnetic stirrer costing $25 against $250–$500 for the commercial version, and a $25 rotator that would usually cost $500. The site is currently running a design competition for equipment ideas. My only question is: How do they tell the difference between those participating labs that are academic facilities and those hidden in the jungle that we read about so often in the news? Perhaps the clandestine drug labs are making so much money that they have no need to resort to DIY equipment.

http://www.teklalabs.org/

Despite some exceptional examples, like those detailed above, I have personally become very disillusioned with public education. I have long been an a strong advocate of thinkers such as Ivan Illich and John Taylor Gatto, who point out that modern schools are more about indoctrination and endless memory tests, rather than preparing young minds for the challenges and opportunities of the wider world. The ultimate aim of education should be that which is relevant, engaging, and provides an edge in the global workplace. That is not necessarily the same as coming out at the top of some arbitrary test rankings. I was always taught that a mind is not a vessel to be filled, but a lamp to be ignited.

After studying for a master's degree in education, I spent many years traveling in Asia and teaching a wide range of subjects at a host of different schools and universities. Eventually, I became so disillusioned with the way textbook publishers enforced their monopolies to the detriment of the students, I decided to pursue a different field completely. In most of Asia, for-profit businesses posing as educators are ensuring that the vast majority of students see themselves as miserable failures by the time they leave school, as only a tiny few will ever reach the top ninety-nine percentile in some pointless examination. Always the maverick, I was able to achieve amazing success adapting traditional board games, only to have my results dismissed by administrators who had vested interests in textbooks and expensively administered tests. Even so, I am still convinced that it is practical, hands-on tasks that make for the most effective learning and look forward to the day when I can go back into teaching without the distractions of overpriced text books and irrelevant exams.

I am eagerly anticipating a time when teachers can 3D print tools, visualizations, and realia that are directly linked to the subjects that they are teaching, rather than simply regurgitating a tired textbook. Imagine the possibilities when we are able to print off any board game and then adapt it to the subject being taught. Think about being able to print building materials such as Lego or Meccano. Of course, it will not be a case of dumping a box of toys on the floor and letting kids play. There should always be specific projects with goals and graded assignments, so they can take it seriously and see the point of the exercize. Almost any toy can be integrated in with lessons in maths and physical science. I know of one teacher who works with Lego-Mindstorms in an after school program, where the kids learn all about gear ratios, velocity, energy, power, sensors, and programming, among other things. They also learn about design, teamwork, and project management. We should give students every possible avenue to experience and experiment with whatever we can and let them determine their skills. I think this is where 3D printers will really revolutionize education. Not every child can become a designer, but all of them can benefit from well-equipped teachers that provide hands on, stimulating classes.

It is well known that universities can be extremely stifling and conservative institutions. When the very first commercial computers were made available, staff and faculties initially showed little interest. It was left up to graduate students to experiment and publish their results. Once the incredible benefits of these new machines were made clear, only then did professors begin to take notice. Anybody wanting a leg up in the manufacturing processes of the future should start playing with 3D printers as soon as possible.

Libraries

Chicago Public Library recently announced that it will be investing in three MakerBot Replicator 2 3D printers, two laser cutters, a milling machine and a vinyl cutter, plus a selection of software. Administrators have been amazed at the public's response, saying that the announcement had generated more buzz on social media than any other single event. It seems that everybody is keen to try out the new machines. Teachers, instructors, and even business owners have reportedly been e-mailing the library non-stop to find out how they can get involved. Despite the enthusiasm, libraries are still playing catch up with community-led makerspaces.

My own Makerbot clone, The General, is now a permanent fixture in the Guangzhou Provincial library, busy helping the next generation of designers and inventors bring their ideas to life. I am not saying that everybody should donate their printers to a good cause, but at least think about taking your machine out with you to do a presentation or a workshop on 3D printing. You will be amazed at the diversity of interested attendees. I was expecting an audience of bespectacled geeks just like myself, but you will find that this technology appeals to a wide cross section of society. I have been surprised to see successful business people mingling with enthusiastic teenagers and even a goodly sprinkling of those being women, many stylish and easily identified as artistic. Such presentations might even become the profitable niche that you are looking for. While you might not be a CADCAM expert, perhaps your communication skills will put you in demand as a much sought after speaker on a tech subject that everybody has heard is moving onward and upward, to take the world by storm.

Creating a 3D printing Jeopardy game for the classroom or lecture hall is an excellent way to ensure that students of any age or nationality are motivated while reviewing a content area. If it is good enough for all the uber-hackers at DefCon 20, then it is good enough for us. Students will problem solve as a group to find answers to many challenging questions, which will allow individuals to benefit from the knowledge of the group.

A jeopardy template is relatively easy to create using either Microsoft's PowerPoint or cardboard cut out frames and once this board is created it can easily be adapted to any study subject. Explain a few basic rules and then launch into the actual game play.

Preparation

Organize the content into four or five topics. For example, at the end of a brief lecture on the subject of 3D printing, I presented five topic subjects: history, companies, techniques, pioneers, and products. I then wrote six questions under each topic, ranging in difficulty from easy to hard. I had previously used this template on many occasions during my teaching career, and so I was very confident that it would go over well as an activity.

If you are creating the template in PowerPoint, then here are some detailed instructions:

1. Type your content topic in the first slide text box.
2. Select "New Slide" from the Home menu. Select the "Insert Table" icon on the slide. Input the number of columns, which corresponds with the number of subtopics, and the number of rows, which corresponds with the number of questions for each subtopic, for your Jeopardy game. Stretch the table to full screen.
3. Enter subtopics in the top text box of each column.
4. Click on "Shapes" in the "Home" menu bar. Select a shape for the action button. Insert this shape into each cell on the table. Right click on the shape in the first cell. Select "Edit Text." Enter the point value for the question in the column. Repeat this for all the shapes on the table.
5. Click "New Slide" from Home menu. Enter the first question in the text box of the new slide. Select "Shapes" in the "Home" menu bar. Scroll down to the "Action Buttons" and select "Action Button: Return." Click "OK" on "Action Setting" pop-up. Repeat this process for each question of the game.
6. Return to the main game board slide with the table. Right click on the first point value button. Select "Hyperlink." Click on "Place in this document." Select the corresponding question. Click "OK." Repeat for all point value buttons.

If you are not familiar with PowerPoint, then an easy alternative would be to hire a freelancer on a micro-tasking site like Fiverr.com to take care of this for you.

Gameplay

Depending on the size of your audience, either select volunteers to play or divide the room into suitably sized groups. If going the group route, explain that each member will take a turn as the group's spokesperson, changing for every topic. Allow this spokesperson to choose the topic and point value the group will attempt to answer correctly. If using PowerPoint, click on the requested point value action button to reveal the question. Read the question as if you are the game-show host. Allow each group time to discuss together what the correct answer may be. Call on the group's spokesperson to explain the group's answer. If the answer is correct, tally the point value for the group. If the answer is incorrect, immediately call on the next group to answer. Do not allow further discussion time, ensuring that each group will be highly motivated to discuss the correct answer for each question posed. Call on the spokesperson for the next group to choose a topic and point value. Continue playing until all questions have been asked. Tally the points and declare the winner.

If possible, have some prizes for the winners, but do not let them know until the activity is over. I considered having 3D printed items as prizes, but eventually settled on chocolates instead, as printables tend to be highly customized items that can be difficult to match to a varied audience. Chocolates, on the other hand, are appreciated by nearly everybody.

Makerspaces

The influence of the modern economy has transformed many educational institutions into businesses that simply pose as schools and universities. Hackerspaces, fablabs, and makerspaces are interesting twenty-first-century alternatives for people seeking a more hands-on experience. They have been described as technological fitness clubs, where members pay monthly membership dues for access to a space and the equipment within it, to work on projects either individually or as a collaborative effort. Makerspaces generally attract people with the necessary skill-sets to assemble, use, and troubleshoot 3D printers currently on the market today. They also possess the skill-sets needed to build 3D printers and other computer-controlled manufacturing systems. Many host monthly workshops that help new people develop basic skills like soldering and programming, or 3D design. There are even group builds where purchased 3D printer kits are constructed with the guidance of a resident expert. Members benefit not only from access to expensive equipment that the average person is unlikely to own, but also from the connections that form when working alongside others.

Such collaboration reinvigorates local economies, solves local problems, and generally improves the lives in the community in an independent and self-sufficient fashion. MakerBot's first 3D printer, the CupCake CNC, grew out of collaborations that began at the NYC

Resistor hackerspace in New York City. At the Noisebridge hackerspace in San Francisco, members have even challenged NASA by launching a balloon to the edge of space that will take high-definition photos and video.

A makerspace can start with just a single table and a few chairs. Shared equipment brought in by individual members can be used during weekend get-togethers with friends. This alone can quickly develop into a full-fledged organization with hundreds of members and global reach.

For more information on existing hackerspaces, the wiki below is filled with useful information including a directory of the thousands of spaces that are already in existence.
http://hackerspaces.org/wiki/

For those seeking inspiration to start their own hackerspace, "Hackerspaces: The Beginning is an free 108-page ebook which chronicles the creation, challenges, and successes of hackerspaces around the world.
http://www.bibliotecapleyades.net/archivos_pdf/hackerspaces_the_beginning.pdf

The Makerspace Workbench: Tools, Technologies, and Techniques for Making by Adam Kemp is a great new book that shows how to design and organize an environment to provide a safe and fun workflow, as well as demonstrating how that space can be used to educate.

These locally-organized institutions allow ordinary people to work directly on advanced modern technology—ranging from computers and 3D printers to synthetic biology and home-brew survey drones. The democratization of this technology is of absolute importance to prevent an increasingly dangerous technological divide between special interests and the masses. For far too long, corporate-financiers have used their monopolies and unwarranted power to influence society unfairly. Many of the largest corporations would have been shuttered and out of business long ago had there not been immense bailouts from ordinary taxpayers. It will be interesting to see if distributed manufacturing can do anything to level the playing field.

Lightning bolt breakthroughs often come from the most extraordinary of places, which is one reason that we should be working on lower cost educational equipment for citizens of the developed world. I look forward to the day when mathematicians at Oxford receive mail from a remote Indian village with solutions for equations that nobody has ever been able to solve. Genius is a sneaky quality that can reside in the most unlikely places.

PART II

Extrapolations: What to Expect Next

Appendices

9

Introduction II

As far back as the 1970s, Isaac Asimov predicted that we would have molecular replicators, essentially 3D printers with molecular precision, by the year 2040. Looking at the state of current technology, his prediction might arrive even earlier than he expected. This is a very exciting time in manufacturing. Machines are suddenly becoming more intelligent than the people operating them. Technology is morphing over time and unexpected convergences constantly usher in completely new use-cases. The concept of an Internet of Things and even an Internet of Everything is slowing making its way into the mainstream consciousness, where connected objects and devices will change the very fabric of society. Automated fabrication will have profound effects on mechanics and bio mechanics. This, in turn, will have world-changing impact because of its enormous capacity to stimulate the collective imagination.

The technology is changing so quickly that making any kind of accurate prediction is difficult. I hope that the following chapters will fire your imagination and open your mind to see many of the possibilities that could be just around the corner. I hope that it will motivate some of you to become directly involved and actually be the changes that others are anticipating. At the very least, I hope that it will offer you a number of different perspectives on the possible outcomes that we could all be facing

10

DLP Printers and More Useful Tools

If 3D printers continue to grow in popularity, it is quite possible that the market for ABS plastic products might start to become saturated, especially if all those printers start connecting over the Internet and sharing jobs internationally. Fortunately, plastic is not the only medium that can be 3D printed, and so it might be a wise move to investigate some of the other mediums and methods that are likely to become available over the next few years. Most enterprise-level printers remain out of the reach of ordinary individuals, but this cannot last forever. Pete Basiliere of Gartner Research recently released a report predicting that enterprise-class 3D printers will be available for less than $2,000 by 2016. The key factors driving the price down are the technology's potential for slashing costs and innovation in 3D printing hardware and software. Sales of industrial-grade printers have been on a steep journey upwards. Machines with an average price tag of $73,000 have risen 31 percent in the last twelve months, which might mean that will soon more and more used models on the second-hand market.

Looking at the performance of plastic extrusion printers, it is clear that prices have dropped precipitously in the last three years. In the image below, the model on the left is the Venetian Lion by Tony Buser printed by Prusajr on a $550 RepRap Prusa; on the right is the same model printed on a $17,000 Stratasys uPrint+.

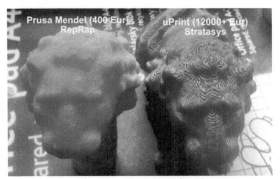

Figure 1. The Venetian Lion by Tony Buser

I cannot put it better than this long time 3D printing enthusiast who has been involved in the industry for more than twenty years:

"The first seventeen-years were exciting—the last three have been amazing. The next ten will be mind blowing. I genuinely believe we are just scratching the surface in terms of uses and applications."

In the field of FDM 3D printers, new designs are being announced all the time. Some of the more interesting entries into the market are moving away from the traditional gantry systems and onto more interesting SCARA (Selective Compliance Assembly Robot Arm) designs. These machines are based on a single pedestal mounting point, a significant improvement in design, bringing with it much greater speed. A good example is the RobotFactory (http://www.robotfactory.it/) where the print head moves only in the Z direction. The build platform itself rotates and moves along the X- and Y-axes, allowing for much greater speed to be achieved by the stable Z-print head. The downside is that this type of design is still much more expensive, and the controlling software far more complex.

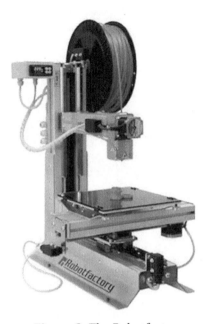

Figure 2. The Robotfactory

It is likely that we will see a lot more commercial SCARA designs in the future, especially now that the open source RepRap Morgan has been vindicated with the $20,000 Gada Prize for Interim Personal Manufacturing. The prize is awarded for simplifying 3D printer design. As we have already seen with more than a dozen threaded rods to be coupled together at various angles using pre-printed brackets and very precise spacing, it can take a newcomer months to assemble one, even with all the parts provided. The Morgan, on the other hand, uses a simple stand made out of any stiff plastic tubing and offcuts of wood, incorporating such economy of design that even the semicircle of "waste" from the stand is used as the Z-axis top plate that is raised and lowered. The majority of the build uses 3D printed parts, including the arms, drive gears, and mounting brackets in a print, snap, and tighten assembly process, for a total materials cost (excluding build platform) of less than $100. The vitamins include the RAMPS 1.4 chosen for its low cost and ease of availability.

Figure 3. The RepRap Morgan

Describing himself as a self-taught hacker from Centurion, just north of Johannesburg in South Africa, Quentin Harley, the designer of the Morgan, is a softly-spoken Siemens engineer and a member of a local makers collective, House4Hack. This is a great example of distributed manufacturing leading to new approaches and ideas. Harley had real problems locating 3D printer parts in South Africa and rather than following traditional designs, he was forced to make something from scratch. "We're just building the tools," he says. "What's really exciting is the thought of putting these things in the hands of people who live in the townships and seeing what they can do with them."

http://reprap.harleystudio.co.za

There is already talk of creating a female counterpart for this new machine. Lilian Vaughan Morgan was the real life spouse of T. H. Morgan and, as it turns out, was a geneticist in her own right, finding time for her profession while also managing her famous husband's affairs so that he could focus on his own work. This means that Lilian will be an even cleaner, simpler multitasking version of Morgan. At the moment, there is talk of the Lilian being able to print two or even three identical parts at the same time using additional arms, with each extruder slaved together mechanically, offering three printers for the price of one. In addition, we are likely to see dual extruders for support structures and auto-eject/continuous printing. And perhaps even a built in scanner if current trends are anything to go by.

OpenBeams are open source extrusion profile beams made from aluminum that offer much higher stability at relatively low cost. http://www.kickstarter.com/projects/ttstam/openbeam-an-open-source-miniature-construction-sys

This technology is starting to see broader adoption with a number of groups working on OpenBeam mendels and rostocks. The first commercial printer to features extrusion profile beams is the Felix (http://www.felixprinters.com/)

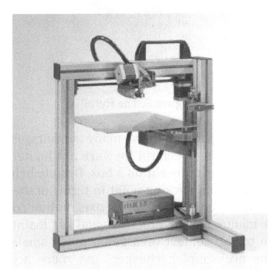

Figure 4. The Felix

Hyrel 3D in Alpharetta, Georgia already offers "hot-swappable" nozzles. This means that a user could print a prototype in plastic, then switch to printing the real thing in clay, Plasticine, or even wax. Founder, Karl Gifford explained the significance of this development by referring to a 3D print of a mushroom. Instead of printing in PLA supported by PVA which requires a hot water bath to remove, the Hyrel could print in clay with wax supports. Once the clay dries, it can be heated up and the wax just flows away. The added benefit is that the wax is easily reusable on the next print. Hyrel also offers a food and dishwasher safe nozzle made of Teflon that can be used for anything from chocolate to peanut butter. Imagine being able to print gourmet chocolates with a full range of extrudable fillings from coconut milk caramel to sapadillo sorbet.

Figure 5. The Hyrel

Robotic arm 3D printers have many advantages for printing larger objects, and being freeform they are not limited to the layer-by-layer approach of printing within a box. Despite being common in manufacturing, the main sticking point in terms of their adoption in 3D printing is the expense involved. Six-axis motion control requires a much higher manufacturing precision, and has maintenance issues over time due to the contact area being much smaller. At present gantry systems are simpler, cheaper, and more accurate than a robotic arm, especially for linear motion.

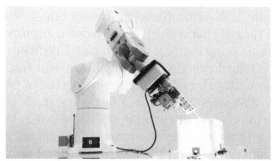

Figure 6. Robotic arm printing

It was hoped that the Baccus open-source robotic arm project, with its USB interface and improved anchoring would bring prices down significantly, but after failing to reach its Kickstarter goals, it is unclear where exactly the next affordable six-degrees of freedom robot arm will come from.

Another problem is that robotic arms are typically viewed as less safe than gantry designs because they can swing rapidly in any direction and therefore require some type of cage or shield. Over the last couple of years we have seen a number of hacks and adaptations of industrial robotic arms into 3D printers by artists and architects. These have shown that it is not so much the robot as it is the heavy industrial environment that is the dangerous factor. In the meantime, robotic arms will certainly make 3D printing affordable by allowing large-scale manufacturers to automate repetitive labor operations when their factories become larger and more automated. We will soon be seeing 3D printers assembled by machines, rather than being laboriously hand built in Brooklyn.

It will not be long now before the big printer brands begin muscling in on this market. The CEO of HP, Meg Whitman, recently announced that they would be launching a 3D printer in 2014, but after the mess that she made of eBay while she was in charge, I will not be holding my breath. At the moment, I am waiting for Kyocera to bring out a printer, as that will be something definitely worth waiting for.

Direct Light Processing (DLP) Printers

DLP printers use a process known as stereo-lithography, whereby a UV laser (usually operating at a wavelength of between 365nm and 420nm) is focussed into a reservoir of a catalyzed acrylic monomer, using a highly detailed dimensional program. The laser polymerizes the liquid into a hard plastic (rather like those quick hardening fillings at the dentist), and is then built up in amazingly intricate layers to form the item desired. Other users have described the FFF printers such as the Makerbot as a stalagmite machine where the material is built up in layers while these DLP printers are stalactite makers, where the object hangs from a platform that slowly moves up a micron at a time. Stereo-lithography, also known as photo lithography, is an extremely precise method capable a going down as far as 100nm.

The most well-known DLP printer at the moment is the FormLabs Form 1. Originally a Kickstarter project, the company asked for a measly $100,000, but it ended up with over $2.9 million in backing.

There was a minor hitch when 3D Systems hit them with a patent infringement lawsuit and also accused Kickstarter of promoting infringing products, but this has now been settled and the first units were shipped in May of 2013.

Figure 7. The FormLabs Form 1

Even experienced printers will find the Form 1 to be an extremely impressive machine. The prints, resin cost ($149 per litre and currently only available in clear), and machine cost soon add up, but it is well worth the investment if you are working in a design lab or engineering environment. At a cost of $3,299, the Form 1 is only $1,000 more than the Makerbot Replicator 2. Formlabs have leapfrogged above and beyond other home and open source printers, but at a price that is within the reach of many hobbyists and small businesses. It cannot match up to some of the more expensive enterprise level machines just yet, but it is certainly a step in the right direction and it is about as close as you can get without sending your designs off to Shapeways.

The complete Form 1 kit consists of the printer, some bottles of liquid photocurable resin, and a cleaning station. In optical stereolithography, cleaning is necessary to remove uncured residue. With the Form 1, this involves two minutes of agitation in an isopropyl alcohol bath, followed by ten minutes of soaking. Be sure to handle uncleaned parts using gloves to avoid getting the resin on your skin. Having a vat of highly flammable isopropyl so close to potential heat sources can be a little unnerving, especially when printing in schools or a home.

The orange-colored shield protects eyes from stray laser light, while also protecting the photosensitive resin from ambient light. Lifting the cowling reveals a build plate hanging over a lucite tank that holds enough resin for a few dozen smaller prints. It houses a build space of 4.9 x 4.9 x 6.5 inches. This is quite tall, but certainly not as wide as the Makerbot's 11.2 x 6.0 x 6.1 inch platform. Even so, the smoothness and level of detail is the machine's main selling point. As I have discussed elsewhere, smaller objects can be assembled into larger items at a later stage.

The printer is whisper-quiet, its only sound being a regular clicking as the laser cures the resin, and the tank tilts focus on the next layer. Other users have compared it to a slow, soothing trance track, while the Makerbot outputs a jagged industrial breakbeat. Additionally there is no apparent odor, meaning that you can have the machine set up in a bedroom and still sleep comfortably while it prints.

Figure 8. Unsurpassed DLP detail

The Form 1 includes a print management software package called "Preform" that runs on an STM32 32-bit ARM Cortex-M3 microcontroller. It has been described as intuitive and easy to use, allowing users to place multiple objects on the platform, duplicate, scale, and rotate. There is even an auto-orient feature that suggests optimal orientation for supports based upon a DFM analysis. FormLabs has now introduced a Mac-compatible version of its PreForm software. The PreForm 0.8.4 release also contains automatic mesh repair, which integrates software from Netfabb.

The objects that come out of the Form 1 look as if they are the result of injection molding or other high-quality manufacturing processes. With a layer height of 25 microns, items come out of the machine looking as solid as any factory-produced item. Print times can be slow for high-resolution prints. A two-inch high chess piece, for example, takes about six hours to complete, although printing at ⬚lower⬚ resolution causes the print times to fall drastically.

For die hard DIYers, Tristram Budel has published plans for a homemade DLP printer over at the Instructables site. The design is based upon a commonly available Acer projector with a resolution of 1920 x1080 pixels. These projectors work by passing a light source through a rotating color wheel and actuated micromirrors to form the image. The higher the resolution, the smaller the feature size, while a high contrast ratio gives a higher resolution with less light contamination. The illumination intensity, also known as the luminous flux, describes the amount of photons per unit of time and controls the cure time. The main downside of DLPs is the cost of resin. An initial filling of the resin bath on some SLA DLP printers will cost \$6,000 to \$8,000. And we complain about ink cartridge replacement! Two popular suppliers for DIY enthusiasts are Spotamaterials and Bucktownpolymers.

http://www.instructables.com/id/DIY-high-resolution-3D-DLP-printer-3D-printer/

For those who are seriously interested in having a bash at building their own DLP printer, perhaps the most useful resource is a Yahoo Group which can be signed up for here: diy_3d_printing _and_fabrication-subscribe@yahoogroups.com. In this group there are dozens of members from all over the world attempting to build their own versions of the DLP technology.

Figure 9. The impressive results of a DIY DLP printer

Some are using projectors, while others are experimenting with

LCD panels. Another useful site is ProjectorCentral.com which brings together reviews and information for projectors, screens, and related equipment as well as an interesting used projector section.

Resin

While many people are looking forward to the introduction of new SLA machines, an equally important factor in the evolution of this technology is that of good, affordable resin. This area of development has its own unique hurdles, starting with the creation of a suitable formula, as polymer-chemistry is still a hugely complicated area of study. Suppliers of the raw chemical ingredients are usually huge industrial corporations with little interest in talking to hobbyist inventors. Most production plants are vast industrial complexes, where even an order of a hundred kilos makes little economic sense. Even if they are willing to talk, buying in realistic quantities at a reasonable price is more than a challenge. Many people have the garage space to develop a DLP printer, but who has the room to store huge drums of industrial chemicals, or even the capital to purchase them?

Fortunately, there are enthusiasts out there designing new resins from the bottom up, not just modifying the gunk that the dentist uses to fill your cavities, or that surfers use to build their boards. These guys are creating resins with properties that fit the purpose of being used on DLP printers. The main advantages of such an approach are that mechanical solutions are not required to solve the shortcomings of the resin and that the price will be far better than anything currently on the market.

Since the early 1990s, UV reactive resin has been produced in large quantities for the furniture industry, mainly for use in finishing the kind of panel furniture seen in stores like Ikea. Basically, it is created from a base monomer, a photo-initiator that acts as a catalyst to harden the resin, and then pigments for coloring, with clear being the cheapest and solid white being the most expensive. This recipe is then tweaked depending on the needs of the customer, whether it is rolled or sprayed, and, of course, UV lamp setups. Of course, this does not mean that there will not be more hurdles to overcome in the future, such as high shipping costs for end users and greedy distributors who triple the price.

Hopefully, any specially designed 3D printer formula will be released under an Open Source License, so that the small DIY printers can make it for themselves and large industrial concerns can obtain it under a "Commercial License," selling it at a price that reflects their huge economies of scale. Of course, there will always be a few guys out there that will prefer to nip down to their local dentist supply store whenever they run out of resin.

The Peachy Printer

The Peachy Printer, developed by a hacker space in Saskatchewan, has been advertised as the world's most affordable 3D printer, although strictly speaking that it is not completely true. This is not a $100 printer, but a $100 mechanism. Even then there were only a few $100 pledges available and now only a few $400 pledges remain. The fully-assembled Peachy Printer Pro, complete with a litre of resin, is actually $1,000 with an estimated delivery time of August 2014.

Figure 10. The Peachy Printer

Despite the hype, the Peachy is still a very interesting open source photo-lithographic printer with a number of refreshingly imaginative solutions. Even though it is not completely clear what is included in the kit package, it is great to see first Form 1 do an order of magnitude cost reduction, and now these guys doing more than an order of magnitude again.

In an interesting twist, the team has created a piece of Blender add-on software that extracts data from a 3D model and translates it into an audio waveform. This is then played to the printer via the headphone jack to drive a pair of electromagnetic mirrors. The higher the volume, the higher the voltage and the greater the movement of the mirrors which in turn reflect and control the path of the laser beam used to draw out the X- and Y-axes of the object.

Refreshing as this approach may be, it has already drawn plenty of criticism. Doubters say that sound cards to drive the mirrors only saves $5–$10 and that a USB connection would be preferable. One potential problem might lie with relying on a sound card with only two channels. This means that one channel is for the X-axis and the other for the Y-axis. What is really needed is a third channel to turn the laser on and off, otherwise it will like drawing with an Etch-a-Sketch because the laser never turns off. In addition, now that laser printers are a commodity item, a rotating, multifaceted mirror on a motor combined with a precision-tilting mechanism might have been a better option. Despite these minor quibbles, it is still good to see radical approaches.

Another feature of the Peachy is that it uses a drip system to control the level of the resin on the Z-axis to determine the height of the object. Salt water in the top container siphons down to a drip feed that passes through two contact points creating an electrical connection that is detected by the microphone jack which then calculates the resultant level of the resin. The drip then continues into the reservoir, where it causes the resin floating above it to rise.

Saltwater is needed to make the simple drop counter work since it relies on the conductivity of the water. Even so. salt water might not be the best match for electronics and metal parts, not to mention the risk of electrocution. Some pundits have suggested using sugar water to achieve a higher density liquid, or even glycerin water mixtures in environments where flies and ants could be an issue. Whatever the case, this idea still represents massive saving, just by the fact that instead of having to fill large vats with fifty litres of expensive resin, users can now fill up with salt water and then just float one litre of resin on the top. It will be interesting to see how they overcome the problems of accidentally knocking the machine, or the possibility that vibrations could cause inaccuracies by moving the floating resin. It has also been reported that the SubG+ resin priced at $45 a litre, is a rather unpleasant and hazardous material.

The team openly admits that the Peachy Printer is not yet at the final product stage and this is why they are raising funds, in order to complete its last leg of design and manufacturing.
http://www.kickstarter.com/projects/117421627/the-peachy-printer-the-first-100-3d-printer-and-sc

Although a great deal of development work is currently being carried out on DLP type projectors, now that major advances are being made in related fields, it will be very interesting to see what happens with LCD, LcOS, and narrow spectrum LED source micro projectors.

Laser Sintering

In February 2014, a number of Selective Laser Sintering (SLS) key patents that currently prevent competition in the market for the most advanced and functional 3D printers, will expire. That said, there are of course twenty years and thousands of improved and derivative follow-up patents related to SLS that will not be expiring in 2014. These will unfortunately continue to block many from the market, and enrich lawyers for many years to come. Even so, the material toughness available to household skunkworks will be going up exponentially. SLS uses a laser to melt particles of powder together. It is faster, cheaper, and often creates more finished-looking parts, since it does not require supports. Because of its high resolution in all three dimensions, laser sintering can produce goods that typically do not require sanding or other finishing processes, and can be sold as finished products. SLS printers can work in many materials, like nylon, metals, and molded polystyrene (the plastic found in CD jewel cases).

An example of a low-cost open source laser sintering 3D printer is the Adderfab. Professor Mark Ganter and his students at the University of Washington have taken the entire X-carriage from a commercial Lexmark Z735 inkjet printer to create an open architecture, powder-based 3D printer, that applies an organic binder to a multi-mode sugar powder. Featuring three powder chambers, the carriage and print head motion is controlled by stock hardware and software, with only minor hardware modifications. Apart from being easily reproducible, printing occurs layer-by-layer, thereby providing its own support material. This technology will allow the printing of materials such as ceramic or glass. Having a powder printer and an extrusion based printer together enables the creation of items that are assembled from parts printed in multiple materials.

On the downside, the process is very messy and requires dedicated equipment to vacuum up the residue, as well as cleaning and finishing the printed object.

Figure 11. The Adderfab

In a separate project, Professor Jordan Miller's lab at Rice University is sintering wax on an SLS printer that will hopefully become cheap to make, cheap to use, and far more accurate in the future.

http://opensls.tumblr.com/about

Other enthusiasts are already working on metal powder machines and claim that many of the necessary subsystems have already been developed for different purposes. All they need to do now is assemble those subtechnologies into a compact, modular, user-friendly design. The team at Metalbot conceptualized a DIY metal printer the size of a small fridge. A commercial ESOSint DMLS Printer still costs about $680,000, but just five years ago an FDM machine was $15,000 and now they are down to $300. Similar price decreases have been witnessed in the open source drone community. Thanks to increased activity in the medical, aerospace, and orthopaedic industries, 3D metal printing is growing at an even brisker pace than plastic printing. Medical companies in Europe are using AM to produce metal orthopaedic implants in the tens of thousands. Perfect bone replacements can be printed in titanium, so that the section touching live tissue or bone is porous and can interface easily with the body. This is called titanium osseo-integration. EOS has reported that their sintered titanium parts are actually stronger than forged equivalent parts. Another common use for laser sintering machines is to make dental crowns out of cobalt chrome powder.

Aerospace companies are putting a lot of resources into qualifying materials and certifying new designs, as well as making the process faster and less costly. SLS has a major advantage over casting and billet CNC machining in that the build integrity can be verified, something that is essential for high integrity components.

Porosity in casting can be overcome, but requires complex techniques such as de-gassing with aluminum, or complicated mold designs with vents, feeders, and risers to reduce atmospheric air pockets and eliminate mold imperfections. Software such as PrintRite3D allows real-time monitoring layer by layer. As AM advances, some metal parts are becoming so complicated and so geometrically intricate that any other method of post-production inspection simply is not effective.

Open source enthusiasts at MetalicaRap (http://reprap.org /wiki/MetalicaRap) and Metalbot (http://www.metalbot.org/) are experimenting with metal sintering. Direct metal printing is still quite rare, and most of the metal models that we have seen are actually powdered metal with an epoxy binder, where a laser sinters a very fragile foam model that must be baked in a kiln and then backfilled with a filler metal such as bronze.

One Direct Laser Sintering machine is the The Matsuura (EOS and Arcam are also big players), which spreads a layer of very fine metal powder in a tray and then uses a 400W YAG laser to melt each particle. This builds up layers twenty micrometers at a time, after which a squeegee type head spreads another fine layer of powdered metal and the process repeats. The Matsuura is also a five axis machining center and, after a fixed number of passes, it goes back over the laser sintered part and cleans it up with a miniature end mill.

The open source communities are experimenting with a number of different approaches in the hope of fabricating full density parts from aluminum, titanium, stainless steel, and nickel alloys in the very near future. The first involves interfacing a regular laser engraver with a slicer program. The engraver would then need to be placed inside an inert gas frame (metal powder in a non-inert atmosphere has a tendency to self ignite and explode) along with a powder roller and a Z-axis. The roller method means that there is no need for complex mechanisms to drop a precision amount of powder. Any excess simply falls into a recycle box at the end. This would mean that the Metalbot would only cost slightly more than a metal engraver. The bad news is that even the cheapest Chinese engravers with 50W/75W Yag lasers still cost anywhere from $5,000 to $20,000. The other main costs will be a gas (argon or nitrogen) tight frame and the fabrication of a high precision powder system that can spread powder layers of 30um.

Another option being considered would be to rig a five-axis head with a MIG welder and then changing the wire size for the resolution desired versus speed. The head essentially builds the workpiece out of weld bead, which would be much faster than direct metal laser sintering, but would have a very coarse resolution.

Using high-voltage electricity to melt metal is preferable to a plasma torch where the compressed gas has an annoying tendency to blow away all the powder. Theoretically, this could be solved by gluing the powder together first with a glue much weaker than the weld produced by the torch. SLS machines usually have heated build volumes, to prevent warping. The laser only raises the temperature a few degrees to transition it from solid to molten. The power requirements on the laser therefore may be a lot lower than one would expect. While a 250 watt CO_2 laser will cut 5 mm steel, a small build volume the size of a minibar might only require a 90 watt laser that could bring the price down as low as $1,500. While there are still barriers such as reflective disruption resonance and heat dissipation to overcome, there is already a great deal of open source software available covering each aspect of the DMLS machine operation, but the breakthrough will be in tying it all together into an efficient package.

While additive manufacturing is making all the headlines, it is well worth looking at the impressive developments that are taking place in the CNC community. There was a time when CNC technology was only affordable to the largest manufacturers. Hobby CNC machines have grown by leaps and bounds over the last few years, and are now coming within the reach of even the smallest machine shops.

For the time being, there remains some animosity between traditional machinists and 3D printing enthusiasts. CNCs have long been complicated, expensive tools that require a PhD in mechanical engineering, a second mortgage, and a lot of hard-earned experience. For this reason alone, there is a tendency for CNC machinists to come across as hypercritical, grumpy old curmudgeons who look down their noses at what they consider to be distinctly inferior AM techniques. Some even claim that 3D printing is a form of heresy. While it is true that 3D printing is a much younger technology, the CNC milling market is still lagging behind in terms of the technologies used, the aesthetics of the machines, and their user friendliness. The tools are five years or more behind 3D printing in terms of ease of use (partly because CNC is an order of magnitude more complex), but this is a field on the brink of a consumer reinvention, just like 3D printing. I do hope that we will be able to overcome some of the generational snobbery and that the two groups can work together. After all, we are all makers, whatever our experience, techniques, or motivations.

Computer-controlled milling machines and lathes are very important and flexible fabrication devices, and prices are coming down nearly as fast as they are in 3D printing. Computer-controlled laser cutters, numerically-controlled milling machines for making big parts, sign cutters, and precision milling machines are all extremely useful pieces of equipment. Tools with CNC variants include, but are not limited to the following: plasma cutters, drills, wood routers, sheet metal turret punchers, wire benders, hot-wire foam cutters, water jet cutters, surface and cylindrical grinders, submerged welders, knife cutters and glass cutters. CNCzone.com is one of the most active manufacturing forums on the Internet and an amazing resource for further research, although Practical Machinist claims to be the largest manufacturing technology forum on the web.

In the meantime, I have space enough to cover just a handful of the very latest and most interesting CNC developments.

The Inventables company sells the Shapeoko desktop CNC milling machine kits that are capable milling plastics, woods, and soft non-ferrous metals such as aluminum and brass. The machines are sold in kit form and require between three and five hours of self-assembly. Prices range from $225 for a basic mechanical kit designed for experts interested in adding their own electronics or making serious modifications, to $999 for a premium 220V Kit that includes all mechanical and electrical components, stepper cable, waste board, assembly tools, and a spindle. In true open source fashion, every nut, every bolt, and every belt is fully documented with part numbers and vendor list.

Figure 12. The Shapeoko desktop CNC milling machine

Popular software includes MakerCAM, Google Sketchup, Autodesk 123D, and TinkerCAD to create 2D part files, as well as a growing number of dxf files that are downloadable from repositories such as Thingiverse.

PocketNC P5

The result of a three-year, four-prototype development effort of husband and wife team Matt and Michelle Hertel (who also happen to be a machinist and mechanical engineer), the five-axis PocketNC P5 is getting ready for market. Five-axis technology has long been available in the industry, but is only just starting to reach levels affordable to hobbyists and home users.

Figure 13. The PocketNC P5

At the recent NY Maker Faire, the P5 spent the weekend machining compound curve turbine wheels out of delrin, a job that is impossible for a three-axis CNC. The P5's two extra axes allow for extremely complex parts to be created in one setup, with the cutting tool moving in the X- and Z-axes while the part itself simultaneously moves in the Y-, A-, and B-axes. This little gem has high precision linear car and rail systems that can travel in increments of 0.0005 and can mill plastic, aluminum steel, and even titanium, all for around $3,000. In addition, it makes a fantastic crystal cutter/polisher and will undoubtedly be very popular with jewelers for cutting waxes. The millable volume is 5 inches in diameter and 4 inches in height and the developers are hoping to add a quick-change tooling system to future machines.

The biggest drawback to five-axis machines is always the programming side. The addition of 4/5 axis programming to CAM software is expensive, with professional software such as Siemens NX and solidCAM from SolidWorks costing in excess of $10,000. Then there is the time spent in learning how to use it properly. The P5 uses a modified Synthetos TinyG board for stepper control. Every sliding axis is on a ball slide, but as of yet it is still unclear whether they plan to offer an affordable five axis continous CAM solution to go with it. CNC-toolkit http://www.cnc-toolkit.com/ is open source and deals with four or more axis. LinuxCNC is also free, but is only a machine controller, not a complete CAM solution. It interprets G-code, plans the axis movements, and executes them. Producing a five-axis G-code from a 3D model can be a real headache. Many enthusiasts are pinning their hopes on Kokopelli, a new piece of code that performs CAD creation in python, but will also generate five-axis G-code. https://github.com/mkeeter/kokopelli

A relatively inexpensive and painless route into the CNC field is the MyDIYCNC Desktop CNC Machine, delivered completely built, tested, and ready for computer connection at just $795. With a work area 7 inches (178 mm) x 13 inches (330 mm) x 3.7 inches (94 mm) and a step resolution of 0.00025 inches (0.00635 mm) per step, this is great introductory machine that includes FabCAM CNC software for PC, Mac, or Linux systems as well as full instructions.

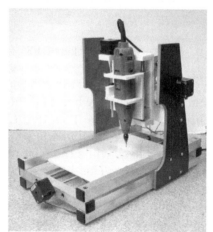

Figure 14. The MyDIYCNC Desktop CNC Machine

The Othermill is a high-density, polyethylene computer controlled mill designed especially for makers who want to cut custom circuit boards that will fit 3D printed parts and produce smart objects, such as wearable circuits and quadcopter electronics. The fully assembled machine is compact, clean, and quiet enough for use at home, yet is precise enough to cut a 10 mm trace and space on FR-1 PCB stock for high level electrical and mechanical prototyping work. Priced at $1,399, the project reached its crowd-funding goal of $50,000 in less than twenty-four hours. The machine comes out of a small incubator and research lab called Otherlab that is housed in a converted organ factory in San Francisco. http://www.otherlab.com/projects.html

Figure 15. The Othermill

While Othermill is optimized for cutting circuit boards, any tool with a 1/8-inch shank can be attached, including all Dremel and Foredom Flex-Shaft accessories. This means that it will also cut metal, wood, wax, and plastic, and so can be used for engraving, routing, and milling 3D shapes. It can create complex and beautiful jewellry out of materials that are as varied as brass and birch. It also cuts machining wax that can then be filled with silicone to make molds. The designers have been making chocolate and ice molds, but it could also be used to make figurines, jewellry, or even cast precision parts.

It uses an open source firmware motion controller known as TinyG that uses a USB that will connect it to any CAM processor compatible with the open source TinyG controller board from Synthetos, including tgFX, as well as several third party CAM interfaces that output standard G-code in arc/mm. In the future, they hope to release an integrated front end called Othercam, which will be able to import both EagleCAD board files and SVG files. This means that it will be compatible with vector based editors such as Adobe.

In a separate development the designer of the MTM Snap design used in the Othermill has released their own snap-together arduino-powered desktop CNC milling machine, the MTM Snap. Milled from

1/2-inch high-density polyethylene (similar to HDPE milk cartons), it has a 5 x 3 x 1.75 inch working area and can be assembled for about $700. Controlled by a custom shield Arduino board running the grbl G-code interpreter, it is designed for easy self-assembly. While the machine is not yet for sale, all the design files are on-line for anybody with a CNC that wants to cut out their own pieces, as well a complete bill of materials, and full documentation for the Arduino shield and software.

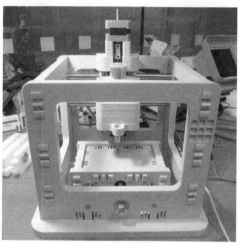

Figure 16. The MTM Snap

Matt Gardner is a 3D printing evangelist with a history of distinctly crazy projects. When not working on his motorized snowboard, he is putting the finishing touches to the Open Gantry system, a Google R&D project soon to be released worldwide.

The Open Gantry is an open source, self replicating CNC, designed specifically for producing wikihouses (www.wikihouse.cc). Simply feed in sheets of plywood, and the machine spits out Ikea–style, flat-pack houses that slot together and do not any require construction experience or power tools to build. Nobody else has been working on an open source CNC with an 8 x 4 feet cut envelope. The cheapest option available is the Blackfoot at $3,200 for a kit. Matt's prototypes have come in at $400–$500 and, with bulk ordering, he hopes to bring this down to $300–$400.

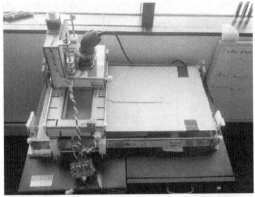

Figure 17. An Open Gantry Prototype

The Open Gantry is designed to be shipped as a kit to a disaster zone along with a couple pallets of plywood and operate for just a few months. To this end, they have sacrificed precision and lifespan in order to reduce the initial purchase price. Even so, with the option of adding screws and a quality router, there is no reason why the Open Gantry could not operate indefinitely.

Their first prototype is a fully functioning 1/4 scale model capable of cutting cardboard and wood. By the time this book is published, he hopes to have released all the source files, a complete bill of materials, and detailed assembly instructions.

Hybrid Devices

It was only a matter of time before the introduction of a combination CNC machine and 3D printer. So far, the three most interesting examples of these have been the MEbotics's "machine shop in a box" Microfactory, the FABtotum Personal Fabricator, and the Powerwasp. Coming out of the same Boston hackerspace as the 3Doodler, the Artisan's Asylum team self-funded five development prototypes of the Microfactory before it was finalized and ready for production at a cost of $4,495. Unfortunately, for all their technical wizardry, their understanding of Kickstarter let them down and they only received a small fraction of the $1 million requested. Despite this flaw, it is still an impressive machine, and we will inevitably see something similar on the market very soon.

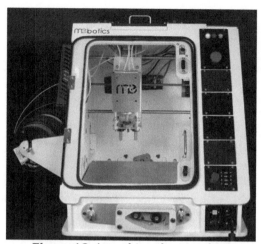

Figure 18. A machine shop in a box

The four extruders on two heater blocks are capable of printing multiple materials and colors. This allows it to print a part in four colors of ABS or a part in two colors of ABS and two of PLA at the same time. The addition of a spindle means that it can mill as well as print, in a perfect marriage of additive and subtractive manufacturing. The machine is entirely enclosed to reduce noise by 90 percent. Opening the door halts fabrication. In addition, it is fitted with a vacuum cleaner connection for easy cleaning. It even has an on-board computer running LinuxCNC, so although fabrication is computer-controlled, meaning that it does not need to be connected to a computer. In many cases it could be faster to machine a complex part section rather than print it, especially if there is a need to create threads, remove otherwise trapped support material, or break movable parts free from the surrounding matrix.

By setting a much more achievable $50,000 on Indiegogo, the FABtotum, a personal fabrication device coming out of Milan, reached its goal in a mere ten days.

The sleek design offers a complete scan-to-print eco-system, including scanning, milling, etching, and printing in one shiny box. The maker community is waiting with baited breath to see the quality of the parts, but at $1,099 for a fully assembled printer, scanner, miller and etcher, this seems like a real breakthrough.

Figure 19. The FABtotum

This hybrid fabrication machine is open source and comes with interchangeable dual extruder/spindle heads. It can produce both very small and very complex objects. The fact that the entire print head is detachable means that other subtractive or additive heads can be attached. In the future these might be a more powerful motor, a small laser diode module for paper cutting, a pick and place clamp, or even a syringe for scientific applications. A larger laser might be capable of milling a double sided PCB or plasma cutting on four-axes, while a separate head could be used for complex coil winding.

Another interesting Italian latecomer to the field is the PowerWASP 3D printer produced by CSP in Massa Lombarda. The brass and steel extruder features an external stepper motor to reduce vibration, improve accuracy, and allow speeds of up to 200 mm/s. A robust aluminum guide system allows milling tools of up to 5 kilograms to be mounted without adversely affecting the precision or speed. Therefore, a quick and easy tool change turns the printer into a CNC mill that uses open source software. The machine has a sleek European appearance, with all the mechanical and electrical components encased in the attractively designed black case. This is a 3D printer combo that I will be watching very carefully in the future.

Figure 20. The PowerWASP

DIY Injection Molding

Plastic injection molding is used to create a large variety of plastic products with different shapes and sizes, from toys and model parts to furniture and building materials. Up until now, injection molding methods that produce mirror smooth parts have always been prohibitively expensive for small users. To produce small, commercial-quality plastic parts or prototypes, it can cost up to $10,000 or more to make a steel mold. This is then sent to China, where large hydraulic molders will make ten thousand parts at a cost of one cent each. The first part costs $10,000.01, but the ten-thousandth part costs only one cent. 3D printed parts might struggle to beat the one cent price point, but can easily beat $10,000.01. If making a thousand components that are very similar, but not exactly the same, then 3D printing wins hands down. With injection molding, it is necessary to invest in a thousand different molds or, at the very least, a thousand different mold inserts which would then need to be manually changed out after each part is manufactured. Fortunately, bench-top injection molding machines are now starting to hit the market.

The PIM-SHOOTER Model-20A, priced at $595 from LNS Technologies (http://www.techkits.com/model_20/index.htm), is aimed at schools, hobbyists, and small companies that already have a drill press and mold clamp. It is a compact unit that fits nicely onto a kitchen counter and operates from standard 110V AC, consuming less than 200W and is perfect for users that only want to create ten parts a week, quickly and on-demand.

Figure 21. The PIM-SHOOTER Model-20A

The PIM-SHOOTER is essentially an injection unit that attaches to a drill press, which tightens the shaft into the drill press chuck. The injector features a heated barrel with a manual ram and a full 0.5 cubic inch resin shot capacity. It works with steel, aluminum, or epoxy molds. To maintain accurate temperature set-points, it includes a dual-display digital temperature controller with thermocouple feedback. The set includes a sample aluminum mold and a 10 ounce supply of polypropylene pellets, as well as pellet dispenser, purging block, safety glasses, and gloves so that users can begin molding as soon as the machine arrives.

For customers who want to make larger parts, the company has designed and built a PIM-SHOOTER Model-150A which molds parts up to 1.25 cubic inches, does not require a drill press, and comes with a manual, screw-tightening mold vice. Offered initially on Kickstarter at $1,500, it is capable of using a variety of materials including Acetal (Delrin), ABS, PLA, polystyrene, polypropylene, polyethylene, LDPE, TPE, and EVA. Although nylon and polycarbonate are not approved for use with the Model-150A, the company is planning to introduce a higher temperature limit in the near future that will make this possible. Users are even able to recycle high-density polyethylene

(HDPE) plastic milk and water containers. Low-cost aluminum molds can be used with the Model-150A, and users can have molds made at local machine shops, or even mill their own if they also have CNC machines. LNS Technologies' website offers molds, as well as plastic pellets. The company's primary business is making electronic and robotic kits for schools, students, and hobbyists, but more than 90 percent of sales of the Model-20A have been to companies or universities. Another popular use has been to mold custom fishing lures.

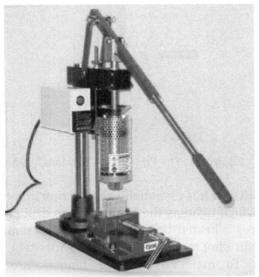

Figure 22. The PIM-SHOOTER Model-150A.

It is quite easy to imagine a 3D printer and a desktop injection machine sitting side-by-side in a small home workshop or makerspace. A plastic part can be created in CAD, then 3D-printed to verify the design or to produce marketing samples. The CAD file can then be converted to CNC for producing an injection mold, and production can be moved to the bench top injection molding process. Eventually, if there is sufficient demand, production can move to full-size injection molding equipment.

A recent blog post by 3sourceful compared the cost of manufacturing using Shapeways 3D printing and Protomold to make two injection molded parts, a very small bracket, less than one cubic centimeter, and the other a much larger fifty cubic centimeter jig. The tooling costs of the molds resulted in 3D printing being cheaper at lower quantities in both cases. But, in the case of the larger part, the cost of the 3D printing material meant that when creating more than one hundred units, Protomold became the cheaper solution. For the smaller part, 3D printing was still cost effective at over one thousand units. Another point to bear in mind is that if there is any level of complexity in the part or strict tolerances, the price-to-injection mold is likely to quickly increase, whereas the price to 3D print would likely stay the same, and would actually be reduced if the complexity is in the form of meshed or perforated features.

11

What Are They Printing Next Door?

I think that Jennifer Lawton of Makerbot said it best when she explained that "3D printing is an ecosystem, not a device." All over the world people are discovering a brand new way to make things, and this new production method is making them think differently about everything they do. This will perhaps be the most important legacy of the current early generation of 3D printers.

When a new product is invented, its design is not set in stone. The early Internet was designed so that a small group of computers located inside universities could share select, important documents with one another quickly and easily. At the time, it did not make sense to transfer hundreds of gigabytes a minute, as we now do on a daily basis, but that did not stop a global web from developing to meet the needs of a wider society. At the moment, we are still in those early days, when computers took up three-story buildings to harness the processing power of a calculator. Nobody can be sure of what the future will bring, except that it will happen at a greatly accelerated pace than ever before.

It is revolutionary because it is the exact opposite way of manufacturing we have done for the last two hundred years. When additive manufacturing is economical enough to be utilized in consumer design, it will radically change design and engineering principles and give designers and engineers a lot more freedom in design and manufacturing. In developing countries where there is a distinct lack of manufacturing, we may see low-cost additive manufacturing gain traction quickly. Africa's deficiency of infrastructure and services have created a very different evolution in the development of telecommunications, for example, where mobile technology quickly leap-frogged the need for traditional terrestrial network infrastructure. Hyper-local manufacturing also has the ability to bypass inefficient and corrupt import systems that are currently the only option available.

I have already talked extensively about the pursuits of hobbyists like myself, but far more interesting is what professionals are doing with the still-nascent technology. All over the world, people are finding interesting new uses for this exciting technology, and more are arriving every single day. There could already be a 3D printer working right next door to you. This chapter takes a brief look at some of the many diverse and fascinating uses that are already taking place.

Cutting edge film industry model-makers are already using 3D printers to design key components. FBFX Ltd. of the UK used an Objet30 Desktop 3D printer to design lead actress Noomi Rapace's space helmet in the recent Hollywood blockbuster, *Prometheus*. Complex geometries were required when creating mating patterns, to ensure the fit and lock of the helmet onto the space suit. A traditional model-maker could typically take weeks to produce such precision; however, armed with a digital toolkit, FBFX was able to quickly create a 3D CAD file of the helmet and 3D print a model in just a few of hours.

Figure 23. An early prototype
Prometheus helmet

Many movie goers are becoming jaded by excessive amounts of computer graphics that no longer assist in creating a suspension of disbelief. Fortunately, many films still use miniatures for large-scale effects scenes and we are quickly reaching a stage where virtually anything imaginable can be 3D printed on a small scale. When the plasticine stop-motion animators get on board with this, all kinds of tiny plastic doors will open up. I am personally looking forward to a revival of the golden age of animatronics, when wizards like Ray Harryhausen and Gerry Anderson were able to smash boundary after boundary with their groundbreaking special effects. 3D printing provides an extremely fast way of sculpting and creating concepts. Instead of going into a mask sculpt blind, FX designers can now print out exact versions by extensively tweaking digital representations until every aspect is perfect. British firm Propshop Modelmakers Ltd. used a Voxeljet to print three, full-size replica Aston Martins—each made from eighteen pieces—for the James Bond film *Skyfall*, at a tiny fraction of the cost of sourcing the real thing. The models serve as doubles for the now priceless original 1960s vehicle featured in the film's action scenes. This is going to be a massive sea of change for movie producers who want to fill their films with expensive or exotic props.

Figure 24. A replica under construction

Prop master Walter Klassen runs a special FX studio in Toronto, where an enterprise level $120,000, Israeli-built Objet Eden 260V churns out dinosaur heads, ninja projectiles, and alien super weapons, complete with extra-planetary hieroglyphs. Most recently Klassen created the futuristic firearms for the upcoming *RoboCop* remake, which finished shooting in Toronto earlier this year. The guns were required to fit neatly over 9 mm Beretta pistols to be able to shoot twenty-four blanks every 2.3 seconds, to add realism to the movie's mayhem. "It's revolutionized the things we can do," Klassen says. "When you start with something in your imagination and an hour later you're holding it in your hand, it's a really empowering technology for many people."

In the last chapter I talked extensively about toys, and it is clear that this is going to be one of the first markets to benefit from 3D printing in a meaningful way. In the past decade, the toy industry has become overly reliant on licensed toys from blockbuster movies, with nine out of ten of the top-selling toys regularly being big-screen-licensed products. The downside for retailers is that toys associated with flops can find themselves consigned immediately to the landfill. The democratizing ability of the Internet means that it is now much easier for independent manufacturers to reach a significant or super-niche audience. The pick'n'mix combination of social media, rapid prototyping, miniaturization, and the Etsy effect (a revival in handcrafted goods), are all opening exciting new doors. We are even seeing a resurgence of retro toys with a "Slow Toy Movement." Cheaper, faster production turnaround and widely available electronica mean there are more flashing, talking, spinning goodies than ever before, although the impact of the maker movement means that items such as DIY chemistry kits for perfumes and makeup are growing faster than ever. Thanks to smartphones, chips, screens, and processors all kinds of titchy tech are now so commonplace that they are amazingly cheap. This is making kits and self-build toys that encourage tinkering, making, and individuality, much more affordable.

Many schools already have a 3D printer, and print-at-home toys are quickly becoming a future inevitability. Some stores are already offering action figures with an exact likeness of the customers own head on the scaled down body. In the very near future, we will see this translate into 3D printed mommy and daddy action figures. Instead of Barbie's impossible ideals, parents will be able to give their child an action figure of their mother and instead of questionable Marvel heroes, how about giving your son an action figure of his father? I think that will result in a decline in military figures and a sharp rise in categories such as emergency service workers, explorers, activists, and nurses. At least I hope so.

With so many artists experimenting with 3D printing, it was only a matter of time before we started seeing all kinds of exotic instruments, strange prototypes, and musical controllers. Amit Zoran of the MIT Media Lab has already created a working flute, but in the future musicians will simply be able to visualize an instrument, a radical new controller, or a custom case and then just print it out. There is already a website devoted solely to 3D printed instruments.

Figure 26. Tri-horn trumpet?

Digital music artist and inventor Onyx Ashanti has created a gestural interface controller for his Beatjazz music system, which is made from 80 percent 3D-printed components. This is a wearable system to help him break away from the confines of the front of a computer screen and create improvised music using wireless gestural interface controllers. His original prototype Beatjazz controller was made from cardboard and featured pressure sensors, accelerometers, and an iPhone.

Based in Berlin, Ashanti has twenty years of experience in the field, having played on the award-winning Basement Jaxx album Kish Kash, as well as three years on tour with Soul II Soul. His new instrument allows the creation of continuous live, improvised digital music by interacting with an array of software synthesizers, each one recorded and looped until he has a complete sonic orchestra. The controls are a three-way wireless network made up of a head-mounted pressure sensor and two hand units that make him look like he is slowly being assimilated by the Borg. Almost 80 percent of the device is 3D printed, making it both durable and lightweight—the headset is said to weigh about the same as an iPhone.

Figure 27. "Resistance is futile!"

Many industries are now beginning to appreciate the benefits of additive manufacturing. I recently spoke to a mining engineer that specializes in the 3D printing of mining supports, a service that is revolutionizing the entire industry. Instead of having parts sent in from expensive third party contractors, some mining companies are already making their own in a fraction of the time and for a fraction of the cost. He also spoke of DLMS parts being used in hard-face mining equipment, resulting in better than original performance.

Even higher up the technological ladder, the European Space Agency (ESA) has launched the €20 million AMAZE project (Addictive Manufacturing Aiming towards Zero Waste and Efficient Production of High-Tech Metal Products), working with twenty-eight partners from across European industry and science including EADS, Airbus, Astrium, Norsk Titanium, and the Culham Centre for Fusion Energy. Their eventual aim is the 3D printing of single-piece satellites, and I am going to talk in detail about this aspect of the aerospace industry in another chapter.

Beyond building parts for spacecraft and jet engines, the technology has very interesting implications for fusion projects. ESA's head of new materials and energy research has already spoken of 3D printing tungsten alloy components that can withstand temperatures of up to 3,000 degrees Celsius, and would be able to withstand conditions on the nozzles of rockets, or inside a fusion reactor. Once we are able to contain the heat of the sun—nature's own fusion reactor design—and contain it inside a metal box, we are well on the way to commercial nuclear fusion.

In what might seem, at first glance, to be a significantly less impressive achievement, Chris Hawkins has developed a fully functional 3D printed stepper motor. Stepper motors are used to control the movement of the extruder head on most budget 3D printers. Obviously, the device was not built 100 percent through 3D printing, but the majority of the parts were. He still needs to add the electronic driver pieces, magnets, wire, and a few nails, but even still this is an enormous step forward.

Figure 28. A 3D printer stepper motor

The coils are regular nails wrapped in magnet wire, while the rotor is a 3D printed framework which accepts neodymium rare earth magnets. The integrated circuit on the upper right is a transistor array that facilitates switching the 20V driving the coils. The board on the lower right is a Digispark ATtiny85 breakout board, that includes a USB edge connector for programming and a linear regulator, allowing a 20 volt as the source. Although it was not specifically designed to be used on a Makerbot, with some improved bearings and some refinement those steps could become much smaller, and we would be one more step closer to a fully replicating 3D printer. I am expecting all kinds of remixes and variations to appear very quickly, as other designers modify the mechanical interface to fit their own stores of spare and salvaged parts.

It is easy to see how this could progress very quickly indeed. Inevitably, we will soon see a design for 3D printed coil winders, and then maybe an adapter for a torque multiplier. The community has already talked about making numerous improvements including the use of electrical (silicon) steel for the motor core, lamination to reduce eddy currents, and shaping to fill the available space, in order to obtain the strongest magnetic field for the wire being used. Some tinkerers are even talking about adding step-down gearing and using it to build another, stronger motor.

Elsewhere, scientists are finding equally practical uses for 3D printers in the fields of environmentalism and conservation. Desert Star Systems, based in Northern California, developed a prototype tracking tag for sea animals using additive manufacturing. Their latest line of SeaTags, are significantly advanced designs that can dive deeper, survive longer, and withstand more environmental abuse than any previous models. They recently printed fourteen PolyJet Otter prototypes and received them within just two days. 3D printing allows them to develop very specific sizes and uniquely shaped animal tags, such as an incredibly low-drag miniature turtle tag, that would otherwise require very expensive injection molding. Their small size means that they have very little effect on the creatures themselves. Desert Star tags use magnetometers to estimate a latitude location in deep water locations, combined with an on board solar cell that acts as a light sensor to estimate longitude. The same cell provides power system to charge the SeaTags. After nearly fifteen minutes of sunlight, the tag retains its charge for up to two weeks in total darkness. SeaTags are used to estimate animal locations around the world. The tags revolutionize sea animal tracking by detailing the temperature of the water, depth of the animal, animal behavior through acceleration measurements, and in the future will also measure oxygen levels in the water, water salinity, and even oil dispersants. This kind of research enables scientists to obtain a much broader understanding of the ocean, and to better protect the life within it.

Figure 29. Sea tags in action

Mansour Ourasanah has created the Lepsis, an attractive terrarium insect breeder that can be 3D printed and used to grow grasshoppers in an urban home. This clever design was recently nominated for the world's largest design prize, the 2013 Index Award. In Canada, Bill Clinton controversially awarded $1 million to a group of MBA students who created an insect farming system that will work toward replacing livestock farms. I myself have been working on a printed bin attachment to farm black soldier flies. The larvae will eat almost anything and leave behind nothing except fertilizer and fat larvae, which make nutritious feed for aquaponic setups or chickens. The adults only live long enough to reproduce, they do not bite or sting and they are not known to be a vector for any human pathogens.

Figure 30. The Lepsis Terrarium

Insects are much more efficient at converting plant cellulose and starches into proteins and fats than fish, chicken, pigs, and especially cows. Only large snakes have been shown to be superior in terms of protein conversion. Feed corn is very inefficient for humans to digest, but insects can convert it at a very high rate. Currently, livestock is fed reprocessed livestock leftovers, which is expensive to reprocess and very inefficient. If done incorrectly, as is the case in many Third World countries, the process can lead to the spread of Creutzfeldt-Jakob Disease or FMD among livestock. Additionally, insect reprocessing enables organic producers to process their own waste, and add a valuable extra layer that can further optimize permaculture harvesting systems.

Apart from being a cheap replacement for animal feed, many insects are very edible and sometimes quite good. We have all unknowingly eaten much worse. Wheat flour, for example, is permitted to contain a maximum average of "74 insect fragments per 50 grams" and the Bible records that bird droppings became a coveted source of sustenance during long seiges. Flour made from insects and mealworms can be very expensive at an upmarket health food store, but there is a big difference between eating ground up insects as part of a chocolate cake and eating a bowl of spiced and sautéed meal worms.

I personally enjoy steamed water beetles and deep fried grasshoppers, but novices might prefer to start with something roasted or chocolate-covered. Human teeth show every sign of being shaped to consume insects, and it is quite possible that long fingers developed to dig them out of cracks and crevices. It would be terribly ironic if God turned out to be more simian that homo sapien, and was looking down on all of mankind's hunger and famine problems yelling, "For My sake, the cockroach is an unlimited food source. You couldn't wipe the little bastards out if you tried!"

Still I do hope that insect consumption remains a personal choice. There seems be a growing number of suggestions from on high about what we, the 99 percent, should do to save the planet. Like the idea that we should ride bicycles so there is plenty of gas for the armored SUVs of the rich, or that we should eat grasshoppers so there is plenty of steak for corporate banquets.

Researchers at Australia's Victorian Organic Solar Cell Consortium (VICOSC)—a collaboration between the Commonwealth Scientific and Industrial Research Organisation (CSIRO), the University of Melbourne, Monash University, and industry partners—

have successfully printed an A3 sheet of flexible plastic photo voltaic cells. This represents an order of magnitude advancement, as previously printed cells were limited to the size of a finger nail. The new cells can generate between ten and fifty watts of power per square meter and could be laminated onto skyscraper windows or embedded into roofing materials.

The team are using a technique similar to the one used in the silk screen printing of T-shirts, in the hope that they can reduce the barrier to entry for cell manufacturing. Unfortunately, their printer is still in the $200,000 range and far too large for an ordinary home. Even so, progress in the field is accelerating. 3D printed solar cells can capture more sunlight than conventional PV models because they are more precise (using copper, indium, gallium, and selenide), less complex, and weigh less. 3D printing may also drop production costs by half by eliminating inefficiencies associated with the waste of costly materials like glass or polysilicon. In addition, the process can generate very thin solar cells that can be printed on untreated paper, plastic, or fabric rather than expensive glass. Now we just need to wait for someone to 3D print a house, print some solar panels for the exterior, and live off printed pizza.

A number of separate teams are, in fact, already working on 3D printing houses. Dutch design studio Universe Architecture has unveiled designs for a looping two-story house that resembles a Möbius strip and will be printed in concrete. They are working in collaboration with Italian robotics engineer Enrico Dini, inventor of an extremely large-format 3D printer that looks like a stage-lighting rig and works like a laser-sintering machine, but which uses sand instead of nylon powder and chemicals instead of a laser. A moving horizontal gantry first deposits a 5 mm substrate of sand mixed with magnesium oxide. Then, via a row of nozzles, the gantry squirts chlorine onto the areas of sand that are to become solid. The resulting chemical reaction creates synthetic sandstone. Dini's machine, called D-Shape, is located in a warehouse near Pisa, and prints at a rate of 5 centimeters per hour over a 30-square-meter area. Working flat-out, it can produce 30 cubic meters of building structure per week.

Figure 31. Dini's large format printer

DUS Architects, also based in Amsterdam, are planning a canal house using a homemade portable printer, located inside an upended shipping container. Called the KamerMaker ("room maker"), it can print components up to 3.5 meters high. Working initially in polypropylene, the architects hope to experiment with recycled plastics and bioplastics further into the build. 3D printing is not going to replace brick and concrete buildings. After, all email did not replace paper. These projects are more about kick-starting debate and experimenting with the huge potential time, labor, and transportation savings.

Figure 32. The prototype KamerMaker

UK architects Softkill Design have announced plans for Protohouse 2.0, a single-story dwelling with a fibrous structure resembling bone growth. Instead of columns and floorplates, it has a fibrous structure similar to the trabecular composition of bone. Unlike sand-based structures, which require thick sections to maintain structural integrity, these fibers can be as thin as 0.7 mm. The plan is to print using laser-sintered bioplastic (plastics derived from biomass rather than hydrocarbons) in a factory and then snap parts together on site. Traditional steel or concrete structures have a very high level of redundancy. They include huge amounts of unnecessary material that is too difficult or expensive to remove, so this new design opens up all sorts of new aesthetic possibilities. 3D printing allows material to be placed only where it is required, and the architects have created an algorithm that mimics bone growth, depositing material strictly where it is most structurally efficient. This method can generate a large volume with extremely thin and porous structures to achieve a strong, fibrous structure using less material than a normal structure, making it much cheaper. The house has a porous exoskeleton with weatherproofing applied to the insides, lining the cave-like living spaces.

More bizarre still is a research team at MIT working on a robotic arm that mimics the way in which a silkworm builds its cocoon. By replacing current gantry systems with a six-axis robotic arm, their design allows free-form printing at a much larger scale, without the need for support structures. Silkworms "print" their pupal casings by moving their heads in a figure-eight pattern. They deposit silk fibre and sericin matrix (a sticky gum that bonds the fibres together) around themselves, acting like a multi-axis 3D multi-material printer. They are able to vary the gradient of the printed material, making the cocoon soft on the inside and hard on the outside. Team leader, Neri Oxman is developing a process to assign different materials or properties to individual voxels (volumetric pixels), creating simple graded materials. These would be useful for printing architectural elements, such as beams or façades that mimic bone, which is hard on the outside, but spongy on the inside.

Oxman is a real pioneer in the field, constantly throwing around terms like "4D printing," "swarm construction," and "CNC weaving" to describe the future of architectural technology. This is extremely refreshing, as the sad reality is that we have been using the same simple stone-on-stone compression technology now, for the last three millenia. We desperately need these new approaches. Lord Norman Foster explained it most succinctly when he recalled an enlightening conversation with Buckminster Fuller:

> I remember, in 1978, showing [Fuller] our Sainsbury Centre for the Visual Arts and being startled when he asked: "How much does your building weigh?" The question was far from rhetorical. He was challenging us to discover how efficient it was; to identify how many tonnes of material enclosed what volume.

Certainly within a decade it will become possible, if not commonplace, to create a habitable structure with a 3D printer, or at least assemble one out of 3D-printed modular components. Unfortunately, the housing problem is much more than just constructing a habitable structure. And anyway, how do we define a habitable structure in the first place? A punishment cell in one of our many jails is a habitable structure, but I would not want to call it a home. A home is an investment that often comes with many running costs, costs which need to be addressed if we are to make truly affordable housing. How can these needs be met by those who need homes the most, those with nothing to invest? Until homes are productive rather than costly, this problem will not be solved.

In most countries, the construction industry employs vast numbers of people, and the entrenched culture of building houses might be difficult to change over a short period of time. If, however, one developer builds an entire subdivision utilizing 3D printing techniques that customers quickly accept, and gains a huge cost advantage in the process, then the movement could take off very rapidly. In the longer term, cost is not going to be the only factor in play here. China already produces humongous housing complexes at relatively little cost to the developer, but this has done nothing to solve the housing shortage. If anything, it has made the problem far worse than in any other country, due to rampant property speculation. Compared to average incomes, China already has the highest housing costs anywhere in the world, and those prices are increasing all the time. China also has more ghost cities than any other country. Locations such as Ordos in Mongolia and Chengong in Kunming are perfect examples of this problem. This is in fact a problem that stretches far beyond Chinese borders. The city of Kilamba on the outskirts of Angola's capital Luanda, has 750 enormous tower blocks that could house up to half a million people, and yet lies almost completely empty.

In the future, architects and developers will need to addresses the basic needs of housing, i.e. what purpose does it serve and what needs does it fulfill? Without a doubt the biggest problem that home printing cannot address is that of location, the problems of where the home is going to be built and who will provide the materials for construction. Building a home can be done cheaply and quickly using a variety of traditional materials, but what about the ever increasing costs of buying the land upon which to build?

Networked Social 3D printing

User friendly social media sites such as Facebook have turned the web into a global communications and publishing platform, by allowing ordinary users to "friend" each other and upload their holiday snaps. A number of start ups are now trying to enable the manufacture and distribution of physical objects in a similarly scalable and global fashion. At the moment the idea of producing plumbing fixtures or gear knobs in the basement of a Birmingham council house, or a high rise apartment in Chengdu sounds improbable, but only ten years ago the idea of buying groceries on-line would have been equally incredible. Only five years ago, the CEO of Microsoft almost fell off his chair with laughter when he heard a rumor that Apple was going to launch a $500 mobile phone. I wonder if he was still laughing when the AppStore made its first billion dollars?

While even our grandparents now have Facebook accounts, it might still sound like a stretch to expect people to be seeking out, downloading, and remotely printing 3D models, but as we can see, stranger things have already happened. Sites like 3D Hub and 100kgarages are already offering individuals the chance to participate in a distributed manufacturing network. Hub members register their printer availability with a map pin, so that customers can find the nearest maker. Customers then select the hub where they want the object to be sent, and ask a local Hubber to 3D print and deliver it. DIY stores and Makerspaces could become hubs, and sell on-demand spare parts and upgrades. Hospital specialists could distribute complex cancer medication in personalized packaging. Garages could deliver replacement parts via your 3D Hub neighbor at a fraction of the cost of keeping warehouse inventory. On-demand network services have already been applied to retail, logistics, public services, entertainment, travel, passports, shipping, and education. Why not to manufacturing? This kind of disintermediation cuts out unnecessary middle-men links in a supply chain, reducing costs at both ends. If manufacturing becomes distributed throughout communities, the concentrated wealth of global business might also be distributed along the way.

One manufacturer is already anticipating this trend by creating a 3D printing fax machine. The Zeus integrates a 3D printer and scanner into one device. This opens the doors to prototyping companies across the world that could send their clients a model in a matter of minutes, without any shipping costs or time delays. This all-in-one-type printer seems to be very much the trend at the moment, it seems reasonable to predict printing and scanning will get both better and smaller.

In what has come to be described as the sharing economy, we are already seeing an enormous growth in companies similar to Airbnb, a site that helps members rent out their unused rooms to other users. Sites of this nature are already spawning their own specialist ecosystems. There are now people who will come clean your home, coordinate key exchanges, cook dinner for you and your guests, photograph rooms for rent, and, through the ride-sharing business Lyft, turn their cars into taxis to drive you around. It will be very interesting to see what secondary services a network of 3D printers begins to generate. Some, such as design and delivery, are obvious, but how long before we start seeing more specialist services? Perhaps these will include finishers who will provide highly detailed painting services for the explosion in miniatures that we are already seeing. It might not be long before we require the knowledge of on-line librarians to help is us navigate through the millions of 3D designs, in order to find that obscure spare part that we are looking for. My own prediction is that we will begin to see "interstitial hardware designers" cropping up, those whose job it is to breathe new life into older items with just a tiny piece of plastic. So many small pieces of otherwise perfectly functioning appliances can be lost, including covers, clips, docks, and handles. Sometimes products become unusable because some other device has changed or has been updated. A good example of this is the custom iPhone adapters for older iPod docks that were recently launched on Sculpteo, allowing users of Bose, Sony, JBL, and other older docks to connect with the new Lightning connector. Instead of having to buy an entirely new dock (or a new baby gate or a new garden parasol) IH designers will provide the necessary replacement design that customers can buy and print.

At the other end of this rapidly developing ecosystem, we are likely to see a lot more people involved in some kind of product reclamation. In a world of short runs and rapid iteration on localized products, the amount of manufactured waste will increase geometrically. In order for such a world to be economically and environmentally sustainable, we will need to see rapid innovation in recycling as well as production. It will be essential to reclaim much more plastic, metal, and other materials. New businesses could arise to prepare products for recycling. Disassembly companies exist already, and their work becomes much easier and more affordable when there are open BOMs (Bills of Materials) from manufacturers to use as guides to disassembly. Manufacturers need to start providing detailed information about metal content and hazardous materials, so that even if one disassembler does not have the tools to remove the copper from a circuit board safely for example, he can at least generate value by preparing the board for the company who can.

While futurists have long predicted replicators, it is less well known that they have also been prophesying the advent of disassemblers, also known as Santa Claus Machines. Imagine a machine that could disassemble old unwanted objects and use the materials to print new objects all from the comfort of your own home. Perhaps this could become a reality if we were to design items with a little more care and attention to their long term existence in the first place.

12

3D Printing in China

In my first eBook on 3D printing, I included many examples and anecdotes taken from my own experience of nearly two decades living and working in China. Many readers later told me that these sections were some of the most interesting in the book, and persuaded me to include a full chapter in this volume relating solely to the future of 3D printing in China.

I would like to start out by stating that the difference between the media portrayal of China and its stark reality is vast. The country's imminent global domination is a constantly repeated theme by journalists ensconced in Beijing's five-star luxury. Although the gleaming of towers of Pudong in Shanghai and Zhujiang in Guangzhou make for impressive glossy full-page spreads, most of China is more akin to Third World sub-Saharan Africa than it is to Milan or Singapore or Palo Alto. China is often described as an economic powerhouse, but what does that really mean in an economic system that is so fundamentally flawed, with most of its main participants trillions of dollars in debt? I recently heard an American comedian describe his home state of Texas as being awash with cash, but absolutely impoverished in every other sense of the word. This exact same description applies very nicely to China in the twenty-first century. Financial stagnation means that the very worst kind of creative accounting has been responsible for those highly contentious GDP figures that authorities continue to conjure out of thin air. The massively overextended lending schemes that led to the huge crashes in Europe and the US have taken place on a far larger scale in China, and yet the dreaded effects of such incompetent mismanagement have yet to have their full effect. Anyway, this book is supposed be focussed on 3D printing rather than serve as a rehash of Gordon Chang's *Coming Collapse of China*, and so I will try to get back to the core subject.

Every year a 3D printing industry report is produced by consulting group Wohlers Associates. The report costs $450 and is well out of my budget, but is regularly quoted by the media in additive manufacturing pieces. They claim that ten years ago, America dominated the global market for manufacturing and selling professional-grade, industrial additive manufacturing systems. At the time, the US industry had ten companies representing its industry compared to just seven in Europe, seven in Japan, and three in China. Today, they state that there are sixteen companies in Europe, seven in China, five in the United States, and two in Japan. This equates to a 38.55 market share for America, while China lags behind with a pitiful 8.6 percent.

Although I was not able to attend the 2013 World 3D Printing Technology Industry Conference in Beijing, I did attend the Toy Expo and the International Toy and Hobby Fair in Guangzhou. While there were a handful of 3D printer manufacturers present, both exhibitions were filled mainly with the low-end plastic tack that we have all come to associate with China. I was the only foreigner in attendance on that particular day and, as I walked around the endless displays of cheap plastic tack, I could not help but think to myself, "My god, these guys do not know it yet, but in just a couple of years nearly all of them are going to be dead in the water!"

3D printing experts Melba Kurman (Triple Helix Innovation) and Hod Lipson (Cornell University) have recently been talking at length about how they believe 3D printing will transform Chinese manufacturing. (http://www.livescience.com/38294-3d-printing-in-china.html

They have written extensively about how they "witnessed first-hand how 3D printing (pronounced like "san D da eeng" in Chinese) is igniting people's imaginations." I could have organized a tour of a dozen first-class organic farms, but that would not have detracted from the fact that China has some of the worst and most widespread food poisoning scandals in the world. Igniting imaginations is something that the Chinese education system actively works to discourage, preferring to produce rote learning exam bots, rather than well-rounded individuals with an active curiosity and critical thinking skills.

They talk about the centrally planned twelfth (and current) Five-Year Plan as if it is the perfect solution for the growth of "distributed manufacturing," without seeing the obvious contradiction. The broad brush goals of the five year plans are all but forgotten at regional levels, when local officials change so frequently and set up their own agendas. The recent spectacular show trials are a good example of how regional and central thinking can be such polar opposites. Li Keqiang, the current Premier, is the first and only member of the CPC Central Committee to have ever earned a university degree, and so we are not talking about a planning committee that is at the cutting edge of modern technology by any means.

One of the important goals of the current five year plan is to build thirty million new, affordable apartments for low-income people. This is what the authorities say, but in reality we see just endless ghost cities. Chenggong, near Kunming, has a huge sports stadium, kindergartens, shopping malls, and a forest of skyscrapers, and yet over one hundred thousand new apartments are still unoccupied. The Kangbashi area of Ordos City was built to house at least three hundred thousand residents, but government figures stated that it had only twenty-eight thousand.

The New South China Mall is not just the world's biggest mall, but also the emptiest. The vast majority of its 1,500 stores have been empty since it was finished in 2005, mainly due to the fact that developers failed to build any highway exits to provide access for shoppers. I could list many other similarly failed projects that I have visited myself, but I am sure that you get the picture. This is why I am little skeptical of any claims that "3D-printing technology will serve as a catalyst to ease China's evolution into providing high-tech manufacturing and related services."

I wonder if it was the red carpet tour of high-end facilities that made them feel obligated to write sentences like "Chinese culture values self-discipline, hard work and respect for authority, beliefs that have enabled China to rapidly transform into the world's largest economy." Many would argue that it was sweatshop labor, lack of regulations, and endemic corruption that have propelled China towards the precipice at which it currently stands. As one anonymous Internet poster put it, "I don't think that Chinese culture values a 'respect' for authority. Fear would be a better term."

Most Westerners judge the Chinese based on the hard working immigrants that they see in their own countries. During the last twenty years of China's mass urbanization, those who can afford it have been emigrating in droves. Reliable figures are hard to come by, but it has been estimated that this brain and skill drain approaches almost a million people a year, few of whom ever come back. In the coastal cities especially, much of the urban population has been replaced by immigrants from rural areas, barely literate with almost no education, coming from conditions of poverty that resemble the Dark Ages. This has been a boon for sweat shops, but has at the same time seriously diluted the urban populations. With little schooling and decreasing opportunities, these newcomers often have to turn to crime just to feed themselves. This mass exodus of the educated demographic and its replacement with "peasants" from another age will have to be addressed before any technological solution can be implemented, and turn China into an information and service economy.

One particularly interesting paragraph that I would like to comment on was this one:

> *"Looking into the future, China's massive population will accelerate the adoption of 3D-printed manufacturing. China's huge domestic market of consumers is becoming more sophisticated in its tastes. This increasingly affluent consumer base will demand novel and custom products that require advanced engineering and manufacturing capabilities.*

While I do not agree that the consumer base as a whole is becoming increasingly affluent, I do think that there will be opportunities in the future. In reality, China has been stagnating for at least the last decade, the numbers being fudged by huge infrastructure projects, such as those that I mentioned earlier. There is indeed increasing affluence for a few, but it is coupled with an ever increasing wealth gap. The rich are getting much richer, while many ordinary citizens are slipping back into poverty. Certainly there will be a demand for novel and custom products, but they will be at the luxury high end of the market, and this is an interesting recurring cycle that I have discussed in more detail in the Mechanical

Assembilies chapter. Selling to the Chinese market will also require more skills as it continues to close up again to the outside world. Not only will you have to print quality 3D products but you will need to be able to navigate sites such as Taobao, Ganji, and 58.com, or at least have someone on the inside that can do this for you.

Kurman and Lipson also claim that "the Chinese government is investing in higher education in anticipation of a shift to a higher-skilled manufacturing economy." I too have seen similar official pronouncements, but the cynical side of me wonders how many of these will actually come into being. A decade ago, I had a great deal of direct experience in the Chinese education system, culminating with a stint at BeiDa, Beijing University, the most prestigious university in the country. It was my experience there that made me leave education entirely, disgusted and appalled with what I saw. Universities were simply businesses posing as education, expanding a system that took advantage of uninformed parents that had never had access to education themselves and simply milking them in their ignorance. The country's antiquated exam system is an enormous bottleneck, doing little except create a feeling of miserable failure in the 99 percent than cannot meet its unattainable expectations. If you are really interested in learning about the true state of education in China then I would recommend a recent Unreported World documentary entitled *Hong Kong's Tiger Tutors* that reveals the inner workings of a system that cheats the students it is meant to serve.

Some challenges have been recognized by Kurman and Lipson such as that of open communication, or the lack thereof. Others are hinted at, such as the "monolithic supply chains," although there was little reference to how the means of production are concentrated in the hands of a very tiny elite. Other observations such as their claim that "China will need to aggressively re-think its intellectual-property laws" are complete folly. How on earth can China open up communication if it is going to "tighten its intellectual-property laws" at the same time? We have seen that the war on digital sharing in the West has been a complete and utter failure, and there is no reason to think that it will be any different in China

Despite our differences of opinion, I genuinely hope that 3D printing technology will enable at least some of the 70 percent of this year's university graduates unable to find a job to have an alternative. As an independent entrepreneur, this year's changes in visa regulations have meant that I, along with many other foreign investors, are no longer welcome in China or allowed to spend the time required to make all the connections necessary to set up a successful new business venture. Fortunately, I was able to donate my own 3D printer to the new Guangzhou library before I left. Local authorities spent a whopping $134.4 million on the new showcase building and I am hoping that they still have some spare change left to include a state of the art Makerspace. I was happy to give them the trusty old General to kickstart the project. Whether it will be locked up and left to gather dust, like so many of the books in most Chinese libraries, remains to be seen. I am hoping that easy access to a 3D printer will prepare locals for an environment of change and enable access to emerging fields of knowledge, but convincing administrators that a library can be so much more than a collection of books has been a tough proposition.

A tightly controlled media has been reporting on the rapidly developing 3D printing industry, but with most of the reports coming from the likes of the *People's Daily* or the famously pro-government *Global Times*, it is perhaps a good idea to take these stories with a pinch of salt.

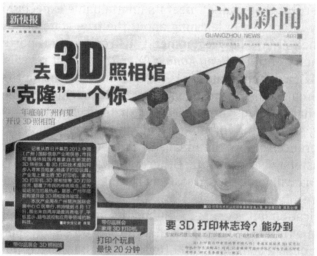

Figure 33. *Guangzhou News* August 2013

Mr. Luo Jun, both CEO of the Asian Manufacturing Association (AMA) and executive secretary-general of the China 3D Printing Technology Industry Alliance, has been particularly active in informing the press about China's 3D printing activities. Mr Luo is a graduate of the Sichuan Provincial Party Committee School, while the

AMA committee includes at least half a dozen members of the CPPCC Standing Committee on its council. So far, Mr. Luo has been telling journalists that 3D printing will play a "very positive role" in upgrading Chinese manufacturing. China hands will instantly recognize this kind of comment as guanhua or "official language," the malleable and manipulative "fruit language" of modern Chinese politics. In a predictable response, consulting firm Deloitte Touche Tohmatsu released a survey of over seventy global executives, many of whom very conveniently agreed that China's current policies are supportive of boosting manufacturing competitiveness. The China 3D Printing Technology Industry Alliance plans to build ten innovation centers for 3D printing technology in ten cities in China in the near future, with a planned investment of 20 million yuan ($3.3 million) for each center.

This should be quite easy considering thirty-one members of the National People's Congress and another fifty-two delegates to the Chinese People's Political Consultative Conference are dollar billionaires. Given the difficulties involved in calculating the hidden wealth of many of China's top leaders and their families, this probably seriously understates the true number of super-wealthy participants in these political sessions. In explaining this amazing situation, (neither the American Senate nor the Congress can boast a single billionaire) Xingyuan Feng, a researcher at the Chinese Academy of Social Sciences, a government think-tank, says, "When business people amass a fortune they need to protect it—so they either find an agent to [do so] or they become an official themselves." The average fortune among these eighty-three wealthiest delegates is $3.35 billion, compared with the average annual wage for Chinese urban workers (note urban, not rural which is far, far lower) of less than $7,000. In March 2013, AMA signed a deal to establish the first of its 3D printing hubs in the heart of the Nanjing Economic and Technological Development Zone. This center will house showrooms and education facilities in addition to a top-of-the-line research and development laboratory. Let us just hope that it is more successful than the South China Mall.

In a rather ambiguous press release, it was reported that the 3D Printing Research Institute of China was "launched" on August 8, 2013 at Zijin Hightech Zone of the Nanjing city, Jiangsu Province. Note the use of the word "launched" rather than "opened," which could mean pretty much anything. As of yet, I have failed to turn up any actual pictures of the facilities, and so I am using my local contacts to verify whether ground has actually been broken on this project yet.

It is also interesting to note that the universities most associated with 3D printing research in China are also those with some of the closest ties to the Peoples' Liberation Army. Xian Jiaotong University and Northwestern Polytechnic University, for example, were both closely involved in the production of China's latest military drones, which looked suspiciously like US Predators. Clearly, the Shanzhai concept extends beyond the civilian world and well into military circles.

China, like many other countries, has a tendency to dictate the location of vast new high tech industrial parks, rather than encourage industry in a more organic fashion. This is perhaps why many of the state sponsored developments remain ghost towns while Shanzhai industries spring up spontaneously in areas where they can best take advantage of existing facilities.

Some might go as far to argue that if this technology really is so ground breaking, then why should the taxpayer need to subsidize it? If 3D printing is going to change the world, then will large government subsidies make any difference in the long term? As I have explained in the chapter on Distributed Manufacturing, government subsidies generally benefit well-established corporations, and yet have little impact on small businesses that require other completely different factors to ensure their success. All over the world, there are many governments already so far in debt that it is questionable whether they should be throwing money at high tech at all and should instead be addressing more urgent problems such as homelessness, poverty, and health. As a 3D printing enthusiast, I am keen to see the announcements that governments are making regarding investments, but I would how much of that money will go to grass roots projects and how much will be siphoned away by powerful lobbyists and their cronies.

Despite these reservations, there does seem to be a definite coalescing taking place in the western cities of Chongqing and Xian, as the coastal cities continue to suffer the effects of a ridiculously inflated real estate market. China Green 3D at the Intelligent Technology Research Institute in Chongqing seem to be making good progress in liquid photosensitive resin UV curing technology. In Xian, military spin offs seem to be benefiting Bright Laser Technologies (http://www.xa-blt.com/) in developing Laser Solid Forming (LSF) or Laser Direct Metal Deposition (LDMD) technology for commercial applications in the Aerospace and Automotive Industries.

Still, it does seem that military funding remains the driving force behind many developments. Cai Daosheng, a former general manager at Wuhan Binhu Mechanical & Electrical Co., which was established as a 3D printing company by Huazhong University of Science and Technology, confirmed the suitability of the technology for producing military equipment such as missiles: "We've had many military projects," said Cai. Issues of "national security" will obviously severely restrict the trickle down impact of such breakthroughs, which is disappointing, when the Shanzhai model has already shown itself to be so agile and effective.

China's research on materials "for 3D printing are much weaker," complained Feng Tao, manager of Beijing Henglong. "Moreover, (despite official proclamations to the contrary) investments by companies and research institutes are small. As a result, China's 3D printing sector is still at the start-up stage and needs more time to mature."

Anyway, take this opportunity to go and make a cup of coffee while I spend a couple of paragraphs detailing three of the officially showcased, state-owned enterprises currently involved in 3D printing.

Hunan Farsoon High-Technology Co. Ltd. was established in 2009 by Dr. Xu Xiao Shu who gained more than twenty years of experience in SLS technology in the US and who, according to Xiangtan University, was rather ironically presented with the Dinosaur Award in 2100 by the Global Alliance Rapid Prototyping Association (GARPA). Farsoon focuses strongly on materials development and, in March 2012, became the second factory in the world after the German-based Evonik to offer nylon powder for SLS 3D printers. Hunan Farsoon now exports the material to the US, Sweden, and Italy, but it is unknown as to whether or not Evonik is considering any legal action.

Wuhan Binhu cofounded by Wuhan Municipal Science and Technology, Huazhong University of Science and Technology, and the Shenzhen Innovation Investment Group is said to be the first in the world to offer models with a printing size of 120 x 120 centimeters, the largest in the industry.

Nanjing Zijin-Lead Electronics Co. Ltd. was founded in September 2008. The joint venture boasts a registered capital of $30 million. Its management and technology development team has thirty members. Nanjing Zijin-Lead can turn out twenty thousand desktop 3D rapid prototyping machines every year. Strange that Makerbot only sold 3,500 in the first two years of production, and yet who has ever heard of the Nanjing Zijin-Lead Electronics Co.?

Dalian University of Technology claims to house the world's largest laser sintering 3D printer with a build volume of 1.8 cubic meters. The printer is said to use industrial grade sand as its print material. At a price of about $160 per ton, this is a considerable reduction on regular materials. I have read about this machine in a few Chinese newspapers now, but that is an awfully bold claim considering the competition that already exists. What about Enrico Dini, the founder of Monolite UK, and the D-Shape "robotic building system," that can print an entire two-story building with stairs, partition walls, columns, dome, and even piping cavities, using a mix of sand and an inorganic binder? And then there is Behrokh Khoshnevis, an Engineering professor at the University of Southern California, who showcased a giant 3D printer that builds housing at a TEDx conference in Ojai, California. And wait, there is more. The Institute for Advanced Architecture of Catalonia have a solar-powered 3D robotic printer that creates buildings. And who can forget Markus Kayser with his Solar Sinter that melts desert sand into cystalline-glass-like structures? Maybe the guys at Dalian University should get out more.

For a more realistic look at the state of 3D printing, perhaps we should take focus upon front line entrepreneurs such as Gu Wei and Eddie Chen, co-founders of Imagineers, based at Tsinghua University in Beijing. Like many Chinese manufacturers, they make a semi-clone of Makerbot's popular Replicator model, taking advantage of the original open source designs. They also provide a low-cost, rapid prototyping service for mainland customers which fills a huge gap in the market, one that is currently filled by Shapaways, Kraftwurx etc. in the West.

They identify the education market as their most important market, something that we certainly have in common. They have already worked with two high schools, but their main stumbling block is that individual schools in China do not have control over their own funds. Chen sums up the general situation in the following sentence: "The Chinese government wants to promote 3D printing, but they don't know how to do it. All they have is money." This is far more insightful that all of the other press articles about 3D printing in China put together. As we have seen, the captains of industry in China are also the same rulers that control the purse strings. In a country where they are quite willing to throw $50 million at a tattooed, washed-up illiterate in order promote the new Chinese Super League, one would have thought that they could have found a few Yuan to open a couple of makerspaces.

Scott Crump, who first invented the technology known as fused deposition modeling and now CEO of Stratasys, recently said of a meeting with party officials in Shanghai:

> *"You could see in the meeting they really wanted to work with us; they needed our help."* But in the end, they *"just want to compete with you."*

Despite this, Stratasys is keen to expand its operations in the mainland. The company, which already has offices in Shanghai and Hong Kong, is keen to open a new office in Beijing and a research and development center in the hinterland.

But if the 3D printing experience in other countries is anything to go by, it is makerspaces and garage hackers who will be the real driving force behind development, and this is very unlikely to happen any time soon in China. A few hipsters are trying to push mini Maker Faires and there was a Global Hackathon recently in Shanghai, but it is going to be an uphill struggle. For example, the Xinchejian hackerspace has two hundred members and is doing great work, but their location, Changle Rd. in the downtown Xuhui District, is a dead giveaway. When I first moved to Shanghai in the early 1990s, that end of Changle Lu was lined with seedy hostess bars and pick-up joints. Like most of Shanghai, it has now changed beyond recognition, and this street is now a much sought-after address for multinationals to locate their China headquarters. On my last visit, I was consulting for the private investment arm of the Porsche family, who were looking for sustainable investments in China. Their first major purchase had been a very desirable villa to use as an office, just yards away from the Xinchejian hackerspace. My point is that a cosmopolitanism metropolis of twenty million people is bound to have at least one hackerspace, but while Shanghai resembles Western Europe, most of China is more like backwater Africa. What happens in ritzy, upmarket Shanghai is simply not representative of the rest of the country. One hackerspace in the most expensive part of town is very different from a national network of spaces all over the country. In addition, Jon Philips has suggested that social innovation in China is still a 150 years behind in China and offers examples of well-known, outspoken dissidents being persecuted and imprisoned. Innovation of any kind struggles in this kind of atmosphere of paranoia and fear.

Earlier this year, during the sixteenth Chinese International High-Tech Expo, which took place between May 21 and May 26 in Beijing, AVIC Laser displayed what they claimed to be the world's largest titanium 3D printed aircraft component. The component in question was for use in China's own J-20 or J-31 military stealth fighters, but representatives of the company said that their 3D Laser Direct Manufacturing technology has been used in producing seven different kinds of aircraft, including the Y-20 Strategic Airlifter, the J-15 carrier-borne fighter, and the C919 commercial airliner. The J-15's chief designer confirmed earlier in March that printable components are being used "in major load-bearing parts, including the [J-15's] front landing gear."

Figure 34. 3D printer fighter parts

AVIC Laser is a subsidiary of China's main military manufacturer, Aviation Industries Corp. of China (AVIC), which produces fighters, nuclear-capable bombers, and 90 percent of the aviation weapon systems used by the Chinese military. An AVIC subsidiary, China National Aero-Technology Import & Export Corp., was sanctioned by the US government in 2008 for illicit arms sales to Iran and Syria.

Historically, forging has been considered to produce a stronger part, but AVIC claims that 3D printing could reduce the cost of expensive titanium parts to as little as five percent of the original value. It costs about 25 million yuan ($4m) to process one ton titanium alloy complex structural parts using traditional methods, but only 1.3 million ($212,000) with 3D Laser Direct Manufacturing.

In a strange twist, they went on to suggest that by using the same techniques, the forged titanium parts on an American F-22 at least 40 percent weight savings could be realized and that overall costs could be reduced by as much as 90 percent.

Over the past thirteen years AVIC has claimed to overcome numerous technical difficulties, winning the 2013 National Technology Invention Award in the process and the intellectual property is now valued at more than a 100 million yuan, according to the Ministry of Finance.

Beijing's University National Laboratory for Aeronautics and Astronautics claims to own a twelve-meter Laser Metal Deposition (LMD), which makes parts, including titanium fuselage frames, for the country's commercial aircraft program. A research team, led by materials science and engineering Professor Wang Huaming, won a second national award from the State Council for technological achievement for a technique called Laser Engineered Net Shaping (LENS) in manufacturing high-density, metallic components.

With funding from multiple sources, including the PLA General Armament Department, the Commission for Science, Technology, and Industry for National Defense, the National Natural Science Foundation and the "973" and "863" programs, they are investigating processes that involve directing a high-power laser beam through a print head while metal powder is simultaneously fed into the build area.

Professor Wang's team had to overcome multiple challenges to produce the printer including developing an inert gas protection system for the extruded metal powder, controlling the rapid solidification of microstructures and preventing internal defects during the laser melting deposition process. The exact measurements of the build area for Wang's LENS printer have not been publicly released, but the team has displayed aircraft parts up to thirteen feet long that were built on the printer. In the United States, smaller LENS printers are being used to produce hardware components for aerospace fighter jets, and NASA is using a similar laser printing process to produce parts for their space shuttles. Optomec, an additive manufacturing company with headquarters in Albuquerque, New Mexico, sell LENS printers such as the LENS 850R, in fifteen countries. European scientists have only been able to print airplane wing sections up to two meters in length and continue to struggle with problems of porosity and rough surface finishing.

Figure 35. 3D Printed fuselage strut

Having spent many years in China, one thing that I have learned about Chinese culture is that outward appearance is often far more important than actual substance. In particular, there are many historical precedents of companies reporting amazing achievements to government officials rather than risk losing the face that is associated with failure. During the famines of the Great Leap Forward, one infamous propaganda photo claimed to show harvests of grain so thick that it could hold the weight of small children. In reality, officials had concealed a bench under the grain and were covering up the fact that mass starvation was ravaging the province.

Figure 36. Shandong province grain harvests

Just last year, I witnessed a particularly bizarre manifestation of this kind of attitude when I visited a $940 million Chinese copy of one of Austria's most picturesque lakeside villages—the UNESCO World Heritage-listed Hallstatt. Built by the Minmetals billionaire, out in the industrial wastelands of Huizhou, Guangdong Province, the project covers more than a million square meters, with cranes and construction sites spread out across barren hills not far from some of the most polluted cities on the planet. The village is a surreal distortion, copied wholesale for the benefit of wealthy industrialists, and located just an hour or so by chauffeur-driven limousine from their grim factories in the smoky distance. A new villa on the shore of the fake lake, (muddy, shallow, and stagnant and some fifty times smaller than the original) costs even more than the real thing in Austria.

Figure 37. Hallstatt and Huizhou

On my visit, I felt as thought I had been transported to the set of the TV show *The Prisoner*, in Portmerion England. Behind the facade, nearly all of the buildings are empty concrete shells, adding to a nationwide blight of empty luxury homes. In Shanghai, more than half of new homes are kept empty, turning moneyed suburbs into eerie bejewelled wastelands, hiding the dirty secret that so much of China's "growth" is paper profit based on empty bricks and mortar. Having seen so many similar developments, I am now understandably skeptical when it comes to extravagant Chinese claims.

Just to show that I am not simply China-bashing here, while I was in Huizhou I was able to visit the much more impressive Legend of Iron factory. Here, Yang Junlin and his ten staff put together full size Transformers from scrap metal, and over the past five years he has designed and built more than a thousand of towering sentinels. Still building giant robots out of scrap metal is one thing, but building a state of the art metal printer many sizes larger than anything that exists in the West is something else completely.

Figure 38. What would these guys do with a large scale 3D printer?
Do we want stealth bombers or Transformers?

American aircraft manufacturers helped pioneer powderized metallurgy back at the end of the 1960s and early 1970s for the engines for the F-15 fighter. GE has since developed manufacturing processes for fuel nozzles in LEAP jet engines that are 25 percent lighter, and five times stronger than traditional parts, but developments in China are allegedly magnitudes beyond this. Some people have said that the pictures of the spar in particular look as though they have been mill machined, although it could have been 3D printed, then finish milled. With some 3D metal printing processes, the only way to make them precise enough is to print extra material, and then mill the surplus away. This leaves a nonclean finish to the parts, as if they were sandblasted or milled.

3D printing from metal powders can leave voids throughout the printed part. These voids eventually become source of cracks that can nucleate due to fatigue loading. The cracks will then coalesce and the part will fail. Wrought metal, on the other hand, is almost completely free of voids in the microstructure, making it the preferred material for lightweight aircraft structures where fatigue life is a high concern. If AVIC really have solved the problem of fatigue using this process, then this would be a major innovation.

Such a development would have massive implications for the company's stock. China's stock market is notorious for being an enormous rigged casino, and so it would not be beyond the realm of possibility for a profit-seeking business to oversell its science and engineering advancements in order to make extremely large gains, especially in an industry as hyped as 3D printing. Many Chinese ventures have in fact seen their stock prices surge to new highs in recent months. It would be quite possible to pass off this kind of thing on journalists that generally would not know any better. I am not claiming to be any kind of metal alloys expert, but I do find it strange that these developments were barely mentioned in the most recent *Economist* article on 3D printing. I was expecting them to have provided much more detail about these breakthroughs. In an article from the September 7, 2013 article, they say only the following:

> *"Some of the world's biggest 3D printers can be found in China. Its astronauts sit in 3D-printed seats which are shaped specifically to their bodies. Engineers working on a Chinese rival to the short-haul jets made by Boeing and Airbus are using giant 3D-printing machines, one of them 12 metres long, to print parts (including wing spares and fuselage frames) in titanium.*

Whenever China makes a major industrial achievement like this, they are usually keen to show off their expertise for all the world to see. A good case in point was the world's largest and most advanced 150MN (15000 tons) heavy-duty hydraulic forging press built by CFHI (China First Heavy Industries) at a cost of 150 million RMB ($.5 million) Reaching a staggering height of almost 25 meters, it can forge is 600 ton giant ingot to an accuracy of less than 3 mm, and is used to fabricate nuclear power pressure vessels.

Figure 39. China's largest hydraulic press

Despite my skepticism, I really do hope that these developments are genuine. If Chinese scientists are successfully pushing the envelope, it will benefit all of us eventually. Such improvements can only be positive, and it certainly brings us closer to the day when we can 3D print our very own advanced fighter jet in the comfort of our own homes.

While I clearly have some reservations concerning official pronouncements (and to be fair I am just as cynical about bloated Western administrations as I am with those in the East), I am very excited about the grassroots 3D printer groups that are cropping up all over the Chinese Internet. The language barrier is preventing more interaction between Chinese makers and their counterparts in the outside world, but there are a number of very active sites well worth keeping an eye upon.

Just as much of the rapid development in the West is taking place under the radar, on private forums and reprap wiki pages, much of the Chinese advancement is happening in Mandarin-only QQ groups. If you are willing to submit to the vagaries of Google's translate engine, I would recommend starting out at one of the following two sites.

http://www.woi3d.cn/

Woi3d (Chinese for I love 3D) is a Hangzhou-based website that provides an on-line 3D design work sharing community, aiming to enable designers, students, and individuals to actively participate. The site has the largest Chinese repository of 3D models.

http://www.3done.cn/

3done features related news stories, but more importantly a wealth of valuable community links. If you are looking for 3D printing contacts in China, then this is a good place to start.

13

To Boldly Print Where No One Has Printed Before

3D printing at various scales is set to push space exploration by magnitudes larger than we have never experienced before. This chapter looks at some of the more recent developments in this hugely exciting field.

In the twenty-first century, plug-and-play concepts are now regularly incorporated into satellite projects. An improved building block system known as Monarch, or "Modular Open Network Architecture," was developed at the Rapid Response Space Works, located at Kirtland Air Force Base in Albuquerque. The Plug-and-Play Satellite-1, or PnPSat-1 design introduced standard walls and hinged panels that looked like pegboards, into which up to eight components could be quickly and easily connected and networked.

Bob Twiggs, a former Stanford professor took the idea one step further with the CubeSat, a tiny satellite design in a standardized one liter cube format (10 centimeters or 3.9 inches per side) and weighing less than 1.33 kilograms (just under 3 pounds). By general convention, microsatellites are between 10 kilograms and 100 kilograms, while pico-satellites or picosats range from 0.1 kilograms to 1 kilograms. Constructed using mainly off-the-shelf components, these microsatellites are so small that they have room for only a few sensors, and burn up in the Earth's atmosphere after just a few months. Despite these compromises, they cost under $10,000, which is considered cheap for the space industry, and which explains why diminutive spacecraft have since become a viral phenomenon, with hundreds of groups worldwide (including high schools and Kickstarter-funded teams) building them. The basic cube design comprises a stack of circuit boards inside, with each face of the satellite covered in solar cells. Two rechargeable batteries split the functions of the satellite into separate parts, one half containing the satellite computer, communications electronics, and altitude control system, the other for payload.

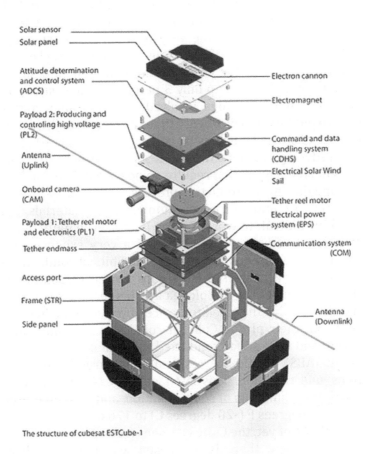

The structure of cubesat ESTCube-1

Figure 40. Cubesat breakdown

3D printing is unlocking great potential for both the Monarch and

CubeSat concepts. Gil Moore, a retired US Air Force Academy professor and stalwart of the space age, who has previously worked alongside luminaries including Wernher von Braun and Fred Whipple, has 3D printed a CubeSat known as the Rampart using Windform XT, a super strong nylon with carbon microfibers. The structure was then plated with a high phosphorus electroless nickel that provides excellent radar reflectivity for tracking purposes. Nylon makes up the satellite's primary structures, its deployable solar cell arrays, and even a propulsion tank.

One manufacturer, Pumpkin, already offers CubeSat kits for $7,000 to $9,000, but even this price is still prohibitive for many, especially when a $40,000 launch price has to be tagged onto this. It is widely hoped that the reusable SpaceX concept is going to make a huge dent in this figure in the very near future. Most people are under the impression that it is the huge amounts of rocket fuel that make up 80 percent of the cost of sending a craft into space. Few realize that the fuel makes up only 3 percent of the cost of a launch. This means that the savings involved with reusable craft would enable us to put ten or even twenty times as many satellites into orbit for the price of single launch using current technology. 3D printing is steadily reducing manufacturing costs, especially by allowing designers to create parts that require no post processing or assembly, streamlining the entire production process.

Aluminum, titanium, or magnesium are light materials, but they are incredibly difficult to work. Carbon fiber is even more of problem in that it requires special expertise and a very expensive vacuum chamber. In space, it tends to flake releasing bits of conductive fibers into the delicate electronics. It is perhaps for this reason that Jacopo Piattoni of the University of Bologna and his team are working with ABS in order to drive the satellites' price down even further. They are confident that their plastic CubeSat could survive launch and low-Earth orbit, and have so far conducted successful tests in near-space conditions. ABS plastic is resilient to extreme temperatures, vibrations, and radiation. This last factor is essential, as a satellite will absorb huge amounts of solar radiation, and its temperature will swing from -4 degrees F (-20 degrees C) to 176 degrees F (80 degrees C) each orbit. As of yet, the CubeSat's sensors and computer chips are not 3D printed, but there is no reason why the metal heat sink required to disperse the electronic components' heat could not be laser sintered in the future. nScrypt of Orlando, Florida, believes that in five years they will have a single machine capable of printing and assembling an entire smart phone, including the electronics, the wireless components, and the display. Once that happens, we will be very close indeed to being able to quickly and conveniently print all the components for an entire Monarch or CubeSat spacecraft.

Figure 41. Cubesat close up

Piattoni's team is working with QB50, which will put fifty CubeSats into orbit at once on a Russian Shtil-2.1 scheduled to launch in 2014. For those not content with just one cube, double- and triple-high CubeSats are available. Developers can go the other way as well: Twiggs's latest project, the PocketQub, breaks up a single CubeSat into eight bite-size chunks.

One of the main reasons for the growing popularity of the CubeSat is the Poly-Picosatellite Orbital Dispenser, more commonly referred to by its acronym P-POD ("peapod"), developed by Jordi Puig-Suari at California Polytechnic State University. The P-POD can house up to three CubeSats, and the ruggedized container can be readily added to practically any launch vehicle, taking advantage of the fact that most rockets have unused carrying capacity. So far, more than forty CubeSats have been successfully launched, with another one hundred planned in the next five years. The CubeSats now in orbit are accomplishing tasks such as studying radio-wave propagation through the ionosphere and measuring cosmic-radiation flux at low earth orbit.

PhoneSats—or smartphone satellites—that cost only $3,500 each, compared to a $1 million price tag of conventional satellites, are already on display in Ames' SpaceShop at their Mountain View

Campus, NASA's hi-tech hackerspace. These off-the-shelf Android smartphones encased in 4-inch cubes, recently hitched a ride aboard Orbital Science Corporation's Antares rocket, and were dropped 155 miles above the earth. During their brief six day stint in orbit, they communicated with ground stations and even managed to send back photographs of the Earth taken from above.

Figure 42. A printed Cubesat

The Arduino CubeSat Satellite is a successful Kickstarter project using a Tyvak Nanosatellite Systems Intrepid system board, at a cost of $3,195 for the system's avionics. A fully operational CubeSat with a 3D printed structure now costs less than $5,000. Without any limitations from machinability, 3D printing allows developers to be more creative with their designs, and new levels of optimization and functionality can be achieved.

In a separate, but equally important development, a team at MIT have developed a benzoic acid inflatable satellite antenna. Given the physical limitations of the CubeSat there is no way that a compressed air canister, valves, and tubing can be crammed into such a small space. There is also the risk that a compressed tank could explode. Benzoic acid is a sublimating powder, which means that it expands into gas form when exposed to low pressure. The team has successfully tested on both cone-shaped and cylindrical, one-meter-wide prototype antennas. In a vacuum chamber the electromagnetic properties of the antennas were measured showing that the new designs were able to transmit data ten times faster and seven times farther than traditional CubeSat antennas.

In even more recent developments, University of Washington Professor Amit Bandyopadhyay, who last year created a 3D printer that could utilize lunar regolith as a feedstock, is now working with Aerojet Rocketdyne to 3D print a coffee-mug-sized picosats from metal and ceramic material, complete with the world's smallest liquid rocket engine.

In a development that might usher in nanosats, Exploration

Solutions have showcased a 3D printed satellite that is about the size of a saltine cracker. Each device is part of a mechanism that can deploy up to three hundred wafer satellites through a spring-loaded mechanism that spins them out into space on a flat plane so as to retain their orientation. This allows them to collect sunlight for power, while still transmitting to Earth. This kind of satellite has the potential to offer ubiquitous WiFi to everyone on Earth. The 3D printed "mother ship" is about 16-inches in height and has 4-inch sides and looks like a mini-skyscraper. The tiny, 10 milliwatt satellites transmitters would use the Code Division Multiple Access (CDMA) encoding scheme, a cellular phone radio frequency, many times stronger than GPS.

NASA has commissioned Made in Space to send a microgravity, 3D printer to the International Space Station in 2014. The initial aim is to print stopgap replacement parts in orbit, for use until permanent parts can be shipped up from Earth. Engineers at the SpaceShop already estimate that some 30 percent of the parts on the International Space Station could be made using a 3D-printer. As the technology is refined and developed, they see a day when large-scale 3D printers could "print" entire habitable structures for use by astronauts, laboratories for conducting science experiments, and even lightweight spaceships, too fragile to withstand a rocky ride into orbit, but fine for operating in a vacuum.

In the meantime, the cost and complexity of space launches continues to fall. The Japanese Space Agency (JAXA) recently launched a SPRINT-A orbital telescope from the Uchinoura Space Center in Kagoshima, southwestern Japan, with just eight people and two laptops. That is not even enough people to put together a baseball team. In fact, it probably takes less people to maintain the Windows server in the data center although, of course, the rocket is slightly less likely to career off-course and explode. A spokesman for the Rebel Alliance in Tokyo said that they were hoping to reduce the crew even further, until only a wookie pilot and an intergalactic smuggler were all that were required for takeoff.

The tiny Epsilon rocket is a three stage solid rocket booster, similar to an ICBM. It does not require fueling, plumbing, cryogenics, or turbo pumps. In addition, an on-board AI for autonomous launch checks the rocket itself. This means that the launch team has a lot less to do than the 150 people needed to launch the previous platform, the M-5 liquid-fueled rocket. Because of the reduced launch team and ease of construction, the production and launch costs of the

Epsilon are roughly half that of the M-5.

With developments like this, the Scaled Composites' White Knight and the SpaceX Falcon 9, we might expect huge hoards of people launching a spacecraft with a massive ground support infrastructure to represent an obsolete technology. Even the United Launch Alliance Delta IV or Atlas V rockets are much smaller than they used to be, thanks to much more efficient rocket assembly buildings. But, in reality, how much of this enormous show has always been a public relations and media event? Seeing a couple of technicians huddled around a laptop is nowhere near as exciting as endless rows of technicians in headsets sitting at subsystem workstations. Of course, launches such as the Saturn Five were highly experimental, which is why they required so much support. Established technology, like these solid rocket stages, is better understood, so requires less people.

Cost savings are arriving from all sides. Earlier this year NASA successfully tested a 3D rocket injector that delivers a fuel mixture of liquid oxygen and gaseous hydrogen into a combustion chamber where it is ignited. The injector was the largest 3D printed rocket component NASA has ever tested and produced ten times more thrust than any other 3D injector made previously. It was made of just two parts, whereas its predecessor, made using traditional metal casting, had 115. By printing objects as a single piece without welding or bolting makes them both stronger and lighter. Using traditional metal casting often wastes the source material and if these are high strength components such as titanium, tantalum, or vanadium, then they are extremely expensive.

For those willing to read between the lines, apart from cost savings, the team at JASC is loudly proclaiming how quickly they can prepare a rocket for launch, which can hardly be coincidental. North Korea has repeatedly flown rockets over Japanese territory in the past, creating a very serious potential threat. Perhaps this could be a camouflaged message to Kim Jong Fruitcake and his generals that the Japanese level of preparedness is improving with leaps and intercontinental bounds.

For the rest of the decade, it will be most interesting to see if all this miniaturization and cost reduction in satellite technology is able to jump start the deep space mining industry. NASA has already mapped nearly a million near-earth asteroids, and now by using "synthetic tracking," or stacking, astronomers are able to identify millions more of these house-sized objects. Previously, they had been difficult to track as they were so faint and fast moving. Instead of long exposures in which near-Earth asteroids show up as faint streaks, stacking involves superimposing multiple short exposures so that the asteroid is a pinpoint composite of multiple images, and the stars become trails. The result is an image in which the asteroid is a sharp point of light against a background of star streaks. Using this technique to obtain astrometry (speed and direction) on very faint objects enables astronomers to identify thousands of new asteroids every single night, using a standard five-meter telescope. It is estimated that there around seven thousand near-Earth asteroids and that nine hundred of those are more than a kilometer across.

Even if we combined the mass of every asteroid in our Solar System, they would only total a mere one-hundredth the mass of Earth. Even so, these resources could support a population thousands of times greater than our home planet. It is estimated that there are a million asteroids orbiting between Mars and Jupiter alone, most of them rich in carbonaceous chondrites and other life-building components.

It has been speculated that a relatively small metallic asteroid with a diameter of 1.6 km (0.99 miles) contains more than $20 trillion worth of industrial and precious metals. Even smaller M-type asteroids (diameter of 1 km or 0.62 miles) could contain more than two billion metric tons of iron–nickel ore, or three times the total annual global production. The asteroid 16 Psyche is believed to contain $1.7 \times 1,019$ kilograms of nickel–iron, which could supply the world's production requirement for several million years. Nearly all of the gold, cobalt, iron, manganese, molybdenum, nickel, osmium, palladium, platinum, rhenium, rhodium, ruthenium, and tungsten in existence came originally from the rain of asteroids that hit Earth shortly after the crust cooled. These are the kinds of interplanetary resources that could become the economic engines which open space to humanity. On the down side, any outside source of precious metals could lower prices, although that might not actually be such a bad thing. And it is also important to consider that much of the value of asteroidal minerals comes from the fact that they are already in space. A ton of asteroid is estimated to be worth $1 million in orbit, but only $4,000 on Earth,

In 2016, the NASA OSIRIS-REx mission will rendezvous with asteroid 101955 Bennu, spend 505 days surveying the rock, and then return to earth with just 60 g (2 ounces) of material. Lockheed Martin estimates that the project will cost in excess of $1 billion. I think that we should take into account that this is the figure given by a defense contractor behemoth, and note their previous excesses that have included $436 hammers, $640 toilet seats, and $7,600 coffee makers. Without a doubt, a small private contractor will be able to do much better, as we have already seen with projects such as those undertaken by SpaceX.

Although asteroid mining was first mentioned in Garrett P. Serviss' 1898 science fiction novel *Edison's Conquest of Mars*, more recent multimillion sponsorships by Unilever and Red Bull, and projects like the Google Lunar X Prize are creating renewed interest in space exploration. This is an especially exciting time for three American companies, Deep Space Industries (DSI) of McLean, Virginia, Planetary Resources (PRI) of Bellevue, Washington, and Tethers Unlimited (TUI) in Seattle, Washington.

DSI has managed to sign up space tourist Dennis Tito, and is now seeking additional funding. PRI, on the other hand, already has a number of high-profile backers with very deep pockets. These include Eric Schmidt and Larry Page from Google, filmmaker James Cameron, Ross Perot Jr. (son of the former presidential candidate), space tourism pioneer Eric Anderson, and X-Prize founder Peter Diamandis. They also have their own wildly successful prototype asteroid-hunting telescope, the Arkyd 100 (http://www. kickstarter.com/projects/1458134548/arkyd-a-space-telescope-for-everyone-0, although DSI is hoping that stacking will offer them a slightly more level playing field. Both start ups plan to survey asteroids, tap them for resources, and shape the raw materials into products using 3D printers in space.

Figure 43. The Arkyd 100

As a first step, DSI plans to launch a number of microsatellites called FireFlies in 2015, to observe near-Earth asteroids and undertake the initial prospecting, identifying which would be the best targets for mining. These will be specially fabricated 25 kg mini-crafts, made from low-cost 3D printed "cubesat" components, designed to make journeys of two to six months, exploring asteroids and other deep space objects that fly near Earth.

In 2016, it then plans to launch the unmanned DragonFly spacecraft, a modular craft that can cheaply hitch a ride with commercial satellites to bring samples weighing between 23 and 45 kg back to Earth, in a time frame of two to four years. By 2020, the company hopes to start harvesting asteroids for useful goods, particularly fuel derived from the ice and methane that make up many astral bodies. DSI expects its first clients to be the owners of the communications satellites which require propellant to stay in their designated orbits.

DSI is also developing a space-based 3D printer called the MicroGravity Foundry, based on a pulverization screw that grinds everything down to grit, and then separates it using a centrifuge separator. A sintering laser would then project 3D patterns in a nickel-charged gas medium, causing the metal to be deposited in precise layers, and then fused into manufactured goods.

Figure 44. The MicroGravity Foundry

"The MicroGravity Foundry is the first 3D printer that creates high-density, high-strength metal components even in zero gravity," company co-founder and MicroGravity Foundry inventor Stephen Covey said in a statement. "Other metal 3D printers sinter powdered metal, which requires a gravity field and leaves a porous structure, or they use low-melting point metals with less strength."

A second challenge that will have to be overcome is the lack of air in space. On Earth, heat generated during any manufacturing process is conducted away to some extent by the air around it. Lack of convection causes major issues as heat does not rise in zero-g, and there may also be fume and lubrication problems. In addition, objects that are in direct sunlight can be hundreds of degrees Celsius hotter than faces that are in the shade. These large temperature gradients can cause materials to expand and contract, which certainly will not help in any fabrication processes.

Other methods under consideration include a number of chemical extraction processes. There again, they might not process in space at all, and just pack it into "freight" containers and send it to a space station. Such containers could also be dropped from orbit to a designated drop site, aka a "Space Harbor" on the moon. The lunar surface could be used as a refining base as it may have enough gravity to use traditional refining processes. The gravity is certainly low enough to allow for easier launching of the processed ore. The lack of atmosphere will make "dropping" freight containers on its surface much easier, since there would be no risk of them burning up in the atmosphere.

According to architects collaborating with the European Space Agency, ESA, (which sounds like an interesting job by anybody's standards,) building a base on the moon could theoretically be made much simpler by using a 3D printer to construct it from lunar soil. The team has devised a weight-bearing, catenary dome designed with a cellular structured wall to shield against micrometeoroids and space radiation. Inside this, a pressured inflatable would provide live support systems for astronauts. Based on a large scale 3D printer building at a rate of around 3.5 meters per hour, completing an entire building would take less than one week.

When considering lunar factories, the power of self-replication is particularly compelling. For example, a 1 kilogram solar-powered self-replicating machine that takes one month to make a copy of itself would, after just two and a half years (thirty doublings), refine over one billion kilograms of asteroidal material without any human intervention. Ten months later, this would be one trillion kilograms which could then be "harvested" at any time. No large mass of equipment need be delivered to the asteroid; in effect, only the information that went into designing the device plus the 1 kilogram device itself. I see no reason why we could not build a Martian base with an automated, solar-powered steel refinery using this kind of reprap based technology.

Competing asteroid mining venture Planetary Resources plans to harvest asteroid ice for rocket fuel, and for platinum-group metals such as palladium, iridium, and platinum itself. They also plan to create a fuel depot in space by 2020, by using water from asteroids, which could be broken down in space to liquid oxygen and liquid hydrogen for rocket fuel. From there, it could be shipped into Earth's orbit for refueling commercial satellites or spacecraft.

A third entrant, Tethers Unlimited, has recently been awarded $500,000 by NASA to put its own spin on space printing. The company is recycling an old science fiction novel theme that was brought to life in the early 1990s by NASA research scientists at NASA's Johnson Space Center (JSC).

The basic idea is to create a SpiderFab, a spider-like robot, with the ability to "extrude" long beams, in the same way that a spider spins silk. These beams could then be joined together using 3D-printed components to form large structures, upon which functional components such as solar panels could be placed. If successful, this would mean far more powerful satellites, with much larger antennae for sensing, and huge solar arrays for unprecedented power. The firm also wants to build orbiting platforms that can beam high-speed Internet and cheap solar energy to anywhere on Earth.

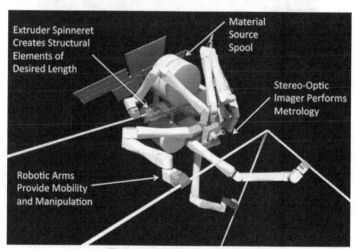

Figure 45. The Spiderfab

An in-orbit fabricator known as the Trusselator, will enable them to create antennas and arrays that are tens-to-hundreds of times larger than are possible now, including kilometer-long solar arrays. By constructing in orbit, the structures no longer need to survive the harsh vibrations of launch and deployment, and can be made with much lower tensile strength requirements.

The original biomimicry design of the JSC Spidernaut made use of the multi-point stance of arachnids, whereby as many as seven legs are stationary during a step, spreading loads more evenly over delicate space structures. Such a system could carry large payloads, transporting structural materials across an extensive solar array or mirrors across a telescope without significant structural loading. This also allows a spider-like extra vehicular robot (EVR) to be deployed in areas too hazardous for astronauts, or in situations that require a level of control that would be difficult for a human in a big clunky space suit. Spidernauts could also utilize their own "web" or space tether technology to move between orbiting superstructures.

Figure 46. The JSC Spidernaut

Such cybernetic creatures were first conceived by one of my favorite hard sci-fi authors, Charles Sheffield, back in the 1979. His novel *The Web Between the Worlds*, featuring the construction of a space elevator, was published almost simultaneously with Arthur C. Clarke's novel on the same subject, *The Fountains of Paradise*.

"The two great ovoid bodies were hanging near the surface of the asteroid, about a hundred meters apart. The eight thin metallic legs were pointed downwards, balanced delicately a few centimeters clear of the surface. Between them, probing deep into the interior of the asteroid, was set the long proboscis. As Rob watched, the great, faceted eyes turned towards him.

The Spiders were aware of his presence. Somewhere deep in their organic components lurked a hint of consciousness.

Corrie had been fascinated by them from the first moment she saw one. "Why eight legs?" she had asked.

Rob had shrugged. "It extrudes material like a spider. How many legs would you have given it?"

On a somewhat darker astro-biological note, asteroid prospecting could provide invaluable scientific data in the search for extraterrestrial intelligence (SETI). Some astrophysicists have suggested that if advanced extraterrestrial civilizations employed asteroid mining long ago, the hallmarks of these activities might be detectable. But what if we find a little more than we bargained for? In Ridley Scott's seminal 1979 sci-fi horror movie, the crew of Nostromo were on a return trip to Earth, hauling behind them a refinery and twenty million tons of asteroid ore, and look at the stowaway that they brought aboard.

14

Military Adoption and Beyond

While those who dare to 3D print guns are publicly condemned by the State Department and congressional lawmakers, behind the scenes, the Pentagon is gearing up to ensure that these high-tech tools shake up traditional supply chains and revolutionize military strategy. Forget geeks printing AK-47s in their garages, the armed forces are already planning a much more systematic implementation of 3D-printed warfare, and is undoubtedly looking at the possibility of printing out weaponry of its own. It is no secret the Chinese People's Liberation Army see 3D printing technology as an easy way to circumvent export controls and trade restrictions on space, military, and defense technology, as well as the currently enforced sanctions on five Chinese arms manufacturers that are involved in weapons proliferation violations.

The digitization process that is central to 3D printing allows the conversion of physical data into things. For the army these "things" could include anything from spare parts for tanks to fully printable drones. Instead of actual parts, an aircraft carrier of the future might be more like floating factory ships, carrying 3D printers and bags of various powdered ingredients. With a hard drive full of schematics technical design files, they could simply print another drone whenever that need arose. Much closer at hand is a distributed global production network in which soldiers send an email with a digital scan or design for a part they need and have it created at the nearest certified printer. The time and money to be saved in terms of logistics alone are enormous. Rectangular packages of powder, which could be printed into bullets when needed, are a far more efficient use of space than stacks of cylindrical bullets. It is estimated that it costs the military fifteen gallons of fuel to put one gallon at the front line. On a frigate or a destroyer 4,000 km from the nearest port the cost of resupplying any item of inventory is exponentially higher. In addition to saving space (extremely valuable when you are confined to a tub in the middle of the ocean) shifting inventory from the physical to the digital world does so much more. This technology can drastically improve the reduction of waste and increase re-usability. Spent casings made from 3D printers, for example, could be chopped up and reused and turned into body armor.

In a taste of what might be coming, researchers at Harvard have been printing incredibly small batteries the size of a grain of sand, using lithium paste, which is hardened to form microscopic electrodes and placed into electrolyte to form a cell. The cells rival the durability, recharge rates, and power density of current mobile phone batteries and can be combined into a large cell, or provide power for miniature devices like the kinds being developed for insertion into the human body. Micro batteries themselves are tried and tested technology. At the University of Illinois, researchers have already developed prototype microbatteries that can recharge one thousand times faster than other batteries and will send out radio signals thirty times faster. Some types of prototype micro-batteries are so advanced they have the power to recharge a car battery. The real breakthrough here is being able to 3D print them. Researchers are now working on printing entire objects with batteries already inside them. Many hearing aids are 3D printed, with the batteries installed later, but researchers want to create fully working units in just one printing session.

Another more sinister use of microbatteries might be the Nano Air Vehicle (NAV). A program at DARPA is developing an extremely small, ultra lightweight air vehicle system (less than 15 centimeters and less than 20 grams) with the potential to perform indoor and outdoor military missions. One of the most impressive flapping wing configurations is the "hummingbird" flyer by Aerovironment to provide warfighters with unprecedented capability during urban operations.

Figure 47. The Hummingbird

A number of difficult design and engineering challenges were overcome such as the challenges of two-wing flapping hovering and fast forward flight, particularly in the wing structure, propulsion, and control actuators. The final prototype includes an on-board power source, and all controls implemented through modulation of the wing strokes and carries and an on-board camera that relays real time video to the pilot.

Combining these achievements with those of the printed microbatteries mentioned earlier could produce some really startling results. Apart from innovative medical implants and tiny cameras and microphones that fit on a pair of glasses and could become virtually undetectable, the same technology could enable flying insect-like surveillance robots. We are all familiar with drones of many different sizes and shapes, but how many of us are anticipating UAVs modeled on mosquitoes. British armed forces are already equipped with the Black Hornet Nano, a tiny helicopter drone that gives troops reliable full-motion video and can be used to peer around corners or over walls.

Figure 48. The Black Hornet Nano

On an ever darker note, a battery that is smaller than the width of a human means that drone-like insects could go beyond espionage and into assassination. Imagine microdrones injecting their targets with neurotoxins or other poisons. Even worse, imagine a mechanical bug that could detonate inside a person's ear canal. Truly the stuff of nightmares.

In 2012, the US announced the world's first openly declared national policy for killer robots, overriding long-standing resistance within the military, and signaling to developers and vendors that the Pentagon is serious about autonomous weapons. Weaponized robot prototypes from four robotics companies—Northrop Grumman, HDT Robotics, iRobot Corporation, and QinetiQ—have recently demonstrated their abilities at Fort Benning, where they were able to traverse rugged terrain, fire machine guns, and take out pop-up targets from a distance of 150 meters. The Northrup Grumman's CaMEL (Carry-all Mechanized Equipment Landrover) can run for twenty-four hours on 3.5 gallons of fuel, and can be equipped with a grenade launcher, an automatic weapon, and anti-tank missiles that can identify targets from 3.5 kilometers away, using a daylight telescope or thermal imaging.

Figure 49. The CaMEL

Recent events such as those in Egypt have shown that the Army cannot always be relied on to gun down a mob of thousands just to protect a handful of corrupt rulers. The idea of autonomous weapons that will protect dictators and governments unconditionally must therefore be very appealing to some. How soon before machines that can vanquish/suppress/intimidate/murder people without those pesky human traits of empathy, compassion, guilt, and regret exist? Convincing people to fight has always been a limiting factor in the history of warfare and it is becoming ever more difficult to find/train/indoctrinate/trick enough psychopaths to suppress an ever-increasing number of disgruntled citizens and foreigners. 3D printing is clearly accelerating the field of robotics and robots are very obedient. Some might even say that democracy ends when the army has no remorse about shooting its own people for unjust reasons.

On the one hand, it can often take decades to bring normal technologies to front lines due to the highly siloed and bureaucratic system of the military. On the other hand, research institutions such as DARPA are often at the bleeding edge of technological innovation. I personally agree with the late Carl Sagan, in that the military should indeed be focused on developing new technologies. After all, the United States' military budget is larger than the combined spending of the next thirteen nations combined. The funneling of hundreds of billions of dollars over the next decade into the advancement of 3D printing technology has the chance to revolutionize the world, and could actually benefit humanity. No other funding source is as concentrated or as risk-tolerant as military funding. There is no need to prove profitability, or even viability. The military will just throw money at it until it works. Referring to space travel, Professor Sagan noted that "exploring other worlds employs precisely the same qualities of daring, planning, co-operative enterprise, and valor that mark the finest in military tradition," and I, for one, am looking forward to these qualities being employed in the advancement of additive manufacturing. After all, technological advancements can be applied to so much more than warfare. This could change the way soldiers build and repair transportation, design shelters, produce food, and treat illness and injury and react during disaster relief operations. We might even see the military become more akin to First Earth Battalions described by Lieutenant Colonel Jim Channon, where soldiers fulfil a role that is more pioneer than palace guard.

When we think about the future possibilities of new technologies, it is important to stretch our imaginations beyond the clichéd fire-base in Afghanistan being attacked by insurgents. Why not instead imagine a world at peace, and think about all the incredibly positive advances for which the military has been responsible? After all, even the Internet was a military network before it was adopted by universities.

One of the less frequently considered benefits of the wars the Western powers have been undertaking recently is the advancement of trauma-related medical technology. So many soldiers are surviving injuries that would have killed them in previous generations, leaving them with missing limbs instead. This, in turn, is advancing prosthetic technology at rates never seen before.

A recent question on popular Internet website *What Would You Look For In a Prosthetic Hand?* While many so-called wits (often under the pseudonym Anakin) suggested a prosthetic bird and others talked vibration and self-lubrication, there were also many enlightening, serious answers. It turns out that there are many people working on this problem and with a varity of different budgets. 3D printed prosthetic hands are often featured in the press as a more positive alternative to 3D printed guns and so in this chapter I wanted to look in more detail at the technology.

Back in May of 2011, carpenter Richard Van As was working at his home near Johannesburg, South Africa, when he lost control of his table saw. He immediately lost two of his left fingers and mangled two more on his right hand. Determined to find a way to get back to work, he began researching prosthetics on-line as soon as he got out of the hospital. Discovering that they cost thousands of dollars, he rigged up an artificial index finger for his right hand with materials from his shop, and began looking for help or collaborators. This eventually led him to work with Ivan Owen, a complete stranger on the other side of the world, (in Bellingham, Wash. to be exact) to create a mechanical hand. Owen is a special effects artist who had been working on a puppet hand which relies on thin steel cables to act like tendons, allowing the metal digits to bend like real fingers. The two began Skyping, sharing ideas, even sending parts back and forth. Finally, Owen flew to South Africa to finish the work in person with Van As.

Van As now has a working mechanical finger, but something else happened on Owen's visit to South Africa. Van As received a call from a woman seeking help for her five-year-old son, Liam Dippenaar, who was born without fingers on his right hand, caused by a rare congenital condition known as amniotic band syndrome. Within days, Liam had five aluminum fingers that opened and closed with the up and down movement of his wrist.

Back in the United States, Owen began working on turning the device into 3D printable parts, until what had previously taken the pair weeks—milling finger pieces, adjusting and tweaking parts— now took twenty minutes to redesign, print, and test. The Robohand is already available on Thingiverse (http://www.thingiverse.com/ thing:44150) along with a dozen remixes of improved individual components, so that anyone can download the plans and, with a 3D printer and about $150 in parts, make a hand.

So far, Van As has fitted more than one hundred children with Robohands. He does not charge anything, not even for the parts, but he does want to train others to assemble and fit the devices.

This example clearly illustrates some of the most important

benefits of 3D printing in any field, not just prosthetics: namely, collaboration and lower costs. The process of fitting and purchasing any artificial limb can be expensive and extremely time-consuming, making them simply unavailable in many Third World countries, where they are needed most.

Although hand technology may not be advancing at the same pace as leg/foot technology, this could be changing thanks to 3D printing technology. Apart from the incompatibility problems of implanted electrodes and human tissue, which I shall address later, the human hand is a marvel of biological engineering that is tough to replicate in a prosthetic. At the moment, gruesome-looking Krukenberg hands are often the only viable option for many people. (I will let you Google it when you feel ready.) Even so, technology is moving very fast and it will be important to retain open systems that are license/patent free and can be disconnected and reconnected without surgery. This would also allow for custom limbs for specific tasks.

For a glimpse of the future, we can look at Dean Kamen's,(the inventor of the Segway) bionic arm, "Luke." http://www. dekaresearch.com/deka_arm.shtml [dekaresearch.com]

At the moment, this top of the line technology still costs around $100,000. http://www.touchbionics.com/products/active-prostheses/i-limb-ultra/. With modular controls, programmable macros, and multiple configurations, this is as light as a female arm (including the battery) and precise enough to pick up a grape without crushing it.

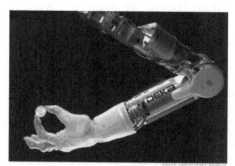

Figure 50. The Deka Arm

German automation firm Festo, famous for its elegantly engineered SmartBird robot seagull, is approaching the problem from a different angle and has developed a prehensile robot arm modeled after an elephant's trunk. The pneumatic robo-trunk is composed of 3D printed segments, and has sensors to maintain its grasp. A second European team is working on a project modeled on an octopus' tentacles, although this might well freak out people familiar with the hentai horrors of the Japanese tentacle menace.

On a more serious note, Bespoke Innovations of San Fransisco are using 3D-printed fairings to make prosthetics look stylish. Keying in on the changing views toward advanced prosthetics, they are creating custom panels that fit over existing prosthetics, and moving us ever closer to the cyberpunk images of fully integrated cyborgs. How long before there will be prosthetics with interchangeable tools like Mannie's in Heinlein's classic *The Moon Is a Harsh Mistress*? Will we ever see Walmart selling custom chainsaw attachments in the landscaping section? If they even come with built-in lasers then there will undoubtedly be some geeks out there signing up for three, and somehow finding the extra room to do so.

Animals are benefiting from these 3D printed advancements as well. Since I wrote about Beauty the eagle in my last book, there has been a prosthetic silicone tail created for Winter the dolphin and the press went all gah-gah over the story of Buttercup the duckling. When hatched in a high school biology lab, she had a backwards left foot, making it hard to walk without getting cuts and constant foot infections. Mike Garey at the Feathered Angels Waterfowl Sanctuary in Arlington, Tennessee, knew Buttercup's foot would have to be removed, and in an attempt to do better than a peg-leg, designed a 3D-printed foot. He took several photos of the healthy left leg on Buttercup's sister, Minnie, combined them in AutoDesk to create a 3D model, and sent the file to NovaCopy, a 3D printer reseller in Tennessee and Texas, who printed out a silicone replacement.

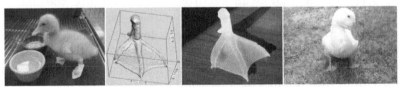

Figure 51. A duck's progress

One of the strangest prosthetic stories to come out of the 3D printing craze is the printing of missing pinkies for reformed yakuzas in Japan. In the oriental world of organized crime, those who commit an offense are often required to chop off a finger and the pinky is usually the first to go. Since everybody in Japan knows what a missing pinky means, many pinky-less former yakuza find that they have trouble getting jobs as soon as a potential employer notices their absent digit.

Shintaro Hayashi, a prosthetics maker in Tokyo, says that the replacements retail for around $3,000 and are sold to three distinctly different categories of customer. The first are those dragged in by girlfriends worried about their reputations, the second are ex-members who are eager to move up the corporate ladder, but worried about the repercussions of their past being exposed, and the third are career criminals who have no intention of getting out, but need to cover up for a child's wedding or grandchild's sporting event.

For years now, we have been fitting replacement hips and knees printed initially from metal, then ceramics, and later polyethylene. 3D printers have also been used to create bone grafts from ceramic, dental crowns from porcelain, and hearing aids from acrylic. New developments are coming out in the field all the time.

Many people suffer pain from walking. Complaints such as back pain, heel/arch, and knee pain are often caused by poor posture and create pain while walking. Doctors can provide foot shoe inserts, or "foot orthotics," engineered to provide support for the foot by distributing pressure or realigning foot joints. However, these devices are handmade, slow to manufacture, and often take between two and four weeks to be delivered to the clinician. These have been an obvious first choice for 3D printers.

A less well-known use has been in printing custom braces and helmets to treat abnormalities. Orthotist Amy Braunschweiger of Infinite Technologies (ITOP), an orthotic and prosthetic facility based in Arlington, Virginia, works primarily with infants suffering from plagiocephaly, or "flat head syndrome," who require the use of a special helmet to correct the shape of their skulls. The use of 3D technology to produce custom medical devices represents a major improvement over past methods, when previous methods of fabricating helmets included taking a plaster cast of a child's head, which often resulted in a big mess and a very unhappy young patient. The 3D scanning system is much less invasive and traumatizing

Plaster casts have always been bulky, obnoxious, heavy, inevitably sweaty, and now they even come in pink. Jake Evill from the Victoria University of Wellington has designed the 3D-printed "Cortex" cast, a plaster cast replacement that is lightweight, ventilated, washable, and thin thanks to its polyamide skeleton. They can even be reused, unlike plaster. A plaster cast takes five to ten minutes to apply, but twenty-four to seventy-two hours to be fully set. The other area is for fractures and joint injuries where swelling is bad at first, but then subsides and therefore a cast cannot be used right away. By using body-morphic data from the unaffected limb and then modeling it for the affected limb, the injured limb could be splinted and ace-bandage-wrapped until the swelling went down and a Cortex could be used. The model could also be used to make clam shells based on morphic data from the diagnostic X-ray or CT scan. This kind of cast is where a top and bottom half are held in place by a wrap. They are used in swelling-prone injuries or in areas where access to wounds is required.

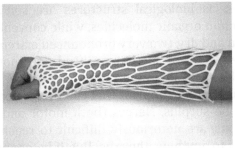

Figure 52. The Cortex cast

Plaster casts never seem to come out in hot pink, but more like a embarrassing shade of dog dick pink, and so this is bound to be an improvement. Plus, and perhaps even more importantly, no more coat hanger scratching. The only downside is that the girls will not be able to sign it. I wonder how long it will be before we are printing full exoskeletons that prevent us from breaking bones in the first place?

Regenerative medicine is one of the most promising areas of 3D printing in biotechnology. The basic principle is to harness the body's natural powers of regeneration to repair or replace the parts that have worn out, so that we can live much longer.

San Diego-based Organovo is printing body parts cell by cell and without the need for a scaffold using the NovoGen MMX Bioprinter. In this way, functional human tissue can be developed in the laboratory. By seeding a prepared scaffold with cells, rat hearts have been created in a laboratory and were seen to expand and contract. Bladders have been made by growing muscle and bladder in a Petri dish. They have been successfully implanted into patients. Because of its relatively simple structure, skin has also been a primary target for regenerative medicine and a number of products are already on the market.

There are some even more ambitious notions out there. Researchers at Princeton University used a modified Fab@Home printer to deposit layers of bovine cells and silicone to create a replacement human ear. Building ears is a common challenge given the complexity of shape and their propensity to become torn off or damaged, but this is a bionic ear that also incorporates a coiled antenna made from silver nanoparticles that can pick up radio frequencies beyond the range of normal human hearing. Bioengineers might one day incorporate sensors into other tissues, for instance creating a bionic knee joint that can monitor strain.

The process of combining electrical circuits with flesh is fraught with difficulties, as biological structures are soft and composed mostly of water and organic molecules, while conventional electronic devices are hard and dry, two very pronounced extremes.

Unfortunately, the average human head does not as of yet have anywhere in which an integrated radio antenna can be plugged. For this reason, a right nipple implant that can be twisted to pick up jazz FM would also be surplus. Nerves (both motor and sensory), for a variety of reasons, are notoriously difficult to regenerate. If nerves are not attached to anything, they die. But, if before amputation, they are connected to skin and muscle that will not be affected, they will remain alive and functional. This obviously has many interesting applications in terms of interfacing with prosthetics. Even so, electrodes of any kind implanted directly into the brain are at an extremely high risk for infections such as meningitis. Still, the ability to combine the electrical and the biological demonstrates that 3D printing has many interesting applications to come.

Organovo believes that three-dimensional human tissue samples could be a better medium for testing new drugs and hopes to begin selling liver tissue next year. Liver toxicity is the most common reasons for a drug to be pulled from clinical trials, and this could be more accurately tested on three-dimensional samples of liver tissue.

Researchers are now hoping to create synthetic coronary arteries that can be grafted onto the heart, a process that has failed in the past due to thrombosis or the enormous tension placed on the wall of the vessels from the circulation. 3D printing may be the breakthrough, offering enormous potential gains as coronary artery bypass is the now the most common operation in the world.

A team at Tel Aviv University is reporting that they have

discovered a way to 3D print tiny, bio-compatible devices known as microelectromechanical systems (MEMS) smaller than a millimeter which will enable the creation of a whole new generation of cybernetic implants and limbs. A new polymer will allow them to incorporate the same types of tiny actuators and sensors that have revolutionized smart phones and computers and will allow developers to create smart limbs.

To all the naysayers claiming that 3D printing will cost ordinary working peoples their jobs, it is clear that in reality, wide fields of work are opening up that we did not even know existed yet. If 3D printers are now being used to make ears, lungs, and other body parts, whose jobs are being cut in this situation? God's?

15

Pushing the Political and Technological Envelopes

One of the main reasons that I wanted to write another eBook about 3D printing was to explore the idea of distributed manufacturing in greater detail. The main inspiration for this has been Mr. Cody Wilson, recently vilified by most of the mainstream media. For those of you who have spent the last twelve months in Pyongyang, Cody's organization built and fired the world's first 3D printed hand gun, sending shockwaves around the world in the process. Unfortunately, guns are an inherently politicized topic, especially with the recent goings-on on Capitol Hill. Defense Distributed knew full well that printing a gun for their project would get everyone's attention.

Of course, we should never underestimate the corporate mouthpiece's ability to hyper sensationalize and over report the fixation of the moment. The media frenzy surrounding 3D printed guns is in one way quite mundane. Simply speaking, we have replicated an invention that has existed for at least eight centuries (explosives propelling a projectile) using twenty-first-century technology, but in reality is it so much more than that.

I personally applaud their work, now that I can more clearly see the longer term goals. Unfortunately, very few others are defending DEFCAD's work, despite the fact that are pushing the envelope of this new technology, but at the same time staying completely within the law.

Even on the Slashdot website, a hangout for coders and assorted techno geeks, the general response was less than positive. Most participants quickly became embroiled in the same old predictable gun debate. One poster was particularly vociferous:

> *[Warning: Large amount of offensive language]*
> *Cody Wilson can go f*ck himself (Score:3, Insightful)*
> *by Anonymous Coward on Friday April 26, 2013 @01:58PM (#43553039)*

This man is single-handedly ruining 3D printing for EVERYONE, just because he's a gun nut obsessed with firearms. He's pushing into a gray area and setting a very early precedent that will impact the availability of 3D printing for the rest of America. Cody Wilson is just what you'd expect from a 25-year old, gun nut, pothead, government conspiracist. He's afraid of having his weapons taken away, he's afraid of having his weed taken away, and he's afraid of his rights being taken away. His entire life is ruled by fear. So how does Cody respond? He perverts a revolutionary technology to make _more_ f*cking weapons with them in violation of the law. F*ck Cody. This is why scientists and engineers f*cking hate people that take what they pour their lives into and deform for their own f*cked up needs. When the 3D printer was invented people envisioned a technology that could help, that could make development rapid, that would improve our lives. Now Mr. Wilson has ruined all that and made it a tool to create weapons. Cody Wilson is a f*cking a**hole.

Although I was always taught that profanity and obscenity are linguistic crutches of the inarticulate motherf***er, this comment certainly struck a chord with many.

The reality is that Cody Wilson does not smoke, drink, or take drugs. Despite the Texas stereotypes, he never even owned a gun prior to starting this project. Thanks to his passion for progressive authors including Proudhon, Baudrillard, and Kevin Carson, he has quickly become a very deep thinker, and an extremely competent strategist. Let us take a moment to reflect on exactly what happened.

Everybody has heard about some kid in high school that blew off three of his fingers playing with fireworks or, worse still, stuck a bullet in a vice and smacked it with a hammer. Although on the surface this looks like the same kind of idiotic prank, these first few shots are actually the opening salvos of what Cory Doctorow describes as the "The Coming War on General Computation." Wilson already has a licence to manufacture and sell the weapon from the US Bureau of Alcohol, Tobacco, Firearms and Explosives. As for exporting the blueprints, he also registered his operation under the International Traffic in Arms Regulations (ITAR), administered by the State Department, and has legal advice that it complies with the rules. DEFCAD went on to do everything that they could to comply with existing laws, including removing the plans when asked (which will in turn be found to be an illegal over-reach). Nobody can say that they were not fully cooperating in all regards. As Bonaparte wisely stated, "never interrupt your enemy when he is making a mistake." By issuing an order that appears to be an illegal overreach of authority, not to mention unenforceable, Uncle Sam dropped a major clanger.

Individual politicians are firmly planting both feet down their throats on the issue, especially in the US where the situation is especially convoluted. If the Republicans support 3D gun printing, they hurt gun manufacturers. If the Democrats ban 3D printing, they confirm that they are indeed the big brother party.

Shapeways has already refused lego ray-guns because the Terms and Conditions and Content Policy do not allow the uploading or the printing of anything that looks like a weapon, although they do make exceptions for miniature weaponry with a maximum size of 10 centimeters. This is annoying as two products I was interesting in printing, that I am sure would have sold particularly well, are forbidden under these rules. I was looking at a vintage ray gun for Star Trek collectors and a novelty sauce dispenser. Both would have been great 3D printables.

Figure 53. An early prototype Federation sink plunger, and a gun acceptable for everyday home use.

Shapeways says that it will not print anything related to air soft guns, or replica firearms that use compressed gas, spring, or electric motors as propellants, even though these do not require any special licensing, and as internal components do not even resemble weapons. They have already publicly acknowledged that the company does not check every user-submitted design. Thingiverse alone is fast approaching some one hundred thousand user-uploaded designs, a number that will explode exponentially when people start buying 3D scanners. All this raises the question: How carefully can companies monitor for the production of gun parts or other weapons? Are there already too many plastic gun replicas in the mix? Thingiverse already carries designs for an entire armory of Star Wars universe weaponry including a Boba Fett EE-3 carbine blaster rifle, Imperial Scout Trooper Blaster, and DC17 Animated Clone Trooper Blaster. User Conseils has quite helpfully collected a list of model guns (http://www.thingiverse.com/Conseils/collections/model-guns/) and it seems to me that at least a dozen of them would be fine for anybody planning a bank heist. Much of the maker community has distanced itself from gun-printing evangelists like DEFCAD, and Thingiverse in particular has removed all their gun designs listed on its site. This genie is unfortunately already out of the bottle. In this chapter and the next, I am going to identify a number of the slow burn fuses that are now smoldering away nicely.

The first thing to realize is that the 3D printed gun is a red herring. Anyone who wants a gun can make a much better one using more traditional tools found in any machine shop or garage or even just buy one. Wilson is in fact challenging the right of authorities to restrict and regulate the incredible technological development we are seeing in the open-source 3D printing community. While I am not a supporter of guns in general, 3D printed guns are actually a good thing, in that experimenters are using a novel technology to do something technically difficult with high tolerances and high forces. This is pushing the boundaries of the technology, which is the only way technology can improve. But this is also about sending a message to lawmakers, letting them know that they cannot simply ban objects or ideas just because they find them objectionable.

Wilson describes himself as a crypto-anarchist and yet hardly any of the media that interviewed him has bothered to explain what this is. Instead, they have simply let readers freely associate and conjure up the usual stereotypes of bomb-throwing lunatics. Most anarchists are simply anti-authoritarians who seek the freedom of self-governance, privacy, and expression. Many people would describe Thomas Jefferson, Henry David Thoreau, the Dalai Lama, and Mohandas Gandhi as anarchists. A crypto-anarchist brings these principles into the twenty-first century and utilizes the distributed nature of the Internet to protect their privacy and political freedom. It is interesting to note that the Electronic Frontier Foundation (EFF) has pledged to support Wilson and, given their record, you can be pretty sure that that they are no friends of the NRA.

In an age where most of us feel that the law is used to restrict our freedoms rather than protect them, most of us are in fact anarchists, without even being aware of the fact. Of course, the governments and other vested interests go out of their way to present anarchists as a danger to society, often just a small step away from terrorists. This is very much the same way in which big media strives to portray file sharers as pirates and thieves and how industry portrays neo-luddites as dangerous subversives. Some of the most respected thinkers in the world today are self-professed anarchists. MIT Professor Noam Chomsky is the most cited living scholar and yet, is all but ignored by the mainstream media. For a slightly less academic example Alan Moore, one of the most interesting contrarians of our time, also describes himself as an anarchist. If you still think that anarchist is a derogatory term then try reading this. http://www.utne.com/politics/anarchism-101.aspx

Despite being lambasted in the kangaroo court of public opinion, Avi Reichental, president and CEO of 3D Systems, says the man behind the 3D-printed gun has done the 3D-printing industry a service. He points out that the 3D-printed gun signifies the democratization of craftsmanship on a larger scale. Equipped with 3D printers, anybody can simply download a file and create an object that, in the past, might require years of training in engineering or manufacturing to build. Wilson has presented us with a gun as a Trojan horse to highlight the perennial issue of the free flow of information. What he has done is highlight in a high profile and dramatic fashion the hugely disruptive potential of 3D printing. Let's take a look at some these subjects on an individual basis.

Regulating Technology

The paragraph below comes from the Google Books synopsis of Scott Shane's *Dismantling Utopia: How Information Ended the Soviet Union*:

> *By the 1980s the Soviet Union had matched the United States in military might and far surpassed it in the*

production of steel, timber, concrete, and oil. But the electronic whirlwind that was transforming the global economy had been locked out by communist leaders. Heirs to an old Russian tradition of censorship, they had banned photocopiers, prohibited accurate maps, and controlled word-for-word even the scripts of stand-up comedians. In this compellingly readable firsthand account, filled with memorable characters, revealing vignettes, and striking statistics, Scott Shane tells the story of Mikhail Gorbachev's attempt to "renew socialism" by easing information controls. As newspapers, television, books, films, and videotapes flooded the country with information about the Stalinist past, the communist present, and life in the rest of the world, the Soviet system was driven to ruin. Shane's unique perspective also places one of the century's momentous events in larger context: the universal struggle of governments to keep information from the people, and the irresistible power of technology over history.

I read Shane's book so that I could compare the censorship of the Soviet Union with that of twenty-first century PRC, but eventually concluded that the co-opted mainstream media of the West does an equally good job of keeping information from the people as the Chinese Ministry of Propaganda.

They key point here is whether prohibitions on a new technology can actually work. Prohibition on alcohol created far more problems than it solved, a situation that has repeated itself with the modern day prohibition of drugs. Despite the ham-handed attempts of the copyright cartels to rewrite the law for their own benefit, culture sharing is growing faster than ever, benefiting even the companies that are trying to kill it. The open source community needs to mobilize and occupy the high ground before a repeat of the file sharing history of the last fifteen years, when the corporate behemoths successfully managed to associate file sharing with piracy in the public and legal minds.

One netizen writes with regard to the DEFCAD take-down notice: "I fear there will be a day that if you want to have a hands-on knowledge of certain technologies, you'll have to move to another country." Unfortunately for the US, this is already true. Who in their right mind would run a torrent tracker, a cryptographic anonymiser or a distributed e-currency on American soil?

It used to be that advances in technology were celebrated. Now they are vilified if they don't fit into a narrow "politically correct" spectrum. This is a disturbing trend in the US where common sense and civil responsibility is giving way to legislation and rule-making. What was once a nation of innovators, risk-takers, and problem solvers is now trying to curtail any type of technology, even knowledge that "could" be used irresponsibly.

In perhaps what is a sign of things to come, the Greater Manchester Police Force made themselves look like blundering plods, when thirty officers conducted a raid on a local toyshop keeper and announced to the media that they had discovered a fully operational 3D printing firearms factory run by organized crime. What they assumed were the next generation of firearms actually turned out to be a spool holder and a spring-loaded Replicator 2 drive block upgrade. The amount of misstatements in the UK media that followed was frightening. They trotted out all the usual garbage that guns could be created by gangs in the privacy of their homes and smuggled with ease because they could avoid X-ray detection. Anybody with 3D printers should now be worried that they will have to prove to the authorities that their prints are not gun or bomb parts. The police claimed that one of the parts was a plastic trigger, but even if it was, then by default that makes every cleaner, weed-spray and insect-spray bottle in my kitchen cupboard illegal. In other news, an eight-year-old grandmother has been released today when it was found that a supposed rocket launcher was just an umbrella stand. I suspect this is more about the fact that hysteria sells, rather than genuine cluelessness, although a major part of this panic could be due to established manufacturing companies beginning to realize that individuals will soon be able to print their $5 items for less than five cents. How long before we see some form of faux outrage to ramp up and 3D printing to be banned or seriously restricted?

Step back for a moment to 1957 and the invention of the laser. Would it have been a wise move to ban this new development? Lasers can be used to guide missiles and could indeed become heavy duty space weapons in their own right. There again, an outright ban would mean no laser surgery, laser pointers, CD and DVD players, laser cutting in factories, the use of lasers in holography, their deployment as a means of bringing about nuclear fusion, and, indeed, their use in 3D scanning and printing.

If 3D printers become regulated, then what is next? Lathes? After all, they can be used to make a barrel of a high-powered rifle. Mills can be used to make land mines. Will we see regulations on sheet metal that is used to make the skin of missiles? Will we go the whole hog and regulate screwdrivers? Everybody knows that they are essential in making IEDs.

Figure 54. Randy Jeffries is now a stringer for Fox News

A perfectly functional zip gun has long been easy to make using match heads and curtain rods, or a lighter and a car antenna. On Northeastshooters.com, a shooting forum in New England, one member details how he made a full automatic AK47 out of a shovel in a just few hours, complete with explanatory pictures (http://www.northeastshooters.com/vbulletin/build-yourself/179192-diy-shovel-ak-photo-tsunami-warning.html). The same kind of work takes place every day in the remote mountainous border regions of Pakistan and Afghanistan, where Khyber Pass Copies are made out of old train tracks and scrap cars (http://en.wikipedia.org/wiki/Khyber_Pass_Copy). This just goes to show that it is a vibrant local market that encourages gun making, not the availability of advanced manufacturing technology. There have been DIY gun construction manuals available for many years, but are they really the cause of gun proliferation?

Figure 55. Not generally available in the children's section of the mobile library.

I wonder how many makers out there, upon being told that they are not permitted to print gun-shaped things, will go ahead and print one just out of curiosity or spite? Does prohibition only increase the long term Streisand effect?

Progress

I am uncomfortable using the word "progress" to describe the rapid improvement of 3D-printed weapons in the same way that I am uncomfortable with the term "development" being used instead of runaway growth, but the process itself still requires documenting. We have quickly seen new and more complex designs, and by the time you read this eBook, I am sure that there will be far more deadly iterations of anything that I have written about here.

The standard Liberator that caused so much press hysteria quickly evolved into the Pepperbox and then into the Trantor 224, a double-action revolver. One YouTube user posted a project that he had be working on in between 3D printing ukuleles. The Grizzly was a low-caliber 3D-printed rifle that, despite having a beefy name, was on par with the kind of rifles used for hunting small game like rabbits and squirrels. Worse still, the whole barrel split lengthwise after just a single shot.

The underlying technology of 3D printers might not be changing here, but the designs are becoming increasingly intricate. Some people are also drawing parallels with the development of firearms in history. One of the more recent designs is the Reprringer. Rather than massively overbuild to withstand the pressures of modern gunpowder cartridges, this pocket pistol is chambered for one of the least powerful commercially-produced cartridges on the market, a

.22 CB aka 6 mm Flobert. Like the 9 mm Shuty that uses a common Glock pistol barrel, the Reprringer uses unrifled steel inserts in the cylinder and comes with an ammo storage case and a tool for unloading the cylinder. It is interesting to note that Archduke Franz Ferdinand of Austria was assassinated with a 9 mm weapon, indirectly triggering WWI.

3D-Printed Ammunition and Projectiles

It might not surprise you to learn there is already a 3D printed bullet. It contains a small piece of metal in the front of the bullet to add weight, but it is still mostly plastic. After all, it was only a matter of time. Now that there is a growing arsenal of 3D-printed guns, a 3D printed bullet could not have been too far behind. Some researchers have said that 3D printing might even make for better ammunition, with manufacturers being able to customize for specific targets.

Industrial technician Jeff Heeszel (aka YouTube user taofledermaus) has uploaded a video of his friend shooting a 3D-printed bullet from a shotgun. As you may have guessed, the bullet worked. Not quite as well as a regular bullet, but, remember, it was made at home on a 3D printer. Heeszel makes videos of himself and his friends shooting random objects like dimes and Tic Tacs out of shotguns. Unlike Wilson, Heeszel is not a crypto-anarchist. In contrast, he is just a guy who loves to play with guns which, in my mind, is probably more dangerous. I will really start worrying when red necks like Ted Nugent get wind of 3D printing capabilities.

Defense Distributed also has a 3D printed .24 cartridge using a printed plastic case, with a sabot-style bullet that seats a ball bearing as the projectile. It seems that every restriction or proposed restriction on guns simply creates another imaginative workaround. Bullets with plastic cartridge cases are already available (http://www.polymersolutions.com/blog/making-ammunition-with-plastic-cartridge-casings/) and only require a metal firing pin and primer. And who needs primers anyway? Why not set off the powder electrically with a 9 volt battery and a bit of .000 steel wool? Compressed air is even easier to obtain than gun powder or primers. Pepper box guns do not need to be incredibly accurate, and so there is no need for huge amounts of energy to send a bullet a short but lethal distance. Admittedly pneumatic systems are more complex than a hammer, but why does a projectile have to be ejected with the hot gasses from an explosion, as in conventional ammunition? Can we expect some as-yet-unimagined hybrid of a firearm and a crossbow that shoots small projectiles with a mechanism placed under high tension? Just look at the wild contraptions Jöerg Sprave creates. Amazingly, plastic slugs can do some serious damage, but as can be seen from Sprave's videos, as does silly putty, bubblegum, and frozen Vienna sausages.

http://www.slingshotchannel.com/
The Slingshot Channel's Official Website

As far back as the 1850s, French engineer Paul Giffard patented a single-shot pneumatic breech-loading gun that featured a pump and air reservoir located under the barrel. In 1872, he received a patent for a new gun design which used removable cartridges containing compressed air, compressed gas, and liquefied gas as a propellant source. In the late 1880s, he perfected the first practical CO2 guns. These arms, which included pistol, rifle, and smooth bore versions in 4.5 mm, 6 mm, and 8 mm calibers, were produced by noted French arms makers Manufacture Francais d'Armes et Cycles de St. Etienne. Later, Giffard's British subsidiary, Giffard Gun and Ordnance Co. in London, manufactured an improved lever-action hammerless version of this gun, that featured an octagonal barrel and a counter for tracking gas usage. Colt even went so far as to pay $1 million to purchase the American rights to produce these guns. During the twentieth century, Paul Giffard's ideas for pneumatic and compressed-gas guns have gone on to find success both as trainers and as smallbore target arms, and several companies, most notably Crosman and Daisy, have built successful businesses based in part on his work.

It is important to note that Giffard patented over two hundred inventions, including a pneumatic telegraph, that used pneumatic tubes for fast delivery of documents, currency, and other small items. He was not a gun nut, but a very prolific inventor.

Figure 56. Two examples of Giffard's work

If the power of propulsion of a fire arm is lowered, the projectile itself might need to change, possibly becoming like a chemically propelled arrowhead. In such a case, if the damage comes from an edge rather than simply the energy carried, the entire "bullet" could be plastic, which would lead to truly undetectable weapons. And what about non-lethal weapons? We have all heard of rubber bullets, and I personally am rather looking forward to the first deigns for a 3D printer pepper spray, for defense purposes of course. By the time this eBook is released I would not be surprised if somebody has successfully created a fully-automatic compressed-air flechette rifle that looks like something straight out of science fiction movie. Actually, forget 3D-printed conventional firearms, just wait until folks get really creative and start designing weapons that are completely novel and unexpected and do not look like anything anyone has ever seen before. Arduino-controlled pipe bombs? Embedded Linux flame throwers? Machete-wielding robots that have a true "kill switch"? Just to make sure, I am being facetious here.

While 3D printed guns still lack accuracy, it is likely that another technological path will soon provide an interesting convergence point. The self-aiming rifle does not actually aim itself, and a person still has to pull the trigger, but it does allow the shooter to tag the target with a laser, and the rifle's computer will process environmental data, along with where the target is located and give you the "ok" when ready to fire. It will even compensate for trigger jerk and other shooter mistakes. A few more esoteric flaws come into play with extreme range too. Many shooters of high performance sporting rifles "float the barrel" to allow for the barrel's natural reflex, or spring-like reaction as the bullet travels it's length. Even the stock can interfere and impede the barrel's response, thus affecting the "fidelity" of the barrel's reaction, which minutely affects the trajectory of the bullet. This is one of the differences between a $500 rifle and a $1,000+ rifle of the same relative caliber and relative "class." Until now, complex and expensive optics and controllers were required for this kind of precision. Even the mass of the shooter holding the rifle can inadvertently affect the rifle's natural recoil. This new self-aiming system has no pulse, it does not breathe, cramp, tire, or even feel the temperature like a human.

Figure 57. High pressure compressed air sniper rifle concept by Rolf Bertz.

Despite these advancements, stopping power is often a more important consideration to firearms designers. This is done by increasing lethality and so logically we will be able to look forward to hollow point rounds, Glazier slugs, and high-capacity magazines. But this is the real world, and we are not talking about facing-marauding zombie hordes here. Army strategists do not care so much about stopping power as they prefer wounding people. An enemy soldier gets a mass grave, but a wounded combatant has to be dealt with, binding medical personnel, supplies, hospitals, transportation, logistics, disability, pensions, and veteran care, all things that hurt the enemy financially. Stopping power can also refer to a visual deterrence. At the moment, most of these 3D printed firearms have the intimidation factor of a super-soaker.

Detection

Much of the media hysteria about 3D printed guns is focused on detectability and whether an all-plastic gun will make it through the X-ray and past the sniffer dogs/trained hamsters/pheromonally-sensitive bees that are trained to smell out the explosives in ammunition. In reality, nearly all airport scanners are "dual energy," which allows them to distinguish between organic and inorganic materials (like explosives in a metal tube) with the newer models utilizing backscattering, so large homogeneous pieces of plastic (like the barrel) will "shine" nice and bright.

The sad reality is that anyone that cannot afford a real gun from illegal sources is unlikely to be going into the areas "protected" by metal detectors. Of course, even if an aromatic tracer is added to 3D printing filament, there will likely be some angry malcontent out in front of the airport giving away 3D printed travel toothbrushes and combs to drive all the dogs crazy, and then adding 3D printed replacement handles to their luggage.

Alternative Weapons

When push comes to shove, just about any every day object can be turned into a weapon. Especially if you have been watching Jackie Chan movies, it is amazing what he can do with a common stepladder. Are we going to go down the route of banning every possible weapon that can be 3D printed, from nunchaku to Mrs. Peacock's candlestick? There is simply no end to the offensive and unacceptable 3D printed murder weapons that will need to be banned.

In February of 2013, a man wielding a Klingon bat'leth robbed two Colorado 7-11s. A number of designs for this alien blade are available from knife outlets on the Internet although retailers only recommend them for strictly honorable and ceremonial purposes. This particular assailant will never get to Stovokor with that kind of disreputable behavior and will probably be sent to work in the mines Rurea Penthea once caught.

Suicide

Some people are claiming that the temptation for manic depressives to take their own lives will be much easier with the introduction of 3D-printed guns. Statistics have so far shown that suicide rates are not affected by firearms control laws. In Japan, for example, the suicide rate is almost twice that of the US, and in both the UK and Australia the suicide rate did not decline after gun bans were instituted. Of course, the very same statistics show that homes with handguns have higher suicide rates than homes with long-barrelled guns, which have higher suicide rates than homes with no guns at all. Despondent people will always find a way to end their misery. In Japan, where guns are uncommon, there was a trend for committing suicide by standing on the rail tracks. Then the railway companies began charging the families with the cost of the delays and so more people turned to gassing themselves, vastly increasing the risks for everyone in the entire neighborhood. Suicidal people will simply find other methods of harming themselves, and attacking the instrument used is just missing the point.

This, of course, brings us to the root causes of the 3D-printed firearms debate and what some would describe as the T-rex in the tool shed. We have all heard the phrase about lies, damn lies, and statistics. Statistics about gun crimes and firearms ownership do make interesting reading, but only really succeed in confusing the whole issue. Fortunately, the advent of 3D printed firearms is making countries such as the US evolve culturally to a point where we begin to address the root causes of violence, instead of the usual hollow grandstanding among politicians.

Laws are passed based on popular support not on actual data. Popular opinion is created and maintained by big media, and we have already seen how little they understand what is going on here. How many reporters focused on the fact that there are already three hundred million regular guns in the US and, even if those of us with 3D printers created one million guns over the next twelve months, that total would be increased by only one-third of 1 percent?

Technology is now becoming available to the general public that is powerful enough to create a serious risk to social stability. If we are to take the "guns don't kill people, people kill people" arguments seriously, then we should be finding out exactly why people want to kill people and do something about it. It is ironic that this dialogue might be inspired by a paradigm shift in manufacturing that also happens to allow for the unfettered proliferation of lethal weapons. The question is no longer, "Why can't we get along?" It is more, "We have to figure out how to get along ASAP, or else!"

Some people are using this opportunity to forward their own agendas. For example, it is obvious that drug prohibition is fueling violent crime, and its removal would be far more effective that any kind of enforced gun control, but that still does not address the root causes.

Looking at America only for a moment, it is clear that the country is weaponizing itself at an unheard of pace, with every manufacturer and importer reporting huge rises in production and sales. FBI background check statistics indicate that, over the last twelve months, Americans purchased a new gun every 1.5 seconds. One report indicates that every major gun and ammunition manufacturer in the country is running at 100 percent capacity, with many so far behind that they have stopped taking new orders altogether. From the outside it looks as if the US is in a fully-fledged domestic arms race. Those who do not have guns are increasingly feeling that they are at the mercy of those who do. Statistically speaking, it is better not to threaten a criminal with your own weapon, but to either hide or run for it. Even the NRA acknowledges that in their "how to survive a school shooter" videos, but the media is sensationalizing the gun issue to such an extent that there is a growing culture of fear.

A recent piece in the *Wall Street Journal* reported that America's police departments have gone from community officers walking the beat to full-on, militarized SWAT operations breaking down the doors of non-violent offenders. The article stated that "in the 1970s, there were just a few hundred [raids] a year; by the early 1980s, there were some 3,000 a year. In 2005, there were approximately 50,000 raids." It continues by detailing examples of aggressive, SWAT-style raids, many of which have ended in unnecessary deaths. Last year, after a Utah man's home was raided for having sixteen small marijuana plants, nearly three hundred bullets were fired (most of them by the police) in the ensuing gunfight, because the home owner believed he was being attacked by a gang of criminals. The US military veteran later hanged himself in his jail cell, while the prosecution sought the death sentence for the murder of one officer he believed to be a criminal assailant. The reports range from incredulous to outrageous; from the raid on the Gibson guitar factory for violation of conservational law, to the infiltration of a bar where underage youth were believed to be drinking, to the Tibetan monks on a peace mission who were apprehended by police in full SWAT gear for overstaying their visas. Then there was the woman who was subject to a raid for failing to pay her student loan bills. It is a small wonder that few respect the police any more. SWAT-style raids are no longer for defense against similarly-armed criminals; it is now seems to be a standard ops intimidation tactic. How much bloodshed will it take for people to realize such a disproportionate response is unwarranted and disastrous?

Not only is there growing polarization within America, but outsiders looking in from other developed nations are aghast at what is occurring. Instances such as the five-year-old boy that accidentally shot and killed his two-year-old sister with a gun that is marketed to kids by the manufacturer Crickett are causing special concern. Here are the comments of one forum poster from Europe:

> *"Perhaps the reason that Europe has drastically less gun crime than the US has much less to do with the differences between European and American law, and much more to do with the differences between Europeans and Americans. If you compare Japanese Americans to native Japanese, we see that they have very similar violent crime rates despite living on*

opposite sides of the world. There's obviously more at play here than the laws. Too many Americans think the best way to defend themselves is to overpower their enemies and that they must own a gun so that they can shoot an intruder or mugger. Europeans prefer to call the police and try to scare the burglar off, rather than getting into a fight. The result is that American criminals come armed, and with the intention of murdering you if they feel threatened. They cannot just run for it if discovered because they do not want to risk turning their backs on someone who is armed. In Europe house breakers they usually flee if discovered.

Of course, these kinds of comments are not well received, as one American poster aggressively replied:

". . . why don't you buy a plane ticket and come take our guns away yourself if the US Constitution irks you so much. Piss off."

Whenever I talk about America, I am very wary of lumping the entire US into a single cultural box. I understand that the country overall may share federal laws and a single language, but beyond that I am uncomfortable wielding such a wide brush. The US is about nine million square kilometers while Europe is roughly ten million. States that border each other will likely be very similar, but the more distance that is put between the states being compared, the more they become dissimilar.

Much of the world remains unarmed, surrounded by unarmed people, but just a few minutes away from armed response. The majority of them live freely without cowering in paranoid fear. Many would argue that crime prevention is far better accomplished by assuring equality and opportunity and decent conditions to all, rather than by gun-toting vigilantes patroling their own little violent fiefdoms. When no one individual's life is so miserable that shooting up a liquor store for $30 looks like an upward career move, then there would likely be far less crime. I personally would prefer to live in a world where people respect one another out of shared humanity, not fear we will end up looking down the wrong end of a barrel.

Perhaps we should stop looking at history and the world as a whole in our search for solutions. History is especially confusing, with phrases like "Abraham Lincoln freed the slaves, but Sam Colt made them equal." I have been unable to find out who originally said this, but I am willing to bet that it was an early Colt salesman. The Second Amendment was framed in a revolutionary distaste for Europe's standing armies, and a resultant animosity toward the arbitrary dictatorship of the state. At the same time, it is also easy to forget that the Ku Klux Klan was one of the first groups to favor gun control, mainly so that it could confiscate the arms from the freed blacks that had fought in the Union army. Much later, in 1967, California became the first state to pass laws against carrying loaded weapons, much to the delight of Republican state assemblyman Don Mulford who was campaigning to repress the armed radicals of the Black Panther movement. The Mulford Act was signed into law by the then state governor Ronald Reagan, a man still revered by America's National Rifle Association.

Both of these examples clearly go to show that America in the present cannot solve its problems by comparing itself to other times and places. The example of Mexico is often given, in that it has a 100 percent ban on guns, where citizens cannot even own a .22, but rarely do you hear about criminal gangs throwing rocks at each other. What is the point in having a ban that is not enforced? Obviously, in this case, all the criminals have weapons and much of the government and police are massively corrupt and part of the criminal gangs themselves. The US is a special case and should be judged as such, without trying to draw worthless comparisons with very different countries and cultures.

At the same time, irresponsible behavior and the socialization of its consequences is actively encouraged. In fact, the hypocrisy is overwhelming. Every Tuesday, Obama famously decides who should become the next victim of a drone assassination attack. Cody Wilson is demonized in the press, while in Salt Lake City, Senator Howard Stephenson, R-Draper, wants to offer gun manufacturers incentives that could include tax breaks to relocate in Utah. Beretta USA is looking at relocating its Maryland operations after that state passed a ban on assault weapons and high-capacity ammunition magazines. The company currently employs more than four hundred people and paid more than $31 million in taxes in Maryland. This is the same government that is on record openly shipping arms, cash, and military equipment to its own listed terrorist organizations from the

Mujahedeen e-Khalq (MEK or MKO) in Iraq and Iran, to the Libyan Islamic Fighting Group (LIFG) in Libya, and to Al Qaeda's Syrian franchise, Jabhat al-Nusra.

Regulating 3D printers is like arresting an old lady at the airport for having nail clippers, while ignoring the state-sanctioned arms dealer walking in with a RPG slung over his shoulder.

The Highly Profitable Small Arms Industry

While the debate rages over 3D-printed guns, it seems that there is little if any effort being made to reign in the large-scale industrial manufacturing of guns, which, if anything, is accelerating at a frightening pace and is on the path to become a worldwide scourge. To me, this is like punishing nicotine addicts with high taxes and increasing regulation, while cigarette makers continue to play the role of untouchable drug dealers, taking in ever-increasing profits all over the world.

The Control Arms Campaign, founded by Amnesty International, Oxfam, and the International Action Network on Small Arms, estimated in 2003 that there are over 639 million small arms in circulation, and that over 1,135 companies based in more than ninety-eight different countries manufacture small arms, as well as their various components and ammunition. The industry appears to be fragmenting, in order to bring manufacturers closer to potential markets. Conservative estimates mention 7.5 to 8 million small arms being produced per year, although according to the Small Arms Survey, "more is known about the number of nuclear warheads, stocks of chemical weapons and transfers of major conventional weapons, than about small arms." To make things even more difficult, more than 80 percent of ammunition trade remains outside of reliable export data.

The majority of these small arms have survived many conflicts, and many are now in the hands of arms dealers or smaller governments, who move them between conflict areas as needed. As if life was not unpleasant enough already for the world's poorest populations, this increasing proliferation is especially devastating for the ordinary people of Third World countries, particularly with those in Africa paying an inordinately heavy price. During the period 1990–2005 alone, twenty-three out of the fifty-four African nations experienced war: Algeria, Angola, Burundi, Central Africa Republic, Chad, Democratic Republic of Congo (DRC), Republic of Congo, Côte d'Ivoire, Djibouti, Eritrea, Ethiopia, Ghana, Guinea, Guinea-Bissau, Liberia, Niger, Nigeria, Rwanda, Senegal, Sierra Leone, South Africa, Sudan, and Uganda.

In countries where food and water are scarce, an AK-47 is only $50. To see what this means for the everyday life of Africans, I recommend the documentary *Black Samurai*, which takes a look at the kendo-like competitions of two tribes in southwestern Ethiopia, What is far more striking, though, is that almost everybody shown owns practically nothing except a loin cloth, a few scrawny cattle, and, of course, a Kalshnikov.

The majority of conflict deaths are caused by the use of small arms, and civilian populations bear the brunt of armed conflict more than ever. The violence becomes more lethal and lasts longer, and a sense of insecurity grows, which in turn leads to a greater demand for weapons. The rate of firearms-related homicides in post-conflict societies often outnumbers battlefield deaths, as small arms become the dominant tools of terrorism, organized crime, and gang warfare. More human rights abuses are committed with small arms than with any other weapon.

This bloody trade generates immense profits for the countries that manufacture and trade in small arms. It is interesting to note that the five permanent members of the UN Security Council—France, Russia, China, the UK, and USA—together account for 88 percent of the world's conventional arms exports. As we have already seen, these are often legal arms sales to irresponsible governments who use them to oppress the people. The United Nation's General Assembly resolution (A/C.1/63/L.39*) has stated very clearly that manufacturers and traders of small weapons should bear partial responsibility for the abuses and crimes that are committed as a consequence of use of these arms, and these are the very same immensely influential organizations that are so vehemently opposed to international standards for small arms trade.

The NRA works hard to suppress opposing viewpoints, and uses the Second Amendment to justify their actions, although the public has not actually appointed them to protect their rights, as they claim to be doing. While the full NRA donor list is a very closely held secret of the organization, the public does have access to the "Ring of Freedom" tier information for corporate donors. This list is a set of contribution tiers and donors that allows people to see a variety of big-money contributors to the NRA. The information twe currently have on its funding shows that the NRA takes millions of dollars a year directly from the largest manufacturers of guns, including Beretta and Benelli USA, as well as companies that make gun accessories and companies that require easy access to weapons (including Xe, the company otherwise known as Blackwater).

The United States is the world's leading weapons exporter by far. America exported $336.5 million worth of firearms in 2011. That is $200 million more than Italy, the next leading exporter. The United States is also the top global importer, and this insatiable American appetite fuels a burgeoning small arms industry around the world. SAS, an independent research group in Geneva, valued global small-arms sales for 2011 at $8.5 billion, more than double its 2006 estimate of $4 billion. American small-arms purchases in 2009 accounted for 38 percent of the global total at $1.8 billion, more than forty-seven other leading importers combined. Private citizens provide the main source of demand for small arms around the globe. Of the 650 million firearms owned by civilians worldwide, more than 41 percent are in American hands. It is no surprise the United States has by far the highest proportion of guns per person, an estimated eighty-nine civilian firearms per one hundred residents. The ATF says US companies increased production by two million between 2006 and 2010, bringing the total to nearly 5.5 million. Three manufacturers produce about a quarter of that total. The top maker of pistols and rifles, Sturm, Ruger & Company, has facilities in Arizona and New Hampshire. Other major players include Smith & Wesson in Massachusetts, which produces the most revolvers, and Maverick Arms in Texas, the leading shotgun manufacturer. Those companies also top the list of American firearms exporters, shipping about 110,000 guns, or 45 percent of total exports, in 2010. Despite decrying gun violence, the current administration is advocating new regulation that would make it easier to export weapons abroad. Washington was chiefly responsible for the collapse of talks last summer on a UN arms trade treaty, a reflection of the vast political influence wielded by the US gun lobby, which is spending tens of millions of dollars to ensure the highly lucrative industry keeps expanding.

Beijing does not report its small arms exports, and has resisted UN efforts to expand reporting of the trade. Deliveries of arms from China to sub-Saharan Africa are estimated to have grown from just 3 percent of the total volume between 1996 and 2000 to 25 percent from 2006 to 2010. Researchers often glean information about Chinese arms from discarded weapons and spent ammunition in war zones.

The birthplace of the Kalashnikov is looking to new markets to make up for shrinking military sales. During the Cold War, Moscow funneled huge stockpiles of small arms to its allies, but sales were decimated by the collapse of the Soviet Union, when former republics came into possession of colossal stockpiles that created a saturation of the market that continues today. In addition, the production of cheap, unlicensed knock-offs in China and elsewhere has helped undercut Russia's foothold in the military arms market. Kalashnikov-maker Izhmash, Russia's largest small-arms producer, is now actively seeking out new civilian markets, with the United States being particularly lucrative, growing at a rate of 25 percent per year.

Authorities around the world are especially sensitive about protests against arms manufacturers. This is clearly represented in an independent UK documentary entitled *On the Verge* (http://www.schnews.org.uk/schmovies/index-on-the-verge.htm. It clearly demonstrates that state run police forces are more interested in protecting the interests of wealthy arms dealers than the rights of ordinary citizens, and the lengths that they will go to do so. The film covers protests aimed at arms manufacturer EDO MBM Technology Ltd. in Brighton between 2004 and 2008. The film is critical of the Sussex Police, showing blatant collusion with the company to intimidate protesters and pursue a High Court harassment injunction that would have banned any kind of protest outside the factory. Since the film was released, the UK police are going to great lengths to prevent the film from being screened at any location. http://www.theguardian.com/environment/2008/mar/27/ethicalli ving.activists

If Cory Doctorow's war on general computing does actually take place, then *On the Verge* may have recorded some of the earliest opening salvoes.

While not directly related to 3D printing, I have included all of this information so that you are properly able to explain the real dangers next time some ignoramus complains the 3D printed guns are a serious terrorist threat.

Gun ownership arguments continue to go back and forth without either side seeming to make any real progress. Gun owners claim that guns prevent several million crimes per year, including burglaries, assaults, murders, and rapes. They argue that a gun not only equalizes a woman's odds of fighting off a rapist, it actually gives her an edge over an attacker twice her size. But just as guns "empower" physically weak good guys, they also empower every scrawny, messed up meth-head on the block. Now, instead of worrying about the one large oversized attacker, our chances of being murdered are multiplied to every cowardly little shit with a firearm. Worse still, the sheer amount of guns available surely increases the odds of being caught in the crossfire when a "good guy" goes paranoid vigilante.

While I would like to remain neutral in these discussions, I am sure that every reader can easily spot my own biases, and so there is little point denying them. When I was younger, the number of my friends that were killed in traffic accidents really frightened me. I was initially surprised to learn that car crashes were the number one cause of death for males my age. My answer was to change my lifestyle so that car ownership was unnecessary. The fact that I am still alive makes me feel, rightly or wrongly, that I made the right decision. I am therefore very tempted to believe that if it can work for cars, why can it not work for guns?

Before I move onto the next chapter and deal with Cody Wilson's real concerns, i.e. the future of distributed manufacturing, I would like to share with you one ray of hope that has emerged from all of this discussion, the 3D Printers for Peace Contest. Alarmed at the media focus on 3D-printed guns, engineers at Michigan Tech recently sponsored the first 3D Printers for Peace Contest. Believing there is far more potential for 3D printers to make our lives better, rather than just killing one another, they asked designers to think about constructive uses of 3D printing and to answer the question: If Mother Theresa or Gandhi had access to 3D printing, what would they print? What kind of designs could help reduce military spending and conflict, while making us all safer and more secure? Of course, there are always smart alecks out there and, when it asked "What would Jesus print?" somebody promptly replies with "nail-resistant socks and gloves."

Seriously though, those in the poorer countries of the world often have problems obtaining spare parts. They tend to have old, no-longer-supported gear, such as tractors or irrigation pumps. Even when the parts are available, they are too expensive to ship, or are pilfered by corrupt postal workers. If a part for your pump or manure spreader arrives two months late, you have already missed the planting season. A printer that can make a part from a spec downloaded over a cellular network would come in very useful. You do not need one on every farm or in every shop, just within a day's walk. Organizers were hoping to see some small-scale 3D printed windmill designs or a 3D printed treadle pump as these are some of the most successful appropriate technologies for lifting farmers out of poverty.

Figure 58. 3D Printers for Peace Contest Winners

When the results came in, human ingenuity surprised everyone again. The first prize was awarded to John Van Tuyl of Hamilton, Ontario, for his immunization beads design, a brightly-colored innovation to help families and doctors in the developing world keep track of childhood vaccine records. Each color and shape represents a vaccine, and the blocks can be printed with a child's initials, date of birth and an identifying number and then strung into a necklace. Putting easily interpreted medical records into the hands of the ordinary people that are more permanent than paper is a very interesting concept. Hopefully, families will be more likely to save the beads than standard vaccination cards.

Matthew Courchaine took second place in the contest for a solar-powered water purification cone, that was designed to be used during disasters or in regions where clean water is a precious commodity. Third prize was awarded to Aaron Meidinger for his design of a Braille tablet, which could let a sighted person leave short notes to a blind person, or vice versa. Plastic tiles with letters in both Braille and the alphabet can be arranged on a platform reminiscent of Scrabble. Even people that cannot write Braille can now can arrange tiles to spell out messages. All the entries are posted on Thingiverse.com, and can be downloaded for free and printed by anyone with a 3D printer.

In the meantime, Cody Wilson's Liberator, treated as both a technological marvel and a terrorist threat has now been designated a work of art. London's Victoria & Albert Museum of Art and Design has purchased two of the originals from Defense Distributed, describing the acquisition as a "permanent cultural provocation."

I personally think that the curator has missed the point

completely. The gun was simply an early proof of concept. What would be much more impressive is a 3D printer continually printing guns, then having them ground into pellets, extruded as filament, and fed back into the printer. Now that is what I call art!

16

A Future of Distributed Manufacturing

To see what a successful distributed manufacturing economy might look like, I would like to share three manufacturing models from around the world that are very different from the current norm. While each has its distinct advantages and disadvantages, perhaps together they can give us some idea of things to come.

Emilia-Romagna is one of the richest regions in Europe, and polls report that its capital Bologna is the favorite city of all Italians. It is a beautifully historic city center, with some of the best-preserved Renaissance palazzos, Baroque porticoes, and soaring medieval towers in all of Italy. It boasts the oldest university in the Western world, founded in 1088, and is home to some of the most respected automotive marques on the planet, including Ferrari, Lamborghini, Maserati, and Ducati.

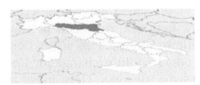

Figure 59. The Emilia-Romagna in Italy

It is one of the most intensively entrepreneurial regions in the world, with ninety thousand manufacturing enterprises, where an estimated one person in twelve is self-employed, or owns a small business. By contrast, New York State, with over eighteen million people has twenty-six thousand manufacturing enterprises.

This entire region of 4.2 million people is the most prosperous in Italy. Unemployment, at just 4.7 percent, is even lower than the jobless rate in Lombardy and Piedmont, northern Italy's corporate heartland. Nearly half of the regional agricultural and industrial output, about $14 billion worth, is exported, chiefly in the form of machinery.

Small to medium enterprises (SME's) predominate and yet, in recent years, the region has produced the highest GDP per capita in the country, now ranking in the top ten of all of Europe. In 1970, Emilia Romagna was near the bottom of Italy's twenty regions in economic performance. Today, it ranks first. Its per capita income is 30 percent higher than the national average and 27.6 percent higher than the EU average.

Apart from being extremely successful entrepreneurs, they enjoy fine food, designer fashions, and a wealth of material goods that provide them with one of the most enviable standards of living in the world. The region continues to cultivate a tradition of fine arts and crafts production which accounts for a major portion of the region's economy. Bologna has the highest per capita expenditure on culture of any city in Italy and public services in health and education are of an extremely high standard.

So what is the secret to this unbridled success? Flexible manufacturing networks of small-scale firms working in co-operative networks, rather than enormous factories or vertically integrated corporations, are the keys to the Emilian economy. They are not simple suppliers of components to a large corporation that lays down the law, but production follows a lean model geared to demand, so there are few significant inventory costs. Small-scale, general-purpose machinery is integrated into craft production, and frequently switches between different product lines. The local economy is not prone to the vagaries of the boom-bust cycle which results from overproduction. In exchange for Italy's highest benefits and wages, workers are flexible. They move easily among firms. Similarly, skills and marketing information travel easily among local suppliers. Nobody talks about productivity anymore, it is taken for granted, like electricity.

As a result, workers are technically very competent. They know how to work machinery, but also have theoretical backgrounds that allow them to become a designer of components. They have the skills needed to run a business and they have a genuine passion for producing quality products. These "artigianati," or self-employed artisans, account for 41.5 percent of the companies in the region. Over 90 percent of these enterprises employ fewer than fifty people, and the average manufacturing firm in Emilia Romagna has only ten employees. Only 1 percent of firms have 250 or more employees. Another key is that they are overwhelmingly geared toward export, not just out of their region, but throughout Europe. They are producing for the Brazilian, the Eastern European, and even the Chinese market.

Of Italy's forty-three thousand co-operatives, fifteen thousand are located in Emilia Romagna, making it one of Europe's most concentrated cooperative sectors. In fact, there are more than sixty thousand workers employed in some 1,800 "red" Emilian co-ops. In Bologna, for example, two out of three citizens are members of a co-operative, with most belonging to several, while 45 percent of the GDP is produced by co-ops and 85 percent of the social services in Bologna are delivered by those very same co-ops. No invisible hand provides Emilian firms with financing, daycare, urban planning, technical assistance, research institutes, and specialized laboratories. Small companies cannot be expected to devote much capital to research and development. They cannot even afford to hire marketing consultants. The regional government arranges for these services, chiefly by contracting with nonprofit economic research agencies like the internationally respected NOMISMA.

Two-thirds of those co-ops are worker owned and while there are only five firms in the area that employ over five hundred, even two of these, SACMI and CMR, are cooperatives. Others range from heavy industry to precision equipment, from gigantic ceramic presses to service co-ops. There are also a number of very important agricultural co-ops, housing co-ops and, increasingly, social co-ops. Coop Italia is the top retailer, surpassing giants like the French equivalent of Walmart, Carrefour, in sales. It has six million owner/members, fifty-five thousand employees, 1,200 stores, and €11 billion in sales. Co-operatives directly account for over 40 percent of the region's GDP. Indirectly, with their economic spin-offs and their involvement in production, distribution, training, and marketing networks, the co-operatives of Emilia Romagna account for a much higher contribution to the region's economy. At the national level, the co-operatives belonging to Legacoop, Italy's largest co-operative federation, employing 202,700 people. In turn, the principles of co-operation, and the adoption of reciprocity and mutual benefit for economic objectives, are the philosophical and social bases of the system.

In the co-operative system, the shareholders of the company are the workers of the company. It is a normal capitalist enterprise, but instead of having bonus-hungry executives and short-term investors, you have workers who are looking for long-term gains, and who are willing to work extra hours or be paid less if the situation requires it.

No less important than the economic structure is the fact that the policies of the regional government actively promote co-operative relations among firms. One reason that few people know about this amazing success story is that they immediately switch off when they learn the whole area is run by communists. Six years ago, the Italian Communist Party renamed itself the Democratic Party of the Left, or P.D.S., but continue to surpass all Italian regional governments by every objective measure.

Actually, it is rather different from the communist system. In a communist system, there is a distinct absence of markets and all companies are owned by the state. The state dictates what is going to be produced, usually without taking into account the knowledge of the local workers, which is coincidentally also something usually valued in capitalist high value industries. There are, of course, many people around the world that will accuse anything to do with co-operatives to be "commie." If they honestly believe that the Soviet Union was all about workers' co-operatives, then their historical insights need not concern us. Emilia Romagna is well known as the "red belt" of Italy because of its unbroken succession of communist and social democratic administrations, which have governed the region since the World War II. Historically, Bologna had always been a center of political and civil opposition to the authoritarian traditions of the monarchy and the papacy. In the 1940s, the anti-Fascist resistance came down from the hills and took power, and this was the only region in Italy where workers actually seized the big factories from their owners and then transformed the region into a working left-wing model of a future Italy. Cities used eminent domain to take over unused land, and would use public money to develop the kind of infrastructure that industry depends on. They would then sell it at cost, below market prices, to small businesses and co-ops. Ever since

WWII, the communist party has been returned to office regularly in free elections with ever-increasing electoral margins: from 34 percent in 1945 to the 57 percent won by Governor Pier Luigi Bersani in the 1995 spring regional elections—the second-highest share won by any of the twenty governors in Italy. The area remains a stronghold of opposition to the alliance of media mogul Silvio Berlusconi and neo-Fascist Gianfranco Fini. In 1994, when Berlusconi tried to cut back the welfare state, demonstrations broke out in cities all across Italy. More than a million people protested in Rome. In Bologna, 250,000 turned out. A demonstration of comparable size in New York City would need to rally five million protesters, but far more inhumane cuts in the city budget never produced more than twenty thousand demonstrators.

It is clear that well-trained, flexible workers employed by financially democratic enterprises are a key to the areas success, but at the same time, the ability of companies to multi-task makes them both efficient and resilient. As we see more and more that technology in the form of tools can accomplish many different tasks, we will hopefully see businesses that are adaptable to changing consumer needs and economic climates. 3D printing represents the beginning of this trend, from huge industrial behemoths capable of producing one product in its countless millions to human scale tools that change their output at a moment's notice. Tools and factories where humans are much more than simple cog-like components, but are instead the valuable, intelligent software that controls the entire process.

Compared to the Adriatic Riviera, the Shenzhen Special Economic Zone is a gritty, industrial city. Just thirty years ago, the place was a tiny fishing village and since then it has become one of China's largest metropolises. Nobody is actually from Shenzhen, and the whole city is made up of immigrants from the rest of the country. Some have likened it to Logan's Run, since there is hardly anybody to be seen who is over forty and college graduatees are lined up outside factories to work for $0.60 an hour. Much of the city is ultra-modern, and yet it already feels like Syd Mead's dystopian vision of the future in *Bladerunner*. It is more cyberpunk-Neuromancer than anywhere else on the planet.

In 2013, well over a billion mobile phones were manufactured here, with about one-third for domestic consumers and two-thirds destined to go abroad. The lion's share were Shanzhai models destined for neighboring countries in southeast Asia and Third World countries in Africa and Latin America as well as India and Russia.

A "shanzhai" product refers to anything outside of government regulations and apart from the big brands. It has also come to mean something that is improvized or homemade and can refer to anything from fashion to pharmaceuticals.

Shanzhai (山寨) comes from the Chinese words "mountain fortification" and refers to a cave or guerrilla-style hideout. In its modern context, this is a historical allusion to the freedom fighters that dwelled in such places. Although most readers will not realize, they actually might be quite familiar with the twelfth-century Song Dynasty legends. Ironically, many Westerners know Chinese classics such as *The Outlaws of the Marsh* (Shuihu Zhuan) thanks to the Japanese cult TV show, *The Water Margin*. Long before George Lucas had relocated heroic fantasy to the far reaches of outer space, many of us grew up with very Oriental versions of Robin Hood, Che Guevara, and General Ludd, in a strange, exotic kind of Tolkien with top-knots. Maybe the introductory spiel from each of the twenty-six episodes will jog a few memories.

The ancient sages said, "Do not despise the snake for having no horns, for who is to say it will not become a dragon?" So may one just man become an army.

I was amazed when I first arrived in China in the early 1990s that I knew so many of the local sayings and proverbs, all because I had watched far too much imported Japanese TV in the form of *The Water Margin* and *Monkey*. While my friends were impressed at my knowledge of Confucius thought, I dared not tell anybody that I had learned everything from 1970s Nippon TV, as they had all been brainwashed from birth to hate anything remotely Japanese.

Modern day shanzhai are more akin to West coast hacker-entrepreneurs, resembling Jobs and Wozniak, back when they were working out of their garage, but with a Chinese twist. The shanzhai economy of China is typically dismissed by popular press as a group of copycats that make knockoff iPhones and other counterfeit electronics, but this is a far richer and much more interesting economic eco-system. Bought to the attention of many computer enthusiasts by Andrew "Bunnie" Huang, who has blogged extensively about the small scale manufacturers, this system exists in many parts of China, including the PC builders of Ganding in Guangzhou (my own stomping grounds) and even the motorcycle industry in Chongqing. Each one can probably be traced even further back to the notorious Wenzhou model.

Actually, assembled is perhaps a more accurate description than manufactured, as most components including application processors, driver ICs, LCD cells, 3.5 inch HVGA displays, logic boards and connectors are all shipped in from overseas. Most semiconductor fabs are located in the same country as the chip designers. Examples include Samsung in South Korea, TSMC in Taiwan, and Intel in Arizona.

The ability of the shanzhai to not just to replicate, but to innovate and riff of (as opposed to rip off) designs is very significant. Shanzhai has been labeled as counterfeiting, but in reality it is more than just copying. They are doing to hardware what the Internet did for rip/mix/burn or mashup compilations. Innovations are much more than simple cosmetics with shanzhai products. Watch-phones, zoom lenses, and 7.1 sound required at least a redesign of the PCBs, custom tooling, and custom firmware. What is more, they understand and meet the needs of local markets and tastes. A good example would be the phones with a built-in UV LED, essential in a country where counterfeit currency is so rampant. Locals are duly impressed that the shanzhai could not only make an iPhone clone, but could actually improve upon it by adding a user-replaceable battery. US law would interpret this kind of activity as illegal infringement, but is protecting the interests of big corporations really more important than meeting the needs of consumers? Even a minor redesign of a phone PCB would be extremely expensive if done by a Western design shop, not because of the custom tooling required, but because of the complicated navigation of all the patents involved. In the shanzhai economy we see people improving on each other's designs, and even outdoing the big corporations.

Shanzhai are collaborative manufacturing groups that suggest "a new approach to economic recovery . . . based on small companies well-networked with each other." According to Chris Anderson, they are increasingly driving the manufacturing side of the maker revolution by being fast and flexible enough to work with micro-entrepreneurs. ⬛Kevin Carson has compared the shanzhai to the household "shadow factories" that emerged in postwar Japan, and the small factories and machine shops of the Third Italy as described by Piore and Sabel. Tom Igoe calls it "situated manufacturing."

These shanzai companies range from just a couple folks to a few hundred employees. Modern cell phones contain sophisticated hardware, software, and systems technology, yet shanzhai companies of only ten people specialize in things like tooling, PCB design, PCB assembly, cell phone skinning, and also rely on a sophisticated, but informal network of product designers, manufacturers, and distributors. Others are broader in their capabilities. One shop of less than 250 employees churns out over two hundred thousand mobile phones per month, with a high mix of products, where runs as short as a few hundred units are possible. Many of the individuals are ex-employees of large corporations, frustrated at the inefficiency and inflexibility of their former employers. They dislike the traditional rules or practices, often resulting in innovative and unusual products or business models. The result is a very competitive price-to-performance ratio and high profit margins, featuring multi-functional capabilities that are able to piggyback on trends and adapt designs accordingly.

According to Mitch Tseng, open manufacturing of this kind builds on open supply chain networks that allow the exchange of resources and capacity between the participants. In the shanzhai, this has been established through open BOMs (bills of materials) and crediting each other with improvements. Even when I was first in China two decades ago, I was amazed that the state-owned book stores were filled with technical manuals for all kinds of appliances, each one with detailed schematics and electrical diagrams. The community apparently self-polices this policy, and ostracizes those in violation.

Shanhzai companies work in a very similar way to US open-source hardware firms such as Spark Fun, Adafruit, Evil Mad Scientist, Arduino, and Seeed Studio, although the manufacturing needs and skills of the shanzhai are still much more advanced, and the vendor networks more complex and interconnected. Even so, both thrive by taking existing tools and products, re-combining them, and repackaging them in more usable ways. The American firms prefer the General Public License to open BOMs, but both revise products constantly and do business based on relatively small runs of products tailored to specific audiences.

Chinese banks have always been reluctant to lend to small private companies and therefore most Shanzhai companies are bootstrapped on minimal capital. This allows new and smaller players to enter the market and produce new products (often for niche markets) faster and with high efficiency. Mitchell Tseng reported that €10.000 is enough to start such a company, that can quickly scale in just a few years to over €50 million revenue per year. Their non-conventional approaches should tell manufacturers around the world that the value proposition underpinning the shanzhai way is one to be reckoned with. For multinationals such as Nokia, it is already too late.

A few, such as Tianyu, sometimes referred to as the King of the Shanzhai, have become so successful that they now market phones under their own brand. The company started off by imitating global brands, but they now enjoy an 8 percent market share in China, more than either Nokia, Samsung, or Motorola. In turn, they now obtain licenses, pay taxes, and sell legitimately on the commercial market.

Thanks to second-generation low-cost handset chips by Taiwan chip designer MediaTek, Tianyu was able to use their knowledge of Chinese users to challenge the multinational heavyweights. Their handset brand, K-Touch, introduced features such as dual SIM card support, and software that enabled users to make purchases on the Chinese shopping website Taobao.com. Responding to the needs of customers in second- and third-tier cities, the brand guaranteed good sales and quickly eroded the dominance of Samsung and Motorola. Other features included built-in business-card scanners and the option to receive phone calls to two different phone numbers.

The shanzhai model is inspiring a new generation of garage builders and innovators taking familiar products and remaking them with peculiar, but innovative twists. In a country where aviation is very tightly controlled, an emerging aviator class is spreading its wings with a plethora of approaches, from the ramshackle to the sophisticated to the potentially revolutionary. Wu Zhongyuan, a farmer from Henan province, built his $1,600 shanzhai helicopter from steel scaffold, an old motorcycle engine, and twirling wooden blades. Xu Bin, a thirty-one-year-old farmer from Zhejiang province, built his own autogyro, which is actually his fourth flying machine.

Despite the thin veneer of communist dictators, China has always been a very capitalist society. The ability to create wealth has historically been limited to those who already possess large amounts of capital. Shanzhai companies have shown that this need not always be the case and that technology can significantly lower the bar for entry into manufacturing. This is part of the greater trend that we are seeing with additive manufacturing. When production no longer requires vast assembly lines and huge factories, then individuals and small groups of workers can finally begin to compete with wealthy investors. Hopefully, this will become clearer in my third and final example.

Local Motors is much more than a next generation American car company. It is one of the most comprehensive examples of a revolutionary approach to car design, engineering, manufacturing, sales, and marketing in the world today. It is also the first disruptive entrant in the US automotive industry in decades.

Local Motors uses an open networked innovation platform to build cars five times faster, at one hundred times less the capital cost of conventional manufacturers. Using the contest model, it received more than forty-four thousand designs from 3,600 innovators for its first project. This beats any one company hands down, who could never afford to hire that size of workforce. Many people still believe that the greatest car designs in history have come from the singular vision of one person and not from the "wisdom" of the crowd, but maybe Local Motors is set to change that. When industries democratize, when they are ripped from the grasp of corporations and governments and handed over to ordinary people, we see massive transformative change. The Internet is already democratizing the fields of publishing, broadcasting, and communications. Could the car industry be next? Maybe Local Motors is fulfilling Cory Doctorow's prediction that "the days of companies with names like 'General Electric' and 'General Mills' and 'General Motors' are over."

Using a virtual space known as "The Forge," CEO John B. Rogers Jr., has built a global community, harnessing a hugely distributed knowledge network from the collective minds of thirty thousand designers, engineers, CAD modelers, and fabricators, each one an enthusiast and passionate about cars. He then releases all that social and intellectual capital into a common pool. Such an open innovation platform sounds counter intuitive at first, especially when we have been conditioned to believe that intellectual property needs to be protected at all costs. Corporations would have us believe that innovation must be locked down with copyright and patents, but all of the Local Motors designs are freely available to access and download. This is radical change in operating and it is becoming clear is that operating under Creative Commons legal framework has exponential benefits that can radically accelerate the innovation process, whilst dramatically reducing costs.

In 2011 over 4.2 million vehicles were built in South Korea—more than double the number built in the US. Worse still, in December of last year General Motors alone had 788,194 unsold cars and trucks on its hands. When we consider that there are around thirty thousand component parts in a modern car, that is an awful lot of surplus inventory. Local Motors uses this surplus in its designs. Rather than building another enormous turnkey car plant, Local Motors is building microfactories in regions where demand is highest, so that money flows into local communities, and creates local jobs. Cars are built and sold from the microfactories on a just-in-time basis, making both the products and process much more sustainable, and very different from shipping thousands of cars halfway across the world, as the major OEMs currently do. This is an open challenge to the existing paradigm of highly centralized manufacturing, embattled dealerships, and dispersed service locations.

Figure 60. The Rally Fighter

Rodgers' revolutionary approach is evidenced in Local Motors' first car: the Paris-Dakar-esque Rally Fighter. Wrought in the creative furnace of "The Forge" by community members from more than one hundred different countries, it is a cross between a Baja racer and a P-51 Mustang fighter plane, built for off-road and desert races in the American Southwest. The aviation inspiration can clearly be seen in the pregnant belly bulge of the fuselage, and the exhaust pipes on the fenders. I personally cannot wait to see one in the old WWII squadron colors, with a pin-up babe paint-job on the hood. Some have described it as a BMW Z8 that has crossed over to the Dark Side, while others expect it to be featured in an upcoming Road Warrior sequel. Forget fuel efficiency, just mount a couple of open source mini-guns on top, and it will be zombie apocalypse, here we come! While there are plenty of critics guzzling the haterade, calling it ungainly, and even ugly, it definitely has a post-apocalyptic feel, and maybe just goes to show that all these wannabe auto designers have been watching way too many Mad Max movies.

For me, the lines are curvy and swoopy in all the right places. Thanks to 18" of suspension travel, it is high enough off the ground to clear big rocks and boulders, yet it is an impressive 40 percent lighter than anything else in its class. It is built for both on and off road, but with the big BMW diesel engine, it is capable of 36 mpg on the highway or 30 mpg in an off-road setting, all the while pumping out 265 HP and 425 pound/feet of torque to the rear wheels. Early critics have suggested that the BMW engine alone is $15,000, with equally expensive repairs, and what could be hard-to-find parts. One suggestion for a more affordable option is the GM Ecotec 2.4L, a tough, inexpensive engine that boasts great mileage on the direct injection version. Even so, there is some irony in the proclamations of how green this car is, with its diesel engine and the lack of paint. I find it hard to imagine your average tree-hugger blasting through the desert and doing burnouts. Still, as an early convert, my real questions are these: Can this "Open Source" vehicle run on "homebrew" fuel? And how long will it be before they are releasing full-scale plans for the entire range of Hot Wheels cars that I played with as a kid?

Every Rally Fighter owner enjoys between three and six eye-opening days building his or her own vehicle at the Local Motors MicroFactory, under the supervision of a professional Builder-Trainer. Building your own car is like having an adult Lego set, and creates a Wonka-like fascination with company products and methods. Users bond with their new purchases, and are far less likely to default on repayments. Not only does it sell cars, but it allows customers to experience their car being "born," which also means that they will likely keep their car for much longer, reducing the turnover in used cars.

The concept of building your own car with factory assistance means that owners become much more confident about their vehicle. Drivers can go from the automotive equivalent of clueless windows users, to black hat Linux hackers in just a few days. Even the garage is transformed from a place of dread, where you expect to get ripped off by sneering salesmen and condescending mechanics, to a hacker-space for car enthusiasts. In the future, these microfactories might even become automotive education centers, where people can show up for a couple hours on Saturday, and spend the day helping other people with more money in their pockets. "Crowd-sourcing" has always been great until you get DOT, NHSTA, EPA, and CFR rules involved, but with this kind of assisted build, customers can skip some government regulations, giving people a connection with their car right off the bat without the long, arduous, and usually problematic process of kit car building. With regards to servicing, Local Motors has pledged a customer experience of loyal, uncompromising, personal service deserving of the largest purchase that many people ever make.

LM's first microfactory was in Chandler, Arizona, but they have already negotiated a second in the Middle East, and more are on the way. Each one is quick and, at $300,000, relatively cheap to build.

They are surprisingly flexible and could potentially house "production lines" for four vehicles simultaneously.

The design contests for new projects continue to come thick and fast. In fact, the company hosts a series of monthly car design competitions aimed at selecting projects for limited series production. These have already included a motorbike design and another for a "Miami Road Racer," where the winner receives a $10,000 award and an additional $10,000 award if the vehicle is eventually selected for production. One of the most interesting projects was a design for an "open tandem," which is a reincarnation of the Messerschmitt, an in-line seated vehicle to be made for under $10,000. This shows that Local Motors is not just another playground for the überwealthy, and is coming up with some ideas that "actual people" can afford. Forge members have even collaborated with DARPA, the US military research agency, to co-design and build a prototype combat support vehicle. I am personally hoping to see them team up with the Open Source Ecology community that is working on projects such as the LifeTrac, a low-cost, multipurpose open source tractor. http://opensourceecology.org/wiki/LifeTrac If Local Motors can do off-road cars, I see no reason why they cannot also do bulldozers, tractors, and back hoes.

Unlike companies like Tesla, with its designs on the mid-size sedan segment, Local Motors wants to work with major auto-makers, not to replace them. Why design an engine from scratch when, like the Rally Fighter, it can use BMW's perfectly good M57 3.0-liter turbo-diesel? Why build a tail light from scratch when you can just use a set from a Honda Civic? It is really impressive to see how much parts-sharing is going on here. This has always taken place, but the scale and declaration of intent here is new. Few people realize that the Lamborghini Countach used Fiat door handles, and the Delorean had a Renault 25 engine in the back. Perhaps we are moving to a time when major car makers become more like Shimano, SRAM, and Campagnolo in cycling, making high-quality components to agreed upon standards, that are installed into highly personalized semi-custom cars.

On the flip side, this presents new opportunities for innovative auto makers with exciting new designs. If you have a compressed natural gas engine then why not work with Local Motors to build a vehicle using your technology in areas with good CNG infrastructure? If you have an E85-burning engine, you could contract with Local Motors to make a small volume car in the Midwest, with its large ethanol production. Wood alcohol has been used in South America for decades and VW cashed in on this local fuel with the beetle engine modified to benefit from this high-energy fuel source. We could see all kinds of high-tech exotica from flywheels to hydrogen fuel contained in nano wadding, to pulverized coal gas in ceramic, oil-free engines. When the cost of entry is reduced from the billions that the big auto companies spend, whole new fields are suddenly opened up. I wonder how long it will be before some steampunk enthusiasts develop a high-efficiency external combustion engine.

Local Motors and the Rally Fighter also raise another question. What is sustainable motoring exactly? Even a Nissan Leaf, which, although clean at of point use, has many skeletons, including battery recycling, enormous inventories, and extra tooling for complex servicing that soon becomes obsolete. The fact is that the private car is an environmental, fiscal, and social disaster. Long before the car has been delivered to the showroom, it has produced significant amounts of damage to air, water, and land ecosystems, through the extraction of raw materials alone. Before any vehicle even hits the road it has already produced 26.5 tons of waste and almost 1,000 cubic meters of polluted air. The environmental impact continues beyond the end of the car's useful life. Disposal of the vehicle produces a further 102 million cubic meters of polluted air and vast quantities of PCB's and hydrocarbons. Does the future lie in low-volume, locally-sourced vehicles that are tailored to the user's needs, which challenge the culture of changing cars regularly, and which are enthusiastically designed and built by the buyer?

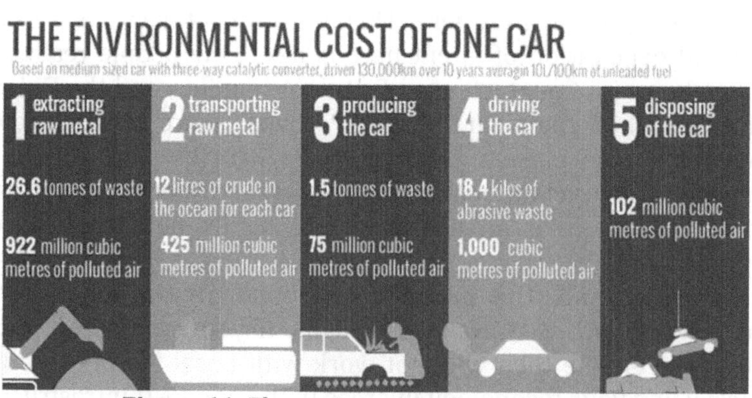

THE ENVIRONMENTAL COST OF ONE CAR

Based on medium sized car with three-way catalytic converter, driven 130,000km over 10 years averagin 10L/100km ot unleaded fuel

1 extracting raw metal	2 transporting raw metal	3 producing the car	4 driving the car	5 disposing of the car
26.6 tonnes of waste	12 litres of crude in the ocean for each car	1.5 tonnes of waste	18.4 kilos of abrasive waste	102 million cubic metres of polluted air
922 million cubic metres of polluted air	425 million cubic metres of polluted air	75 million cubic metres of polluted air	1,000 cubic metres of polluted air	

Figure 61. The environmental cost of one car

Maybe Jim Kor's 3D-printed city car project, the Urbee2, gives us a clue to the future. Produced in the RedEye on-demand 3D printing facility, using ABS plastic, the three-wheeled hybrid weighs just 1,200 pounds. The diesel hybrid power train under the hood can take it from New York to San Fransisco on just ten gallons of gas with a top speed of around 40 mph.

Figure 62. The Urbee2

A Future of Distributed Manufacturing

The maker community is hopeful that maker entrepreneurial approaches can fill the vacuum left by the enormous plants and factories of yesteryear. Dale Dougherty of *Make* magazine has pointed out that Detroit is suffering from a lack of jobs, but not of talent. Instead of government subsidies going to monolithic car companies, what would happen if microfinancing was channeled into small networks of mom and pop auto-manufacturing set-ups? Surely either the state or federal government could bootstrap a selection of peer-to-peer investment schemes and crowdfunded projects in order to sow the seeds for a grass roots recovery.

There has been an inordinate amount of innovation in software and services thanks to the ubiquity of the web, the development of software tools for rapid development and employment, and open sharing of code, tools, and methods. It is high time that this approach is applied to the manufacturing world. Suddenly, the tools are becoming available at reasonable prices, allowing micro-factories and small companies to cater to smaller, local markets and niches. Could this represent the next step in industrialization, where smaller, more agile companies entirely replace the centralized Fortune 500 corporations of Detroit, many of which barely cling to life with their unsustainable, antiquated business models? Dinosaurs such as Ford and the other big-auto giants would have already been shuttered and out of business had it not been for their unwarranted influence and power buying them immense bailouts from America's taxpayers.

As the giants fall, thanks to alternative business models undermining their monopolies, we will finally become aware of the lies that built them up in the first place. It is at this point that we need to dispel a few myths about what actually constitutes industrial efficiency and the dominance of large corporations.

Four enormous lies are propping up the current industrial complex. Once these are dispelled, we will have a much better understanding of how distributed manufacturing can offer a superior alternative to our current problems. I want to look carefully at these lies, one at a time.

Lie Number One: *Small-scale production can never compete with the vast assembly lines of cheap labor that are essential for producing affordable products.*

According to conventional wisdom, Henry Ford gained his place in history by inventing the mass-production assembly line, thereby making infinitely more products available to everybody. Most people are quite surprised to learn that this is a complete falsehood. In August 1913, Ford was one of the earliest large-scale manufacturers to take advantage of recent advances in machine tools, thereby enabling the employees to work on pre-hardened metal. This meant that, for the very first time, they were able to produce standardized parts that remained constant throughout the manufacturing process. Prior to this, armies of fitters were required to "fit" all the non-standard parts together. This innovation of precision and interchangeability could have been introduced just as well into small scale production, (as it is in Emilia Romagna and shanzhai operations) radically increasing outputs and drastically reducing costs. By eliminating the old job of fitter, Ford managed to reduce assembly times from 514 minutes to an incredible 2.3 minutes. When the moving assembly line concept was introduced in December of the same year, it only reduced cycle time from 2.3 minutes to 1.19 minutes. Contrary to public perception, the assembly line was not even Ford's idea. They had been implemented as long ago as the early 1500s, when the Venetian Arsenals were capable of producing one galley per day, enabling the first great maritime empire.

Desktop manufacturing means that the real innovations that made Ford so efficient are now becoming available on a micro scale. Rather than a workshop full of lathes, presses, and power tools to cut drill-precision interchangeable parts, we are fast approaching a time of laser sinterers that will build them from scratch, just as easily as an ink jet printer churns out a sheet of A4.

Ralph Borsodi utilized a detailed system of careful cost accounting to establish the costs of producing his own food. Even with home labor added, their canned goods cost 20–30 percent less than store-bought canned goods. He conceded that factories, with their elaborate division of labor and economies of scale, could produce a can of food for less, but the addition of advertising, management, and distribution costs significantly raised the final price. Added to this, there were many factors that could not be included in a financially-based accounting system, such as the fact that home-grown food was of higher quality, provided better family nutrition, and offered improved health and resistance to illness. Production itself replaces idleness and the need for expensive gym memberships, encouraging a strong as well as healthy body.

He went on to demonstrate that two-thirds of the average family household items could be produced more economically at home than they could be made in a factory. What is really interesting is that he made this claim way back in the 1920s, long before the introduction of all the home appliances and labor-saving devices that we take for granted today. The enormous advances in consumer technology in the century since Borsodi has created a new breed of homesteader. The thrivalist thinks life is about much more than simple survival, and is keen to take advantage of every convenience to make their lives as comfortable and sustainable as possible. The truth is that we do not need enormous factories to meet our immediate needs. Much of what we consume, we can produce cheaply by ourselves while the remainder only requires small-scale manufacturing networks.

Lie Number Two: *We live in a meritocracy where anybody can become a successful entrepreneur.*

Researchers David Blanchflower and Andrew Oswald have discovered that entrepreneurial success has almost nothing to do with personality traits or educational achievement. It turns out that the single biggest factor in predicting self-employment is not creativity or inventiveness, but access to start-up capital. Their results demonstrated that the greatest single predictor of self-employment was having received an inheritance or a gift. Should it be any surprise that success in a capitalist system is restricted only to those tiny few who have access to large amounts of capital? This revelation leads directly to the next enormous lie that we have all been forced to swallow.

Lie Number Three: *The modern industrial world was built from scratch by a generation of business-savvy, innovative young men, such as John D. Rockefeller, Cornelius Vanderbilt, Andrew Carnegie, Henry Ford, J. P. Morgan, and Thomas Edison.*

The myth goes that twentieth-century progress can be attributed to the innovative genius of these Captains of Industry and their free market capitalism. This conveniently ignores the fact that, without massive government intervention, state-subsidized infrastructure and specially granted privilege, none of their achievements would have been possible. Their success was only possible by piggybacking upon centralized transport systems first in the form of railways and then, later, state highways and civil aviation. "For example, under the terms of the Pacific Railroad bill, the Union Pacific was granted twelve million acres of land and $27 million worth of thirty year government bonds. The Central Pacific received nine million acres and $24 million worth of bonds." This was later repeated in the building of the highway system and the network of national and international airports.

General Motors is the perfect example of how corporate welfare on a massive scale enabled these companies to succeed. GM began by deliberately destroying the world's finest public transportation network in a short ten year period, so that they could replace the trams and trolley buses with private cars and coaches. In 1932 they were fined just $5,000 for what was estimated to be $300 billion dollars of damage to the national streetcar system.

The National Highway Users Federation was created and headed for twenty years by GM President Alfred Sloan and quickly became the most powerful lobby in Washington. Sloan was followed by the next GM president Charles Wilson, who later became Eisenhower's Secretary of Defense in 1953. Wilson immediately began pushing highways as a national security necessity, appointing Francis Dupont, whose family money created General Motors, as head of the Federal Highway Commission. He then created the President's Advisory Committee on a National Highway Program, also known as the Clay committee after Lucius Clay who was also on the Board of Directors of General Motors. Members included Steve Bechtel, owner of the largest construction company in the country, Bill Roberts of Allis-Chalmers who made earth-moving machinery, and Dave Beck, the corrupt president of the Teamsters Union who was later jailed for embezzlement. Somewhat unsurprisingly, the committee immediately recommended the national highway system. In just three months, the committee raced through testimony from twenty-two organizations, then delivered a proposal to the United States president: forty thousand miles of high-speed divided highway linking every city in the country. The largest corporations in the country effectively externalized the cost of a nationwide transportation network to the ordinary tax payer. Ever since then, they have been reaping the profits of the world's largest infrastructure project, without which their businesses would have been untenable, allowing society at large to foot the bill.

Think for a moment about all the energy production and distribution networks built by the state to provide industry with the cheap power that was essential to make factories competitive. Not to mention the huge changes in the country's legal framework to benefit corporations. Modern America was not built on innovative genius at all, but on government-assisted cronyism, without which the entire model would fail tomorrow.

Lie Number Four: *Society requires enormous production capacity to meet its ever-increasing demands.*

Modern manufacturing is based on planned obsolescence, and without the ability to cheat consumers into buying goods that will either fall apart or become irrelevant in a very short time, industry as we know it would collapse. If we stop and think about this for a moment, it quickly begins to make sense. Huge sums are required to build large factories and equip them with complex machinery. To ensure a good return on investment, larger and larger quantities need to be sold to the buying public. Most consumers will only buy as fast as they consume any particular product. The factory owners know that if they make quality products that last, then they will be consumed slowly. If it makes low-quality products, then the public will be forced to buy them more often and so it makes them as poorly as it can get away with. Manufacturing was off-shored not only to take advantage of cheap labor, but so that our complaints about cheap plastic tack could be leveled at the Chinese, half a world away, rather than the people selling it to us. When products are made and sold locally, the maker is much more careful to protect their reputation. As 3D printers of all kinds improve and more and more people become able to produce items for their local markets, will they really be happy to produce the same plastic junk that China churns out, or will they be making items of quality that last for a lifetime? Detractors of additive manufacturing claim that the process could never match the output of existing factories. The reality is that much of that demand is simply manufactured by producing shoddy goods that need to be replaced every five minutes. Start focusing on quality items that are meant to last a lifetime and the need for factories with such enormous capacities quickly begins to dwindle away.

Our modern industrial society is built on a handful of bald-faced lies and as soon as this corporate hucksterism is revealed to the public at large, the entire structure will topple to be replaced by something that is a vast improvement. My hope and prediction is that this will be distributed manufacturing. The promise is that it will bring about a much greater equality in terms of industrial and economic democracy (as opposed to political democracy which is currently being subverted by the economic power of big business) and a better, more stable model for society.

It was inevitable. A technology like 3D printing that essentially puts cheap labor, manufacturing, and retail all in the same place, upon one's desktop was bound to happen. It spells the absolute, utter, and permanent end to the monopolies and unwarranted power and influence of the top tenth of 1 percent who have lorded over humanity since human civilization began, That is the good news. The bad news is that this is a permanent end which the vested corporate interests will fight against with the total summation of their ill-gotten power and influence. The first time around this came in the form of penal transportation and the hangman's noose to execute the British Luddites. Business analysts Gartner have already predicted that by 2020, "the labour reduction effect of digitisation will cause social unrest and a quest for new economic models in several mature economies. A larger scale version of an 'Occupy Wall Street'-type movement will begin by the end of 2014, indicating that social unrest will start to foster political debate."

Over the last two decades, there has been a near global conversion of regional economies to the ideology of corporate capital. Some of this development has been forced by institutions such as the IMF, and some has been freely adopted by those who have been led to believe Margaret Thatcher's claim that "There is no alternative."

Of course there are alternatives, but the problem is that those who have done extremely well for themselves on other peoples' sacrifices and efforts are blocking, undermining, smearing, and destroying any alternatives which are not in their self-interests. This happened throughout history where the elite of the time and place always protects the system and their own. We can reasonably expect guns to begin appearing in much larger numbers when the power of ownership, essentially the right to buy power, is threatened.

Eventually, everybody is going to have access to this technology and, therefore, the ability to print on their desktop what Fortune 500 corporations have held monopolies over for generations. This will include everything from arms manufacturing to automobiles. The age of empire, corporatism, and elitism is coming to an end, but apparently not without one last battle.

If we look at the recent history of South America, the rich and powerful always seek to maintain their positions and any movement that is felt to be a threat to the power of the right wing tends to let loose the butchers. If distributed manufacturing is seen as some sort of socialist or communist tainted notion then violent conflicts will surely follow. Even the idea of sharing with others may offend some of the old, stuffed-shirt aristocrats.

Attempts to restrain this disruptive power will first come in the form of legislation and red tape. Similar ploys can be seen in the legislative and sociopolitical gauntlet that has been introduced to slow the organic food movement. The so called Captains of Industry are slowly being revealed as little more than Captains of Greed, with the majority having little understanding of the real meaning of industrious. Current strategies of exploitation are moving away from technological inequality to intellectual property extortion. The loss of IP would make many large corporations irrelevant, and so they will fight tooth and nail to preserve it. Tastes of this can be seen in the attitudes of the MPAA and RIAA. Whether this will actually work is debatable. Any kind of ban will be virtually impossible to enforce. We only need to look at how the music industry has tried to vilify file sharing by banning particular sites or devices. They would have had more chance of stopping a tidal wave with a bucket. Napster was a mere ripple. 3D printing will be a mega tsunami.

This challenge to the traditional top-down economics of mass production will ultimately lead to the creation of a hard-to-imagine new socio-economic order, just as the Industrial Revolution itself did.

For the zealous partisans of distributed manufacturing, we are looking forward to far more equality and social justice.

Just for the record, I am not a utopian techno-idealist believing that a scientific broom can sweep away all of our messy problems. I am clearly looking forward to a better society for all, but I do see the possibility that we are heading towards techno-totalitarianism with the rise of a digital oligarchy more powerful than anything that has gone before. Open source programming has driven enormous innovation in software, but huge computing firms still dominate the market and reap the benefit. On-line music sharing was supposed to put independent musicians on a level playing field, but the big music labels are as powerful as ever. Every new technology has the potential to help unlock more human creativity but I worry that our current version of capitalism is actually much more akin to medieval feudalism, and only does the opposite. New inventions can be used to de-skill work and cut costs, ultimatel leading to mass unemployment or menial drudgery. Unless we overthrow a system that reduces everything to the needs of profit, no technology will ever provide a path to freedom.

Not only could new technologies be co-opted by those who need them least, at the same time they can be downright destructive. Short term technological casualties are sometime inevitable. If we look for a moment at the era described by Vaclav Smil as the Age of Symmetry, a golden age of innovation, that lasted from around 1867 to 1914, we can see from the entire history of innovation—from the early domestication of animals to the rise of the Internet—that it is possible that more innovation occurred in the half a century than the rest of history put together.

Even so, this period was quickly followed by the Great War and just fifteen short years later, America entered the Great Depression, causing economic recession around the world. This could have been coincidence, but it would seem that innovation can also lead indirectly to economic hardship. Innovation clearly increases productive potential, but in our current economic system, without a corresponding rise in demand the result of innovation may be fewer jobs. Fewer jobs mean less demand and the economy can quickly deteriorate.

Under certain circumstances, innovation can have negative impacts, especially if the markets are given completely free reign. Surely I am not the only one who thinks that this might have been happening lately. A great deal of modern technology has left two types of jobs: the very highly paid skilled jobs and the dirty menial jobs, with precious little left in between.

17

Legalities, Legislation, and Lawsuits

The predictions of the analyst group Gartner are usually well thought out, accurate prophecies of what lies just around the corner. Even so, when I read their claim that by 2018, 3D printing will lead to "intellectual property" losses of at least $100 billion per year, my BS meter went completely off the charts.

I personally see an entirely different scenario, one which was repeated at the Inside 3D Printing Conference by John Hornick, an IP attorney with Finnegan, Henderson, Farbow, Garrett & Dunner LLP in New York:

> *"IP will be ignored and it will be impossible or impractical to enforce."*

As anybody living in the information age knows full well, removing anything from the Internet is like trying to take the pee out of the pool. Companies can attempt to sue, but if people are merely printing one or two unauthorized objects at a time, this makes little economic sense. To this end, how long will 3D printers be viewed in the same light as VCRs, tape recorders, or firearms, in that the manufacturer cannot be held accountable for the wrongdoings of individual users?

If we look for a moment at the early history of the USA, English manufacturing and textiles was off-shored to take advantage of cheaper costs and the slave labor available in the colonies. American companies copied as many British and European products as they could, and only when they were on an equal footing did they adopt the same rules. Benjamin Franklin blatantly reproduced the works of prominent London booksellers without paying any royalties. When Charles Dickens complained, he was mocked for his ancient views and told that he should be glad of the publicity.

Despite their protests, the English were hardly in any position to take the moral high ground. The British Empire was founded on piracy, starting with the capture of Jamaica by Sir Henry Morgan and Sir Francis Drake. The resulting war reduced Spain to a mere shell of its former self. Despite the high falluting titles, both were little more than common bandits. Drake took every opportunity to buy the affections of the Queen by showering her with gifts, paid for with plunder and pillage. While he desperately sought the esteem of the court, most saw him as nothing more than a wretched criminal. Even his men despised him, deserting on numerous occasions as a result of his mistreatment and treachery.

Going back even further, it is important to realize that the term copyright only tells half the story. Copyright monopolies were not initially created to protect authors, but to suppress and censor. Shortly after the invention of the printing press, the French authorities banned both bookshops and the use of the machine under penalty of death. The ban was a failure and so the Queen of England, Bloody Mary, who was clearly not known for her tolerant attitudes, tried a different tactic. On May 4, 1557 she issued a complete copyright monopoly to the London Company of Stationers. In exchange for the very lucrative rights to all English printing, the company agreed not to publish anything deemed politically subversive. This copyright monopoly was, and remains, a censorship instrument to suppress political dissent.

Vietnam recently passed an incredibly broad new censorship law so that blogs and social media cannot "quote, gather, or summarize" information from the media or government websites. Officials claimed the restrictions were necessary to "protect intellectual property." In Russia, the government has used copyright restriction to censor activists by raiding their offices and shutting them down with bogus claims that they were using infringing copies of Microsoft software.

When authoritarian governments see large corporations abusing their power with such ease, it makes sense that they will use the same tactics to stifle public participation in the political process. This is the perfect excuse to hide behind when they censor the public. Simply claim that they are protecting intellectual property, and frame it in the same language used by corporations, and they have a free ticket to censor nearly anything.

According to Google, almost half of the take-down notices received are not valid copyright claims, and so the Digital Millennium Copyright Act (DMCA) is being used for censorship purposes ranging from doctors removing negative reviews and businesses silencing competitors, to the removal of war crimes video footage. With so many Western governments kowtowing to incessant demands of the copyright monopoly, a growing number of Third World regimes are enacting stricter copyright laws to justify the censoring of political and free speech.

The recent digitization of audio and video gives us a clear picture of what is likely to be the most disruptive element of 3D printing.

"Napster really did leave a bad taste in everyone's mouth. It was such an oversimplified and Draconian reaction [by the music industry]," concludes Melba Kurman, an acclaimed 3D printing author and technology analyst. The music labels fought tooth and nail to prevent digital music from even existing, and only begrudgingly joined in when they realized that their businesses were failing. Despite this hostility, MP3s are now their bread and butter. The music industry was completely unprepared for their digital revolution, and the manufacturing industry seems similarly behind the curve. Big media kicked and screamed with the advent of the TV, cassette recorder, and the VCR. Remember the ridiculous "home taping will kill music" claims? On each occasion, they were completely wrong in their predictions, and they were equally mistaken when it came to digital music. They have concocted lies and propaganda about "piracy," and commandeered copyright laws as a bludgeon to abuse, oppress, and persecute an entire generation that has grown up far more technically savvy than its predecessors. The MPAA/RIAA regularly blackmail ordinary users by threatening to reveal their filesharing activities to the authorities and because the legal system is so heavily stacked against the individual, most people cave in to this kind of extortion. And yet all of their attempts to stifle the sharing of knowledge and culture have failed. Trying to restrict the freedom of information always fails in the long term.

Of course, the problem was never so-called piracy. That was simply a term hijacked by lobbyists in attempt to criminalize the act of sharing, in the same way that they co-opted the word "stealing." as taking the actual physical copy, (disks, books, etc.) while so-called copyright criminals simply make an exact duplicate without altering anyone else's. The real problem was competition. At first, the Internet allowed easy access to secondhand CDs on sites like eBay, and the labels could no longer maintain their ridiculous profit margins. Rather than react accordingly, they tensed up even further, until widespread digitization became a devastating body blow. Now they have to face up to the fact that their monopoly of music is over.

The music industry conveniently ignores the fact that the advanced technology made them rich in the first place. Until recording devices came along, the only way to make money was playing live. The advent of records suddenly created a massive gravy train for the music industry, enabling them to sell their product to the masses, instead of being limited to live audiences. The technology has now come full circle. Will the manufacturing industry take similar actions to suppress the advancement of technology, without which they could not exist?

The gazillion dollar recording artist is a phenomena that only exists because of mass audience broadcasting on TV and radio. There are vast amounts of talent out in the trenches, but the "millionaire musician" has been a historical outlier, a quirk of physical media bottlenecks and copyright restrictions. Music was not scalable until the first recording devices, when it suddenly transferred 99 percent of the wealth into the hands of just 1 percent. Now the pendulum is swinging back towards normal. The Internet has forced musicians to ask, "Am I really worth $100 million?" and reassess their real worth.

The record companies are reaping the seeds that they themselves have sown. Quality of mainstream music has been inexorably dumbed down from Mozart to Miley, until quality musical performance is no longer a requirement. The mainstream studios are now facing real artists and losing. From the Sex Pistols and The Ramones, to the steady stream of "hits" that are advertised so heavily that they drown out any real talent, popular music has degenerated into just a few basic chords, a catchy hook or chorus, and some non-confrontational, regurgitated lyrics. This has resulted in generations of unsophisticated listeners that do not know the difference between the top forty artists and their next door neighbor and his laptop. Did they really think that they could churn out half-assed simpleton music forever, without being out-competed by bedroom producers? These days, Garage Band on an iPhone is as good as $100/hour trip to a recording studio was twenty years ago. Mainstream music requires very little musical mastery and has very little appeal to people that are intellectual, or at least deeply interested in the actual content of their music. Audiences are looking for artistic vision and a love of music rather than a love of profit. Many will be happy to see the "professional music business" die, especially if they can dance on its grave, to music it could have never imagined.

Add to this the way in which new bands are financially screwed by the industry so that they routinely make less than a 7-11 cashier, and we start to wonder what copyright is actually protecting. Is it the right of a greedy music industry to ruthlessly exploit artists, just to keep its cash cow mooing? Maybe it is the cult of personality that allows a few decadent super stars to be filthy rich at the expense of everybody else? Is it the artificial scarcity of an outdated economic model? The anti-piracy jihad of the parasitical music industry is only succeeding in turning more and more of their best customers against them. It is difficult to feel any sympathy for an industry that has been screwing musicians for years.

In reality, more competition broadens the market. There will undoubtedly be fewer multi-millionaire recording artists, but the total amount spent on music can only grow as supply grows. The music recording industry may be taking a hit because it is so slow to adapt, but the music culture is going through a renaissance. They claim to be losing imaginary billions, but in the end this will trickle up to the record labels as well.

Perhaps you can see some parallels in the world of physical goods. Have you noticed how cheap Walmart goods have driven smaller retailer and manufacturers out of business? It is interesting to see how retail and banking, for example, have become so much more concentrated in the hands of fewer companies. Does this kind of unfair competition ensure that a state of artificial scarcity ensues? Could there be some connection between the fact that just a few musicians, athletes, CEO's, and bankers make millions of dollars, while everybody has to scramble around for crumbs?

Hollywood seems to have its head buried in the same sand pit as the music business. Few people realize that the early American film industry was initially forced to move en mass from New York and New Jersey to Hollywood, at least partially to escape Edison and the heavies he sent out to threaten filmmakers and "confiscate" cameras in the name of patents and intellectual property. Nowadays they have adopted the same violations that first threatened them. Jeff Cusson, a spokesman for HBO, openly admitted that "we're indifferent to the technology," clearly displaying the siege mentality of the industry. He was commenting on the corporation's decision to prevent the *Game of Thrones* iPhone holder that I wrote about earlier. This is a very different refrain from the actual creators. David Petrarca, the show's director, noted that widespread sharing actually does more good than harm. During a panel discussion at the University of Western Australia, he said that shows like *Game of Thrones* thrive on "cultural buzz" and benefit from the social commentary they generate. Every viewer—paid or unpaid—is a potential ambassador for the show and therefore a valuable part of the marketing cycle.

Overall, the theater business continues to grow, in spite of the trash they shovel out these days. According to the MPAA, revenues were up last year up by 6 percent, the year before up by 12 percent. Few of us will weep if Batman #26 is canceled. Hollywood accounting ensures that costs are massively inflated, primarily by greedy producers and actors with overinflated egos. It is interesting that the public is appalled by the news of another multi-million bonus paid to a banker or company director, while the salaries of A-list actors are kept top secret. It might actually be a good thing if the big conglomerates step out of the movie making business so that real filmmakers who have a passion for the craft have a chance to screen their movies at theaters, instead of the Hollywood drivel currently crowding them out.

Of course, this is not only about enormous profits. As the copyright industry continues to globalize, profits are increasing. This fight is about them retaining the gatekeeper position of determining what culture and knowledge is available to the masses and, by extension, control of the political discourse. And if you thought the whining of the content industry concerning the unauthorized copying of imaginary property was loud, the screams of the much larger manufacturing lobby will be deafening.

California-based Authentise has already designed a software that allows designs to print, but which then disappear once the job is complete. This kind of Digital Restriction Mechanism (DRM) is actually a violation of existing copyright law. Copyright is for a limited time only and then that work falls into the public domain as a contribution to the collection of human works. During the period that the copyright monopoly is granted, the right of fair use must always be maintained. Publishers do not own the content, in the same way that a parent does not own a child. A parent has rights and responsibilities over a child until the limited term of parenthood has expired. Abuse of children is illegal and parents who chain up their offspring in the basement are prosecuted. When a copyright holder engages exclusive rights, they are not fulfilling their responsibilities. And that needs to change. In addition, region locking is simply discrimination. What makes an Australian less worthy of being able to view content than an American? Furthermore, the publishers need to be held to task, and even sued for material that has already been lost. Significant amounts of human culture and history are being lost all the time due to copyright abuse and this needs to be urgently addressed.

In the West, patent laws stunt innovation by forbidding designers from incorporating new features, when even the most simplistic and obvious things are patented (rounded corners, anyone?) preventing them from ever realizing the devices they dream about. Inventors are likely to get sued over some obscure submarine patent that most people did not even know existed, part of a legal system that has been co-opted by corporate interests to protect their own needs. It is an antiquated model that favors the privileged, but one that will inevitably lose traction in the digital age. When 3D printing allows anyone to scan an object and create it, the concept of intellectual property and trademarks will simply be revealed as irrelevant.

Industrial Protectionism laws, a combination of copyrights, design patents, and trade-dress protection have always been slow to change, especially when compared to the speed of technological innovation. To file a patent costs anywhere from $1 to $10,000 and they are much more expensive to prosecute, often hundreds of thousands of dollars when going up against large multinationals. This means that the odds are always stacked very heavily against small designers and backyard inventors. 3D printing excels in catering to a market of one, but that kind of design can never be lucrative enough to involve costly patent mechanisms. The only thing guaranteed about a patent is that the owner is forced to keep pouring money into it. The Chinese will ignore it, while wealthy companies can afford to drag their competitors through the courts for years on end, until their competitors are bankrupted by legal fees.

Just as the copyright monopoly has been used to stifle culture, patents, and other IP fallacies, it will also be used to prevent all kinds of innovation and development. If there is one thing that prevents 3D printing from becoming a mass market, it is patents. Machines could be so much better and easier to use if designers could think freely about how to solve technical problems. In reality, all the obvious ways of solving these problems are patented. A thing as seemingly simple as making multi-color printers, are next to impossible without breaking several existing patents. Many bad patents were granted that actually covered prior art, and the next ten to fifteen years could be wasted enriching the lawyers. Whenever lawyers are involved, it is always the consumers who end up footing the bill. The best ideas should always be in the public domain if we sincerely want to create a better world. Try to imagine what society would be like if basic building blocks such as the alphabet were restricted under copyright.

For the Internet generation, the copyright monopoly is something that the establishment uses as a bludgeon to extort, abuse, and oppress. It is used to prevent them from educating themselves, to censor their protests and voices, and to prevent their art from reaching a wider audience. Rather than rewarding artists, copyright is used to silence them. None of the fines that are being extorted from this sharing generation are actually going to artists, they are simply lining the pockets of entrenched executives and overpaid lawyers. The law is manipulated so that it kills innovation, silences any challenges to the status quo, and ensures that multinational corporations can continue to buy political power.

Rick Falkvinge has suggested that the teenagers of today who have grown up in this abusive environment will kill this monopoly construct the first chance they have, to the thunderous applause of their peers. But will it really take that long? The manufacturing industry is already using the same tactics to silence artists and shut down competition. In a world where the wealth gap grows steadily larger by the day, most teenagers are already disenfranchised, their voices counting for little against those of older generations who already control most of the resources. Makers, by comparison, are a much different demographic. How long will they put up with scaremongering and deceit of the "3D print piracy panic" press and their lobbyists before they simply tell them to go fabricate themselves?

One interesting development that I will be watching very carefully is the WTO's authorization of Antigua and Barbuda to make $21 million per year by ignoring their agreement to honor copyrights. This is meant to be reparation for the USA's prohibition of cross-border gambling, which violates their WTO commitments. It has been estimated that this form of protectionism costs Antiqua and Barbuda approximately $1 billion per year, although considering the GDP of Las Vegas alone is almost $100 billion a year, it could well be much more.

An announcement regarding the opening of tenders for private sector participation should be announced shortly and it will be very interesting to see if any 3D model repositories chose the small Caribbean nation as a base. The US has already responded in kind by blocking Antigua businesses from exporting to the US. We should note that the WTO set a $21 million limit on how much profit can be made from this activity, but not how much it could cost the US in lost sales. Antigua could feasibly set up a BitTorrent-based, all-you-can-download service for, say, $1 per year, with a profit level of 4 percent, and make up their $21 million in profit with just five hundred million subscribers. Kim Dotcom and the Piratebay must be considering their options very carefully.

Events such as the Snowden debacle and the NSA revelations have been a watershed. Previously, most nations were quite happy to cooperate with the US to ensure that Mickey Mouse stayed well protected. However, with the growing anti-US sentiment, this might change very rapidly. It remains to be seen how long the over-reaching greed of large corporations will negatively impact the fate of ordinary American citizens.

18

Anticipating a Paradigm Shift in Mechanical Assemblies

Technology in the twentieth century has been dominated by our recently discovered ability to automate complex mental functions using programmable computers. By harnessing electronic brains, we have been able to accomplish tasks that would have been unthinkable just a century ago. Now that we are beginning to automate manufacturing tasks with 3D printers and CNC machines, this is destined to have an even greater impact on our physical world than the computer revolution. So far, many of the key advances have been digital, but additive manufacturing is now allowing us to improve upon our analogue devices, and we are suddenly seeing a complex mechanism renaissance. We shall start by taking a look at how this all started.

Complex adding machines have been around since before the seventeenth century, but Babbage's Analytical Engine of 1837 encountered a stubborn mechanical bottleneck that would not be surpassed for another hundred years, until the early 1940s. During World War II, there was an acute shortage of human computing power to calculate the complex firing tables and trajectory angles required for heavy artillery. Much of test firing was conducted by women at the Aberdeen proving ground in Maryland. Variables including wind, temperature, and pressure made the work enormously difficult, and extremely time-consuming for a devoted team of mathematicians at the nearby Pennsylvania University. One single trajectory, at just one angle took anywhere from thirty to forty hours of laborious handwritten human calculation. At this rate, it took one person four years to complete just one set of firing tables. Desperate for assistance, the officer in charge, Captain Herman Goldstein, contacted Moore's School of Electrical Engineering, which quickly built a monster calculating machine containing eighteen thousand vacuum tubes and half a million soldered joints. ENIAC was suddenly capable of completing five thousand additions per second, and calculating the trajectory of a shell in a period faster than it took to reach the target. While the giant brain was developed too late to be of any real use in winning the war, scientists were soon lining up to obtain valuable computing time. This breakthrough meant that electronic computers now far outperformed their mechanical counterparts. This suddenly allowed complex calculations which in turn opened up many new areas of science, especially those requiring analysis of vast amounts of data, such as stress analysis in engineering, or parsing the data from large networked telescopes in radio astronomy.

Early mechanical calculators had reduced the time it took to complete the US census from eight years to just six weeks, but the introduction of more powerful electronic computers has affected almost every branch of human endeavour. In fact, it might now be easier to ask which field has not been radically changed thanks to computing. It has revolutionized the basic tool kit in most areas of science. In physics, computers and particle accelerators are changing our understanding of the very fabric of reality and, in genomics, computers allow us to compare sequences thousands of base pairs long from a hundred samples to make a phylogenetic tree. Of course, the humanities have benefited too. Archaeologists and geologists for example, are now able to leverage maps from satellites, while linguists are able to parse immense datasets of written works. Computing power has changed forever the way that we handle, analyze, and process information. Just imagine the changes that are going to take place when we are able to improve our physical manufacturing abilities in the same way that we have improved our mental faculties.

Just as Babbage's Analytical Engine was an early attempt which promised to automate complex mental tasks, so the 3D printer will automate and simplify the skills of expert craftsmen and highly trained artisans. This trend has already with projects such as the turbo entabulator (http://www.thingiverse.com/thing:101105), a fully printable mechanical computer, and other machines that hark back to the earliest clockwork mechanisms. Chris Fenton, the designer of the Entabulator, who humorously describes himself as a cunning artificer, has also built Jacquard-type card readers, which were some of the very first programmable devices. And though it may be in jest, the Turbo Entabulator marks the beginning of using 3D printing to make complex objects, showing what happens when you mix a little bit of imagination with new technology. The possibilities truly seem endless.

When early clockwork mechanisms were first popularized, they changed Western society beyond recognition. Some of the first really complex devices were the automated bell towers of the monasteries, often made in wood, and which amazingly still run today. The Beauvais Cathedral (1305) and the Salisbury Cathedral clock (1386), for example, are now the oldest working clocks in the world.

We must not forget that seemingly simple clockwork mechanisms had culture changing impacts on entire societies. Without the development of clocks and the notion of accurate time measurement, the Industrial Revolution and mass production would not have been possible. Without the accurate measure of longitude, maritime navigation and globalization would have been unthinkable. John Harrison's Longcase Chronometer, built in 1713, was originally made entirely of wood, including all the gears. From these beginnings, mechanical clockwork miniaturization led directly to machine programming and a computer revolution. Accurate time keeping was a keystone technology for Renaissance Europe, and the technology that allowed this development soon moved from public, practical usage into the realms of art and entertainment. It is hardly surprising then that clocks remain the best selling machines in all of human history.

By looking at three landmark creations from the golden age of clockwork automata, we can go on to speculate about similar landmark points in 3D printing technology:

1. Karakuri ningyô (からくり人形) are mechanized puppets or automata from Japan, dating from the seventeenth to the nineteenth century, and perhaps the ancestral family of today's Sony Aibo and Asimo robots. The word karakuri literally means "mechanism" or "trick." Tea-serving dolls date

from 1659 at the beginning of the Edo Period, but perhaps the most famous piece is the Young Archer (yumi-hiki doji) created by Tanaka Hisashige, that accurately shoots arrows at a miniature target.

Figure 63. The Young Archer

1. Jacques de Vaucanson (1709-1782) specialized in sophisticated automata that were the first attempts to reverse engineer separate parts of human biology, what we now call bionics. In 1737, he completed "the transverse flute player," a shepherdess that played eleven different tunes using a complex, mechanized tongue on a real flute. He went on to work on a second model that played twenty tunes, and a rather less successful "Digesting Duck," sometimes rather disparagingly referred to as the "Defecating Duck."

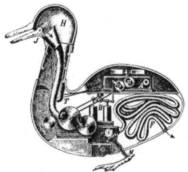

Figure 64. The Digesting Duck

1. In 1774, Jaquet Droz fabricated the Writer (the automata that inspired the principle "character" in Martin Scorsese's clock-punk movie *Hugo*). This was an amazing piece of bio

mechanical reverse engineering, with a total of six thousand moving parts, and was followed shortly after by the Draughtsman (similar to the Writer, but which drew pictures), and the Pianist (a female-style android that played an organ-style piano).

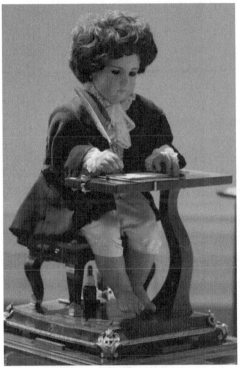

Figure 65. The Writer

Amazing as these creations were, just compare them to the current complexity of everyday dolls and figures. At the time of construction, these the three pieces above were considered masterpieces of art, and wonders of the mechanical world. For just $10 it is now relatively easy to find an action figure on eBay with thirty or more articulated joints. Clearly the shape of things to come, Thingiverse makers are already putting the Guangdong injection molders to shame, having released an 18-inch, open-source action figure, with a massive seventy points of articulation.

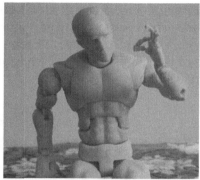

Figure 66. Open Source Action Man

http://www.thingiverse.com/thing:116571

The creation of clockwork automata entered into its first golden age in the 1770s, but the work was hard and painful labor for a vast artisan workforce. When we look back at some of the classic automata of the eighteenth century, we see that every single part had to be hand forged and crafted to the most minute detail. Screws less than a half a millimeter had to be hand crafted using the arduous process of forcing the steel through a tiny screw plate.

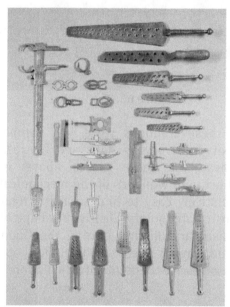

Figure 67. A selection of handcrafted screw plates

James Cox was an entrepreneurial craftsman working in the 1760s–80s, claiming to employ between eight hundred and one thousand workmen, producing a great variety of lavishly ornamented articles for trade with the Far East, first with India and then with China. The reception for his luxury "toys" or "sing songs," (singsong is an anglicization of the Chinese word "zimingzhong," meaning "the clock that plays by itself"), was outstanding and a huge financial success. Some, like the automaton in the form of a chariot pushed by a Chinese attendant, were gifts to the Chinese emperor Qianlong (r. 1736–95), who had a special fondness for clocks of both Chinese and Western origin. Another was a beautifully bejewelled pineapple which, upon suddenly opening, would reveal a nest of birds that immediately began to sing. Many of these are still in the collection of the Palace Museum in the Forbidden City in Beijing. In 1793, Lord Macartney calculated that the collection of English clocks and watches kept by the Chinese emperors at Jehol was worth more than £2 million. Artifacts produced by Cox for export is evinced as early as 1766 when the *Gentleman's Magazine* published a description of two curious clocks with moving figures, and set with diamonds and rubies, intended as a present (what we would now call a bribe) from the East India Company to the Emperor of China.

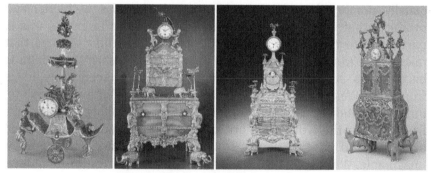

Figure 68. A selection of sing songs

The objects that Cox sought to export to the Far East were part of a very selective trade in luxury goods that had developed in the wake of Jesuit missions from the late sixteenth century and later diplomatic visits, with their accompanying elaborate gift rituals. Especially favored were clocks and watches, not for telling the time, but as status symbols. The artifacts made by Cox were dominated by the motifs of Chinoiserie and clearly reproduced Western stereotypes of Chinese cultural identity. For the Chinese consumer, however, all these pagodas, mandarins, chiming bells, and dragons were attractive because they appeared representative of European taste, and flattered their illusions of self-import. Eventually, a ban on exports of luxury goods from London to China in the late 1770s forced Cox into bankruptcy.

Concentrated in London's Clerkenwell district there are still thousands of craftsmen and designers, heirs to the vibrant artisan crafts of the seventeenth and eighteenth century. Clerkenwell Green was famously a hotbed of British radical and socialist movements. Wat Tyler took his followers to Clerkenwell in 1381, as did the Tolpuddle Martyrs and the Chartists, who fought for political reform in clashes with police and Horse Guards on Clerkenwell Green in 1848. Lenin plotted against his capitalist foes by printing his underground journal *The Spark* in 1903 opposite the Green, in a former Welsh school that was to become—and remains—the Marx Memorial Library. New skills brought into the area by domestic and foreign immigrants such as the Huguenots, turned Clerkenwell into a center for clock and watch-makers, jewellers, printers, enamellers, engravers, gunsmiths, furniture, and cabinet makers.

Modern day Shenzhen has in many ways been compared to seventeenth-century Clerkenwell. Although shanzhai products are usually portrayed as low-cost, poor-quality copies of higher-end products that illustrate China's alleged inability to innovate, this is partly due to the American cultural bias that anything strange that takes place in China must be bad. In reality, the Pearl River delta is becoming a self-sustaining economic ecosystem, seeded by ideas from the West that have taken root, and are now nourishing innovation and entrepreneurship. The region is drawing in specialists from all over the world who are keen to take advantage of the local expertise and ease of access to almost every kind of component imaginable. While China is racked with constant protests, Guangdong province is especially vociferous in its criticisms of the government. Even as far back as the Opium Wars, it was Cantonese mercenaries who sacked and looted the Summer Palace in Beijing, as a reaction against the opulence of their oppressors. Shenzhen now boasts a skilled workforce that can copy just about anything from artworks of the great masters to the very latest high tech gadgets.

A distinctive feature of Cox's work was the way in which he often brought together complete components to create larger and more impressive objects. He himself described this as exporting "the superfluities we received from other countries, worked up by our artisans." This is probably a reference to the import of escapement mechanisms for Cox's automata from master craftsman Jaquet-Droz. This modular approach to design and manufacture is in clear evidence today, with 3D printers being limited by their relatively small build envelopes.

Even as I write this, automaton clocks at Sotheby's are drawing increasingly serious demand from Asia. One example that last came up for auction at Bonham's in 2002, where it fetched £250,000, found an Asian buyer this time around at a price of £1.4 million. There were three other clocks included in the sale, all geared towards Far Eastern interest, being either Chinese-made or Chinese market pieces, and all exceeded their estimates. A George III period, ormolu-cased musical automaton table clock made by Henry Borrell c.1795 for the Chinese market realized £620,000 and two Chinese ormolu-cased and paste-set clocks of Qianlong period made in the Guangzhou workshops went for £380,000 each.

The relevance of all of this detail is that that balance of trade at that time was an enormously unequal balance of trade in favor in the Chinese Hongs. Porcelain and tea were the height of fashion in Europe and boatloads of opium were being imported as an all-purpose ready remedy. Aspirin and other modern medicine had not yet been invented, and so opium was being imported in prodigious quantities, while imported rhubarb was a hugely popular constipation cure for the upper classes, brought on by overindulgent excess. Imports from China reached unheard of proportions, until the exchequer was literally drained of silver. This particular page of history has largely been rewritten. Sun Yat Sen accused the Western powers of smuggling opium into China, a tactic that proved invaluable in uniting the country against the "white devils," a term that is still used on the streets of Hong Kong and Guangzhou to this very day. Cox's products were exceptional in that they were actively sought after by the Chinese, who arrogantly dismissed every other item produced by the newly industrialised West.

Everybody now knows that China is about to overtake Japan and become the world's largest consumer market for luxury goods, having surpassed the United States in this regard many years ago. China alone accounts for nearly one-third of the world's luxury goods sales. Eighty percent of Chinese luxury goods buyers are under forty-five, compared to the thirty percent of luxury goods buyers in the United States and just nineteen percent in Japan. And the trend continues. In April 2013, sales of gold and jewellery were 72 percent higher than in April, 2012. Any recent visitor to Hong Kong will have seen the long queues of Mainlanders outside European watchmakers and designer boutiques. Domestically, very little is imported, and while the demand for Western goods is actively suppressed, the advent of additive manufacturing could change all of that. Could an era of 3D printed luxuries kick start a consumer market in China that is still a small fraction of its Western counterparts?

In the BBC4 documentary *Mechanical Marvels: Clockwork Dreams*, Professor Simon Schaffer shows clearly that all these kinds of intricately designed mechanisms required very labor-intensive conditions, and extremely skilled workers. One expert, David Rooney, Curator of Timekeeping at the Royal Observatory in Greenwich, agreed strongly with this, and even went as far as to say that these kind of exquisite micromechanisms simply do not grow organically. While they may not yet fall from the boughs of fruit trees, they can now be conjured up very quickly and almost effortlessly with a 3D printer. In fact, the whole situation has changed dramatically with the advent of distributed additive manufacturing. Suddenly, we can print extremely complex devices, just as early computers allowed scientists to tackle enormously complex mathematical problems that would never have been considered before.

3D printing is already opening up completely new ways of manufacturing items that would have seemed impossible just a decade or so before. One of my favorite examples is the Parametric Involute Bevel and Spur Gears. (http://www.thingiverse.com /thing:53451) Frustrated that spheres do not adhere to the 45 degree rule, and the resulting fact that ball bearings tend to print poorly, Emmett Lalish went ahead and designed a new kind of bearing that can only be manufactured by 3D printing and comes fully pre-assembled. The planetary gear set, as this is also known, functions like a cross between a needle bearing and a thrust bearing. There is no need for a race or cage, because the herringbone gearing keeps the individual gears perfectly spaced. Best of all, the design is fully parametric and made to be adjusted in the Customizer app for any and all needs. Normal gears use a small pressure angle in order to transmit torque, but here a large pressure angle courtesy of the herringbone, transmits force much more efficiently.

Other advantages include high-power densities, large reduction in a small volume, multiple kinematic combinations, pure torsional reactions, and coaxial shafting. Most of us have seen this mechanism in a tabletop pencil sharpener, where the planetary gears are extended into cylindrical cutters joined at the pencil-sharpening angle. Apart from its compactness and outstanding power transmission efficiencies, a typical efficiency loss in a planetary gearbox arrangement is only 3 percent per stage. Because the load being transmitted is shared between multiple planets, torque capability is greatly increased.

This clearly demonstrates that it really is possible to create a 3D printed object, with moving parts, that requires no assembly, and that works to an extremely high standard. It might just be a geared wheel today, but tomorrow this could be part of a highly complex machine. Emmett has a knack for improving on everyday items, something that will become much more common as more and more tinkerers buy themselves 3D printers. As an aside, I would also recommend his Moines Soap Dispenser, a household item that is far superior to anything that comes out of any factory.

Just as seventeenth-century clock makers kickstarted innovations that helped push along the industrial revolution, we are currently seeing the same spirit of invention with newly purchased 3D printers. The main difference is that clock makers were, for a long time, limited to one simple mechanism, while now makers can be universal with a plethora of open source tools available.

So what evidence is there that this is an actual trend and not just a figment of my imagination? The remnants of the clockwork era still fetch admirable prices among tinkerers and hobbyists. Lever-wound cylinders for music boxes, antique clock parts, and governed spring driven motors all regularly fetch between $100 and $200 per piece, even though they are essentially spares to be used for repairs.

Figure 69. A prototype printatble clock
Thingiverse users have gradually been perfecting 3D-printable

working clocks. Rrustedrobot's videos are a true testament to how well collaboration works on the site.
http://www.prototribe.net/vidplay/testjig2.html
And the clockwork library and printable clock script are available here.
http://www.thingiverse.com/thing:7976

In America, simple automata already fetch ridiculously high prices. The Unwelcome Dinner Guest, a simple wood automaton depicting a backyard scene of a bird scarfing down the chained-up dog's dinner, by Automata Artist Dug North (who eccentrically describes himself as having a BA Giz. in Applied Gizmology with a specialization in Kinetic Gizmology from the International Institute of Gizmology) fetches an astonishing $2,850.00.

Figure 70. The Unwelcome Dinner Guest

http://www.dugnorth.com/automata-unwelcome-dinner-guest.aspx

While the hobbyists are making admirable progress, academia is coming at the problem from an entirely different angle. Researchers at Birmingham City University have used high-resolution scanners to recreate an early seventeenth-century pocketwatch that included alarm and calendar functions. The gilded brass Ferlite watch (named for its creator) was an enormous technological achievement at the time. The level of detail that went into its design—including intricate gold leaf floral designs—made it the iPad of its day.

In a separate, but even more astonishing development, a team of coders at the research and development labs of the Disney Corporation have created a computational design system, allowing non-expert users to design and fabricate complex animated mechanical characters. The mechanical assemblies of the character are generated automatically and then connected to each other using gear trains. The system automates all of the tedious and difficult steps, until the resulting mechanical characters can be fabricated using 3D printers.

http://www.disneyresearch.com/project/mechanical-characters/

This is an amazing set of software tools that allows a designer to create characters with complex internal driving mechanisms that would have previously been extremely cumbersome to assemble. Now they can be manufactured in a single print.

As we have seen, mechanical characters have been part of the toy industry for hundreds of years, but until now, the design technology has changed little, and was strictly limited to a small handful of expert designers and engineers. Even then, the design process was largely trial and error, with much iteration needed to produce an acceptable result. Creating mechanical characters, whose motion was determined by physical assemblies of gears and linkages, has always been an elusive and extremely challenging task. Even an artisan as accomplished as the great Vaucanson worked for four solid years just to create one of his flute playing automata. In the past, this has meant that mechanical characters have been limited in scope and complexity, which in turn limited the range of possible movement and the creative freedom of the designers.

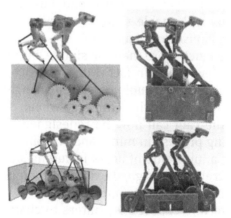

Figure 71. EMA gallop

Even at this early stage, the team at Disney have made some incredible achievements. The EMA gallop above features an external gear box, consisting of six driving mechanisms, ninety-three separate components, and an amazing 122 individual connections. The framework also allows the user to design mechanical assemblies with internal gear boxes, as seen below in the Froggy character, with its four driving mechanisms, forty-three components, and forty-seven individual connections.

Figure 72. Froggy the mechanical frog

As I have clearly demonstrated, toys that exhibit mechanical movement have always been extremely popular consumer products. This new software is a breakthrough technology of major significance that will go far beyond simple animatronics, and usher in a long awaited age of highly sophisticated robots that can at last become household items. Although the early automatons that we have looked at were extremely complex feats of engineering, they lacked any form of environmental awareness. Nowadays we have a plethora of electronic sensors that will allow the rapid design and manufacturing of customized robots that can sense and interact with the world around them. This will enable them to carry out tasks so complex that they were previously undreamed of.

I expect to see much more than the simple bearing revolutionized in the next short few years. In fact, I dare predict that many of the keystones of mechanical technology will be changed almost beyond recognitions. Components such as the gear wheel, the lever, the joint, the switch, and the cam can now be redesigned with a completely new manufacturing process in mind, and we can expect to see rapid improvements in a multitude of areas including size, efficiency, ease of production, strength, design, flexibility, complexity, modularity, availability, ease of use, and distribution.

In the short term, I expect 3D printers to change from one-trick plastic ponies to thoroughly universal fabbing machines. Just as the first computers were little more than complicated adding machines, the multifunctional PC could not have been anticipated until we designed and built fully programmable computers. Now a PC can perform a multitude of tasks from playing chess to creating databases to writing documents. When we made the jump from mechanical calculators to general purpose programmable computers, we quickly saw a processing speed increase of a thousand fold as we changed from relay switches to vacuum tubes. What kind of exponential growth will we be able to harness when we switch from plastic based 3D printers to fully programmable general purpose fabricators? Once 3D printers are efficiently combined with CNC devices, suddenly we will have not just additive printers, but fully variable fabbing units, and that is where the real fun begins.

Fabber combos are already in development, and a good place to start research is on the Linux-CNC mailing list. Some of the issues being worked through at the moment include interfacing the print head temperatures setting and feedback, and matching the high axis speeds of 3D printers. Fortunately, it is not all that difficult to take a Wade extruder and plunk it onto a CNC machine.

And so, the question remains, what will be some similar landmarks in 3D printing to those that we saw in automata and early robotics? Creations such as the Young Archer, the Flauteur, and the Writer were certainly milestones in art and craftsmanship, but what similar breakthroughs can we expect from 3D printing?

On considering this question, I first began thinking about future technology breakthroughs, such as when would we have our first 3D-printed, underwater gill breathing prosthetics. Then I began speculating about all the open source tools that we will be able to download and assemble at home. I am so much looking forward to having my own linear book scanner or a fully printable, open source Dremel-type multi-tool, preferably with a detachable laser guided press as an option. I soon realized that I was simply creating yet another wish list of printables, and I had already done that twice in my previous book.

A much better way to look at this future scenario is to approach it from a different angle completely. 3D printers are accelerating prototyping speeds as well as bringing down costs of production. Therefore, rather than dream of products that I hope to see developed, I began to realize that reductions in the cost of current items is going to be a far more influential factor in the short term. Skeptics are still complaining about the lack of items to print, but once we see a greater number of $1,000 items reduced to a cost of just $100, those complaints will soon evaporate. This will represent a significant tipping point in the evolution of the technology and something to which I am very much looking forward. My own top ten list of the goodies that I am hoping to see reach this much more accessible price point will probably differ quite significantly from that of other people and so I have tucked it away in the appendices.

19

Opportunities for Big Business

After watching Michael Weinberg on the PBS Off Book show entitled *Will 3D Printing Change the World?* I began thinking about how this technology could benefit large companies, as well as the individual entrepreneurs that I have focused upon in this eBook. Specifically, if I were the CEO of a large multinational, what would I do to anticipate the impact of 3D printers, and what business strategies would I adopt to ensure that my organization would profit from the changes that are inevitably going to take place? Existing manufacturers and producers will need to be proactive and consider options that might at first seem counter intuitive.

One of the first areas to research would be the cost of lawsuits against the sharing community compared to the profits that have been generated by iTunes in the last five years. While I am sure that many misguided companies will go the Games Workshop route and mimic the actions of groups such as the RIAA and MPAA, in long-term this will be very costly and ultimately self-defeating. I have already written about the highly attractive demographics of the 3D printing community and alienating this group with threats and intimidation would likely result in a very unpleasant backlash, not to mention the loss of a potentially very profitable market segment.

Different markets will certainly require different strategies, but it is important to note some of the early battles that have been lost in the copyright war that has been waged so far. There is a valuable lesson to be learned from George Lucas' over extension, specifically his attempts to close down small-scale producers of Stormtrooper outfits in the UK. Not only did the lawsuits fail, but he generated a great deal of bad feeling amongst some of his biggest fans in the process. It is difficult to put an accurate price on this kind of negative publicity, but other companies can certainly learn from George's mistakes and avoid those costs from the very start.

There will be so many opportunities for companies to embrace the work of their greatest fans. Another good example of what not to do comes from Square Enix when they discovered that Digital artist Joaquin Baldwin had a range of Final Fantasy VII figures stylized to resemble the characters' low polygon-count blocky look in the original PlayStation game. Fans raved and Baldwin was selling them for between $14 and $30 on Shapeways. Square Enix does not sell such models nor do they intend to and so they reacted with cease-and-desist demands threatening six-figure penalties for each figure manufactured. Rather than work with a designer that has created a completely new line, Square Enix simply killed the venture. Instead of making easy money from a line that they did not have to design, manufacture, or ship, they generated hundreds of pages of negative press coverage and the lasting ill will of many fans. Perhaps they had hired consultants from the music industry.

As the head of a large studio or production company, I would work to embrace my fans, not try to put them in jail. To begin with, I would encourage and even sponsor fan clubs that were related to my products. I would initially invest in ten very desirable 3D models to make freely available for any use on Thingiverse and then begin producing more models to be made available on subscription basis to be paid by fan club members. There are thousands of really talented 3D designers out there and commissioning these guys to create custom pieces of related artwork and memorabilia would cater ideally to the requirements of any fanclub. As a manufacturer, my costs would be limited solely to the design of the models. All production and distribution would then be taken care of by the fan club, which could either use their own printers to produce the items, or order them in the materials of their choice from a firm like Shapeways. If we look at George as an example, the choice of artifacts from the Star Wars universe is almost infinite. Just stop for a moment to think of the selection of vehicles, spacecraft, uniforms, armor, equipment, accessories, weapons etc. that are available from that one story alone. I imagine that the best way to approach such a wide choice would be to use the contest model. Every six months George announces a new contest, whereby he offers a few hundred thousand dollars in cash prizes for the best designs in a particular category, preferably categories that have been suggested and chosen by the members of the fan club. Those same members are then able to vote on the design entrants and the winners are made available as fan club exclusives. Based on an annual subscription of $50, the sheer amount of Star Wars fans would quickly make a scheme pay for itself, as well as generating large profits for George.

I am loathe to offer any suggestions to Lars Ulrich, after he did so much to destroy Napster and then received a cool $1 million for his efforts in the process, but the same model would work equally well for him, assuming that Metallica has any fans left. The same annual subscription model, followed with modeling contests to create some really amazing merchandising and memorabilia. I am sure that initially we would see "And Justice for All" statues and 3D representations of other album covers which would be quite predictable, but the beauty of holding design contests is that they bring together a design team that is far larger than the band or their management could ever afford to hire. The only problem is that Metallica and Dr. Dre are so hated as sell-outs to the recording industry (doubly ironic for a thrash metal act and a gangster rapper), that their fan clubs might only attract a half a dozen teenagers that are too young to remember Napster.

Metallica is probably a poor choice to use an example. Most of the maker community is very pro-open source and despite the fact that a large majority of them are indeed metal fans, Lars and the boys are so universally despised that we would quickly see a huge explosion of the most unflattering, mocking statuettes imaginable. If we were to apply this model to a band that still retained a shred of respect among its fanbase, then we would see some interesting developments.

During their heyday, Kiss was the undisputed master of tacky merchandising, selling everything from key rings and pencil toppers to lunch-boxes and poseable action figures. In fact, the selection goes a long way beyond such simple items. As I write, there are more that twelve thousand Kiss-related items of memorabilia listed on eBay, everything from Kiss condoms to logoed car seat covers, from full-size Kiss burial caskets to Kissopoly, the bands specially authorized version of Monopoly. Is it so hard to imagine a young and upcoming rock band offering a range of open source CAD files to their fans, so that they could create their own customized merchandising and memorabilia? Just think what the mash up generation would create with scans of the band members, their albums, and the logos. Not to mention the value of interacting with their audience.

Gene Simmons and the boys show no sign of retiring gracefully to make way for a new generation of artists, so maybe it will be Kiss that pioneers a new range of 3D models made available to their many fan clubs and tribute sites.

There are many ways for musicians to make a living beyond CD sales. These days even a simple thing like a ringtone can sell more copies than the original song. Most working musicians make their money playing gigs and selling merchandise. Only the very lucky get big money recording deals. Lady Gaga is one of the first artists to have adopted the popular "freemium" business model. She gives away billions of free views of her music videos and collects the ad revenue that YouTube pays. Then she sells a much more limited commodity, seats to hear live shows, at a premium. I wonder how long it will be before she starts offering 3D models of her outrageous designer outfits for fans to download. With Internet technology she would only need ten million people to pay 99 cents a download, and she has made an extra ten million dollars. Alternatively, she might choose to sell it at just 10 cents or just 1 cent and become even more famous in the process.

What works for musicians could work equally well for Hollywood. I wonder how long it will be before some forward-thinking movie producer decides to license 3D models rather than a range of physical action figures produced in a Chinese factory. I bet that the producers of the Lone Ranger are wishing that they had done this, instead of being stuck with containers full of masked 1/6 sale masked men and surly Tontos. In the future, the next blockbuster movie could license models at a range of different scales from 28 mm for role players, 1/6 and 1/4 for collectors and even full size for the rapidly growing cosplay and convention communities.

3D models are quickly going to become so ubiquitous that some players might have to adopt radical tactics to rise above the chaos and successfully interact with their audience. I have already talked about a number of far-sighted companies that have developed a clear understanding of the crowd sourcing model, but I also expect to see a revival of the approvals schemes that were once popular among philatelists. Every month, a collector would receive a book of fifty to one hundred stamps. He or she could simply choose to keep the ones that took their fancy and return the rest, only paying for those retained. This could work for a jewellery designer for example. They send out ten designs a month, but the customer only pays for those that they turn into actual physical copies that can be worn.

It will be important for many companies to interact with and pay closer attention to their existing customers. At the moment, the BBC carefully monitors a number of torrent sites that specialize in TV shows. It is reported that they will even release shows on those sites first so that they can gauge the response and decide whether or not it worth doing a physical DVD release.

Unfortunately for us, most of the copyright monopolists that are hoarding the cultural legacy of our generation are far too conservative to recognize the value of this new medium. Rather than embracing their fan art and fan literature, most publishers are still trying to restrict access and forbid fair use.

Is it so hard to imagine that Lego would sell digital files that allow users to print lego sets on their own 3D printers? Clearly they would not be able to charge as much as they can for physical Legos, but the margin would be so much better, without all of the materials, manufacturing, and distribution costs. Some people would still want to design and print their own Legos, but if they could buy the designs for $10 and save a few hours in CAD software, how many would choose to pay?

While I agree the lawyers will become rich fighting IP battles, I have little doubt that some companies will embrace the idea of selling designs directly to consumers, so they can dispense with pesky things like employees, production, storage, shipping, and so on. If some users want to 3D print products, manufacturers should embrace it, sell or give away the CAD files, and provide customer support, not lawsuits.

It only takes a little imagination to see how many companies could leverage this sea of change to their advantage. Car companies could be forging closer links with enthusiast clubs by providing 3D designs of sought after parts. Museums could soon be doing a roaring trade in virtual reproductions. I could see institutions such as the Royal Armories and the Imperial War Museum doing especially well in this field.

Any physical item that is widely appreciated has suddenly developed an extra form of value as a 3D model. Companies should be thinking about all of the items to which they have access and how to monetize their digital counterparts.

This might in fact be the last chance for many companies. The rapid development of home scanning technology might soon mean that the entire back catalogues of some companies will be available on-line before they have a chance to release them officially. With all the bad feeling that Games Workshop has already created, it is quite plausible that the advent of $100 scanners will allow the global community of gamers to scan all of the company's existing miniatures and upload them to a new repository in Antigua. It would be ironic if Games Worksop were to miss the 3D printed boat as they have so much to gain. The market for designs of their early AD&D ranges would be huge, as would be twenty-first-century upgrades for the classic boardgame Talisman.

Scale model kits from companies like Airfix and Revell are still very collectible. How will this market react when hobbyists can simply download a kit and print it off themselves?

Businesses have always handed out freebies at trade shows and exhibitions. Now with 3D models, marketing departments will be able give away umpteen more key rings, miniatures, and other assorted knick-knacks that bear the company logo simply by releasing STL files.

This is an important time to act as the value of 3D models has already begun the same precipitous decline that was suffered by music tracks as they were digitized into MP3s. There was a time when half a dozen or so songs were worth $20. Now it is easy to fit hundreds of thousands onto a single iPhone hard disk. There could quite possibly come a time when CAD models come with everything we order.

Appendices

Recommended Reading List

Music for 3D Printers

$100 Tipping Points

About the Author

Attributions

Recommended Reading List

I have touched upon so many interesting and diverse subjects that a "further reading" list could quite easily double its length. Instead, I have restricted myself to just a few favorite discoveries that I have made. This is by no means an exhaustive listing, as there are new books on this subject being released all the time. What follows is just a small selection of some of the most interesting discoveries that I have made while doing my research. The first section contains traditional dead tree books, while the second details a selection of interesting documentaries.

Mechanisms and Mechanical Devices Source Book by Neil Sclater and Nicholas P. Chironis (Third Edition, 2001)
Mechanical Assemblies have tremendously changed our way of life since the industrial revolution. For a comprehensive introduction into mechanisms and mechanical devices I would like to refer the interested reader to this fascinating textbook. Filled with fascinating diagrams from obscure, out of print works, this is a work of inspiration for inventors, tinkerers, and gadgeteers.

The Homebrew Industrial Revolution: A Low-Overhead Manifesto
by Kevin A. Carson

From the Reprap front and center on the cover, this is clearly essential reading for anybody interested in 3D printing and distributed manufacturing. It is a deeply researched investigation of networked local manufacturing, garage industry, household microenterprises and resilient local economies, introducing the casual reader to a wealth of new concepts not usually revealed in more mainstream sources of information. Best of all, it provides an optimistic view of a new economy emerging from the neverending recession to which we are being subjected at the moment.

English Clocks for the Eastern Markets: English Clockmakers Trading in China & the Ottoman Empire 1580-1815 by Dr. Ian White

A large format, cloth bound volume with hundreds of color photographs, diagrams, and illustrations over 398 pages published by the British Antique Horological Society. It looks in great depth at both the Anglo-Ottoman and the Anglo-Chinese trade as well dedicating three full chapters on James Cox and his amazing works of art, that are increasingly being recognized as an important facet of eighteenth-century English art, rather than just ingenious contrivances. Availiable to AHS members for £ 50.00, but £ 75.00 for non-members.

As yet, I have been unable to obtain a copy of "The Role of Automata in the History of Technology" by Silvio A. Bedini published in *Technology and Culture*, Vol. 5, No. 1 (Winter, 1964, pp. 24-42), The Johns Hopkins University Press, but it has been praised by a number of sources and I would recommend readers with better access to Western materials than myself.

By far the most interesting source that I have seen on the subject of shanzhai is the research conducted by Lyn Jeffery, director of the Technology Horizons Program at the Institute for the Future. In early 2011 he began recording a group discussion of the subject with some fascinating luminaries in the field, including Bunnie Huang, David Li, founder of Xinchejian, Eric Pan, founder of SeeedStudio and Jon Phillips of Fabricatorz.com. Their conversation really is "a remarkable, free-wheeling conversation among a set of pioneering thinker/makers in China, Singapore, and the U.S." and well worth seeking out. Highlights include a new set of shanzhai rules and the model's impact on the Arab Spring. For a more in-depth, academic look at the subject, I would recommend, *The Business Model of a Shanzhai Mobile Phone Firm in China* by Jin-Li Hu and Hsiang-Tzu Wan of the National Chiao Tung University, Taiwan published in the Australian Journal of Business and Management Research Vol.1 No.3, June 2011.

A new quarterly peer-reviewed journal, *3D Printing and Additive Manufacturing*, will launch around the same time as this book, in the autumn of 2013. The editor-in-chief is Hod Lipson and the publication will include original articles, exclusive interviews with top professionals and innovators in the field, commentaries, opinion pieces, industry reports, a debate section, webinars, videos, and podcasts.

Rise of the CNC - Ultimate CNC Design Course($60.00) is an interesting 450-page overview written in a non-technical manner by Jon Cantin of CNCKing.com. Apart from discussing the fundamentals of table routers, 3D printers, and laser cutters, it also features sixty-four projects demonstrating how to successfully design for these CNC machines. In addition, there are industry interviews and an in-depth buyers guide.

There is a growing body of 3D related speculative fiction coming onto the market, and the works that follow are just a taste, something to occupy those spare twenty-six hours while your Makerbot trundles away spitting out a Dizingof work of art.

Cory Doctorow is the co-editor of the Boing Boing website. His latest novel is *Makers*, but I think that it is also worth reading his short story collection, *Overclocked*, where he posits a world in which 3D printing technology had crashed the world economy. Both are available as free downloads from his website. In true mirror-shades tradition, Makers Perry Gibbons and Lester Banks are typical brilliant geeks in a garage, trash-hackers who find inspiration in the growing pile of technical junk. The characters are simultaneously completely geeky and suave, lovable and flawed. Even the suits—marketing people and lawyers—are interesting. If you are a cyberpunk fan then this is a great introduction to Doctorow's work.

Rule 34 by Charles Stross is a futuristic police procedural set in a near-future Edinburgh, in which 3D printing has become boringly ubiquitous. It is a loose sequel to *Halting State*, which I personally preferred, but that was more about virtual realities than 3D printing, but only one character, Detective Inspector Liz Cavanaugh, returns from that story. The entire novel is written from the characters' perspectives as it moves from character to character. Some people find this second-person narrative voice irritating, and even literally tiring, but I recall enjoying its novelty. It extrapolates everything excessive in our current culture and creates an almost dystopian Scotland of 2035. Though very grisly and sexually explicit in parts, there are many humorous interludes and the whole thing is very cleverly put together, but readers new to Stross might want to start with *Halting State*.

Voyage from Yesteryear is a 1982 science fiction novel by James P. Hogan and I have included it here because it is an interesting comparison between authoritarian regimes and post scarcity societies. The human species has re-established itself far away from a global conflict that has engulfed the whole world. Far away on Chiron, a small habitable exo-planet in the Alpha Centauri system, complete with limitless robotic labor and fusion power, has created a post-scarcity economy run as an anarchist adhocracy. Money and material possessions are meaningless to the Chironians and social standing is determined by individual talent, which has resulted in a wealth of art and technology without any hierarchies, central authority, or armed conflict. When new settlers arrive from Earth bringing with them all the trappings of the authoritarian regime, bureaucracy, religion, capitalism, and militarism, more conflict is inevitable.

In Mechanical Mice by Maurice A. Huigi (aka Eric Frank Russell), Robot Mother is a very early use of the concept of self-reproducing automata. The story concerns a machine that constructs duplicates of itself using available parts, in this case by stealing them from watches.

Documentaries

With the abilities of the modern internet, I highly recommend quality documentaries for educational fair use purposes. For far too long, this kind of resource has been kept out of the hands of the ordinary public. Extraordinarily high prices, limited broadcasting regulations, and vastly overreaching copyright restrictions are finally being overcome and there are some fantastic video resources now becoming accessible to individuals. Here is a brief selection of a few that might interest readers that have made it this far.

Mechanical Marvels: Clockwork Dreams was a brilliantly

entertaining and informative documentary from BBC4 on the history of automata, originally shown in June 2013. Professor Simon Schaffer charts the incredible story of automata and demonstrates how such brilliantly designed, sophisticated, advanced automata were crucial to the development of modern programmable computers. Traveling around Europe, Simon uncovers the history of these machines and shows us some of the most spectacular examples, from the beautiful Hellbrunn Palace and Water Gardens to the "intelligent" chess-playing Turk. All the machines he visits show a level of technical sophistication and ambition that still amazes today, revealing that these long-forgotten marriages of art and engineering are actually the ancestors of many of our most-loved modern technologies, from recorded music to the cinema and much of the digital world.

Great Experiments was a science series shown on BBC2 in the autumn of 1985, presented by highly respected scientist Professor Heinz Wolff from The Great Egg Race series. It is difficult to locate, but there are VHS rips of the show on a few specialized torrent trackers. This particular twenty-five minute episode entitled "Number Crunching" tells the story of Charles Babbage, a mathematician who, in the 1840s, became impatient with the mathematical tables of the time and built his own "difference engine"—a precursor of the modern computer.

How a Watch Works is a very enjoyable short film that was commissioned by the Hamilton Watch Company and produced by the Jam Handy Organization in 1947 as a training tool for its sales and marketing staff. It highlights the details of the manufacturing process such as how steel was painstakingly alloyed into Ellinvar Extra to make hairsprings and how the factory in Lancaster, Pennsylvania used to make a huge batch of bread dough every morning to use for removing dust from watch movements in the era before synthetics like Rodico putty used by modern watchmakers for the same purpose. It gives simple and fascinating descriptions of the theory and principle that drives a simple manual mechanical watch in easy-to-understand terms, with some excellent visual aids like a 7.5 foot working model and a garden hose-driven mock "clock" to help make the inner workings very clear, even if you have no previous understanding of what makes watches tick.

Masters of Fine Watchmaking is a collection of documentary films produced by the Foundation for Haute Horlogerie in Geneva in 2005 to promote the innovation and technical expertise involved in fine Swiss watch-making. The series showcases both centuries-old and cutting-edge expertise through eleven portraits of specialists and artisans, including the designer, watchmaker, stone-setter, movement designer, the guillocher, and enameller. Each episode is a wonderful if brief peek into a wonderful world of which most of us remain completely unaware.

NHK is the state-run Japanese broadcaster, renown for their quality documentaries. The network has a twenty-four hour English language channel and for this reason many of the better shows are available dubbed or with subtititles. NHK has a tendency to vacillate between two extreme poles, Japanese culture shows that are painfully infantile in their presentation at one end of the scale, but at the other, in-depth scientific shows that are still relativity uncommon on Western mainstream networks. A good example and particularly relevant show for this book is the Edo Robots episode of the *Last Artisans* series. It explains how mechanical dolls are often seen as the forerunners of Japanese robotics. It focuses on the work of ninth-generation doll maker Shobei Tamaya who loves to surprise the crowd with original creations, as well as classic restorations such as the Young Archer.

For a much more modern example of Japanese technology I would recommend a recent episode of the J-TECH series that investigates the development of microsatellites. It focuses on the work of Professor Shinichi Nakasuka of Tokyo University, who is considered as the father of microsatellites in Japan and one of his former students founder of Axelspace, a venture company that is building the world's first commercial microsatellite, for Weathernews Corporation, the WNISAT-1.

Shift Change: is a new independent documentary that highlights worker-owned enterprises in North America, and the remarkable Mondragon co-operatives in the Basque region of northern Spain. At the time of writing, it has not been officially released, but I recommend it as the co-operatives of the Basque have much in common with the counterparts in Emilia Romagna, and should therefore be a useful insight. The examples covered in North America should give an idea of an alternative for cities such as Detroit.

Music for 3D Printers

The first thing that strikes many new Makerbot owners are the charming chirps, beeps, and whistles that the machine makes while it is printing. This electronica has fascinated some hackers so much that they have written software that uses the stepper motors to play music. I prefer to go the other direction and keep a play list of suitably electro music queued up for while I am printing. I see that it is now possible to print vinyl with a 3D printer, so maybe I will put this together as a K Tel type compilation. All I will then have to do is print one of those antique gramophone contraptions so that I can play the damn thing.

Here is my top ten 3D print-along tunes at the moment:

1. Born To Be Wild - The Moog Cookbook - Ye Olde Space Band - Plays Classic Rock Hits
2. Outta Space – Billy Preston
3. It's Fun to Smoke Dust - Lobsterdust
4. Iron Man - The Cardigans
5. Richard Cheese - Star Wars Cantina (Barry Manilow)
6. South Park of Whatever – The Pessimist
7. Koyannisqatsi – Philip Glass
8. Popcorn – Hot Butter
9. The Diggers Song - Chumbawamba - English Rebel Songs 1381-1914
10. Donna Summer – I Feel Love

Born To Be Wild - The Moog Cookbook - Ye Olde Space Band - Plays Classic Rock Hits

Roger Manning and Brian Kehew adopted space-suit disguises and the aliases of Meco Eno and Uli Nomi to cover a number of classic rock standards from acts such as Kiss, Boston, and Led Zeppelin. These bizarre examples of electronica never fail to freak out any friends when I play them for them. This particular synthesizer tribute cover version is pure feel-good music, and will bring a huge grin to the face to everybody in your makerspace.

Outta Space – Billy Preston

Billy Preston created the intergalactic sounds of "Outta-Space" long before synthesizers and samplers by running the sound from a clavinet through a wah wah pedal and then improvising a groove, while calling out chord changes to the backing-band. He later added organ and hand claps to the track. As always, the clueless record execs thought that they knew better than the artist, and consigned this classic to the B-side of "I Wrote a Simple Song," but Radio DJs began flipping the single and, while the A-side only reached number seventy-seven on the Billboard Pop Singles chart, "Outa-Space" climbed all the way to the number two spot. In the 1990s, Intel Corporation used the song to promote their MMX-enabled Pentium processors, and for me there is not a superior track out there that represents the high-tech wizardry of 3D printing.

It's Fun to Smoke Dust (Queen vs. Pastor Gary Greenwald vs. Midfield General) Lobsterdust

For many of us, 3D printing is all about mixing, remeshing, and mash ups, sampling the physical world and then recreating different versions using the latest technology. Perhaps that is why we love musical mash ups so much. The problem is that most mash up music is still way under the radar thanks to the music industry taking a serious "get the eff off my lawn" stance about what it still considers to be sole property. Anybody that has seen documentaries *such as* Downloaded, *RIP - A Remix Manifesto and Good Copy Bad Copy* will know exactly what I mean, and if you still have not, then I seriously recommend that you study these hard as the copyright war is only just starting to heat up, and as 3D printer enthusiasts, we are going to be right on the front lines. This particular track is remix genius, and I am not going to spoil it by detailing the contents. Suffice to say that the irony, wit, and technical brilliance of this song leaves Girltalk, Norman Cook, and Dangermouse standing in the dust.

Richard Cheese - Star Wars Cantina (Barry Manilow)

While we are still talking about mixing and mashing and technological tributes, I would like to recommend that you all sample a bit of Dick. How on Earth he has not had a team of ILM Storm Troopers kicking down his door in the middle of the night, I will never understand, but much kudos to the guy for coming up with this truly inspired parody. There seems to be a large crossover between 3D printing enthusiasts and sci-fi fans, and so I am pretty sure that everybody reading this will enjoy this hilarious mash up. I especially recommend it for the printing of those obligatory Yoda busts.

South Park of Whatever – The Pessimist

This is a tough one to find, but it is well worth the effort as it is quick, clever, and to the point. One of those, "Damn, I wish I had thought of that" tracks. Actually, the idea is so simple that I am sure it will inspire many people to come up with something along similar lines. Same same, but different, as my next door neighbor would say, god bless him.

Iron Man - The Cardigans

Here is a track that just goes to show how covers can sometimes knock spots off the originals. I know that the mass media treats Ozzy as a rock deity, but let's be honest, he is a drug-addled old fart with the IQ of lard, who just happened to be the vocalist for three really talented musicians. I am sure that if my Makerbot could sing, it would be belting out Iron Man and the Warning at the top of its extruder, but Nina Elisabet Persson's dulcet tones really take some beating.

Koyannisqatsi – Philip Glass

For those of you who do not know, this strange word is Hopi Indian for "world out of control." Just about any composition by Philip Glass would be suitable as a 3D printer soundtrack, as well as any other form of additive manufacturing. This one is the first part of the famous Quatsi trilogy of groundbreaking documentaries, but most of his minimalist compositions, with their radical consonant vocabularies, would be appropriate for an FDM printer.

Popcorn – Hot Butter

Long regarded as an electronica classic that was originally released in 1972, there are now literally hundreds of remixes out there based on the original Hot Butter version. Some of the more hardcore techno remixes would have been great if The General's extruder could have sprayed out liberal amounts of party foam and turned the entire apartment into an Oliver Klitzing-type Ibiza mega rave, but I am not sure that the neighbors would have been too happy.

The Diggers Song - Chumbawamba - English Rebel Songs 1381-1914

It was initially suggested that my Makerbot was female in gender and that she should have a name like Wanda because she was skilled at magically creating something out of nothing. I suppose that she could have been a mechanical version of the that sexy Marvel femme fatale, Wanda the White Witch, rather than her namesake from the Muppets, but the whole mechanistic nature of the device just screamed out to me that it had to be a male. From then on, he was affectionately known as The General. Assuming that he was the first of his kind that was going to bring down the entire Military Industrial Complex, this seemed quite appropriate. And, anyway, if a couple of southern rednecks can name their car after a general, then I see no reason why I should not do the same for my 3D printer. That being the case, this has to be the machine's official theme tune. I suppose that logically it should have been track number four, "The Triumph of General Ludd," but that was just too damned obvious.

Donna Summer – I Feel Love

Dating from way back in 1977, the heavily electronic sound of this track has stood the test of time far better than much of her back catalogue. Combining operatic vocals with a surprisingly contemporary backbeat, this has been described by some as the Bohemian Rhapsody of the disco era. I am not sure that I would go that far, but it does sound quite good while your hot ends are warming up.

$100 Breakthrough List

Here is my top-ten list of thousand dollar items that I would like to be able to print with a maximum of hundred of dollars worth of raw material. By printing just these ten products, I will have made a saving of $10,000, and about covered the cost of an intermediate enterprise-level printer. Please excuse me while I indulge myself for a few paragraphs. Hopefully it will inspire you and fire your imagination to create some ground breaking 3D printer projects.

Costume Armor

In my previous book I talked a little about the growing rise in popularity of 3D-printed armor for LARPers and conventioneers, and I am still convinced that these are going to be significant products for additive manufacturing. I keep seeing 3D-printed dresses on fashion websites, but what I really waiting for is a fully bespoke set of Imperial Stormtrooper armor, complete with all the very latest attachments and some oversized, jaw-dropping kind of exotic, advanced plasma repeater. Used suits still fetch up to $1,000 on eBay or http://www.whitearmor.net, but they are generally the more basic models, in standard sizes. I would really like to see these outfits come down to the $100 price point, not just so that I can have one, but so that I can kit out all my friends at the same time, preferably with oversized BlasTech DLT-19 Heavy Blaster Rifles. Going to a convention is all well and good, but here in Asia, it is very much a group activity, and it would be great to attend such events as a small squadron with five or six close friends. I can just imagine marching in as part of a heavy weapons unit, and setting up one of those ion cannons, as used by the Stormtroopers in the ice caves of Hoth, in *The Empire Strikes Back*. In our case, it would be fully retrofitted to fire smoke rings and giant bubbles. I really admire all the charity work that the 501st Garrisons do, and I could see our Special Bubbles Unit being a big hit at hospitals all over the region. Anyway, it is always handy to have a spare suit handy, just in case you run into problems at the Laundromat.

Figure 73. I hate it when this happens!

If this technology works for Stormtrooper outfits, then why not a full range of party and convention garbs, from Starship Troopers to Sorayama Android outfits? Of course, it need not be sci-fi outfits all of the time. Sports such as jousting and kendo could suddenly become much more accessible if I can remove the cost of having to spend thousands of dollars on armored protection, and print off a suit for just $100.

On an individual basis, an even more impressive cosplay costume for next year's Shanghai convention would be a towering Space Marine outfit.

Figure 74. Halloween on steroids

I personally would prefer a full set of Inquisitor of the Ordo Malleus armor, complete with a heavy bolter and oversized holy tome. Not only do these costumes look awesome, but a really good one will make it much easier to gain the attention of the growing numbers of Sisters of Repentia that I see at various cosplay events. I could then offer to assist them in their quest for absolution.

For a taste of things to come, I was really impressed by the robot suit commissioned by *Wired* magazine at the 2013 Comic-Con. Although it looks like a mecha, this is actually a suit with an exo skeleton made up of two sets of arms. Much of it came out of a 3D printer and it will be interesting to see if the new editor decides to release any of the design files.

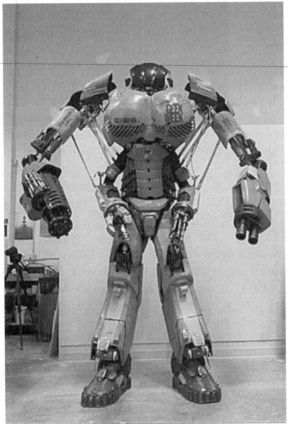

Figure 76. The ultimate 9.5 feet tall attention seeker

Gaming Sets

As a long-time fan of role playing games, I find it great that I can now download rulebooks, scenarios, and expansion kits quite easily. All I need now are a few miniatures, and some props to organize a fun evening of dungeoneering for my friends. Imagine if I could print off a full dungeon adventure set, say 250 miniatures covering all the PCs, NPCs, monsters, denizens, and encounters, as well as a modular set of subterranean room features, including 3D floor tiles, artefacts, and walls. What role player has not dreamed of an Advanced Dungeons and Dragons adventure set on this scale? At 250 pieces, this could also include plenty of all room furnishings and fittings including unholy alters, LED cressets, and the occasional treasure hoard. Possibly a few ingenious but deadly tricks and traps and definitely a few dark and claustrophobic oubliettes, complete with the skeletal remains of previously unsuccessful explorers. All of this would cost me a small fortune if I were to buy it from Games Workshop, but just think if I could print it all at one go, everything I could possibly need for one full adventure, everything for just $100 worth of ABS. A few purists might like to DM with just a rule book and some character sheets, but I have always wondered what it would be like to run a small campaign with all the miniatures needed to show every detail of the setting. If I could grind them all up at the end of play and feed them back into the printer, well, that would be even better.

While I am at it, what about a five hundred piece Warhammer 40K expansion kit. OK I admit it, I am not really a Games Workshop fan, and I would print out a huge set like this just to piss them off, just like I used to download Metallica albums out of pure spite. As a youngster growing up in Nottingham, the home of Games Workshop, we spent nearly all of our money on White Dwarf Magazines and heavy metal LPs. I helped make Games Workshop the industry giant that it is today, just as much as I helped make James Hetfield and Lars Ulrich into multimillionaires, and so it really grates on me to see them turn on the same fans that made them so rich in the first place. In reality, I realize that I am just helping to publicize these overly-litigious morons by downloading and disseminating their products, so I would probably go for a set of creative commons Eclipse Phase adventures instead. Games Workshop simply charges too much for their miniatures, The next thing is they will be requiring COAs and proof of purchase to play in sanctioned/shop level events.

Bespoke Track Bike

Made to measure track bikes, the really sexy aerodynamic frames made popular by the likes of Chris Hoyle and Bradley Wiggins, still cost thousands a dollars, as each one has to be hand built by experienced craftsman. Just imagine how track racing would be revitalized if anybody could print off their own custom-fit track bike for just $100. If you have never experienced the excitement of a

Madison or a Devil Take the Hindmost, then 3D printable track bikes will soon introduce you to some of the most exciting races in modern sport.

Figure 77. Super cool concept bike

During the 2011 Asian games, Guangzhou invested nearly $80 million into a world class velodrome. If I could print myself a bespoke, low profile, fixed-wheel frame and bits, then I would be down their every week, training hard to see if I could beat Graeme Obree's new land speed record. Even better would be if I could rediscover a tandem design that I saw when I was younger, for a pair that were hoping to break the 100 mph mark. It was a strange configuration with the riders facing away from each other and some highly complex gearing, to ensure that the pair created maximum torque and the highest possible speed.

Norwalk Juicers

Figure 78. The Norwalk Hydraulic Press Juicer

Norman Wardhaugh Walker was a British pioneer in the field of vegetable juicing and nutritional health. He was also the designer of Norwalk Hydraulic Press Juicer, still the most advanced model on the market and one that is still popular with entrepreneurs starting up their own health farms and detox clinics. Walker was a leading light in the raw foods, juicing, and vegetarian movements, long before they hit mainstream consciousness. The Norwalk Juicer is one of those rare high-end products that China has not as of yet, been able to reverse engineer. My budget does not currently stretch to $1,000 for a high-end drinks maker, but if I could print most, if not all of the parts on my desktop matter compiler, I would certainly be drinking passion fruit and snow peach nectar for breakfast lunch and dinner most of the year.

Oculus Add-Ons

Most of us in the tech arena are eagerly awaiting the arrival of the Oculus Rift, the HD headset that will finally make Virtual Reality a reality. While the goggles are currently priced at around $300, that price will drop quickly as word of their awesomeness quickly spreads. Let's be honest, most us have been waiting since our early teens for just this kind of device. Rather than print a pair of goggles, I see the real saving in printing a stereoscopic, 180-degree field-of-view camera rig, capable of capturing and post-processing HD images that can be adapted for VR. Professional camera gear is notoriously expensive, but a huge range of shoulder rigs and time lapse adaptors are quickly becoming available on Thingiverse. How long will it be before all the parts, mounts, and housings are available in a single, zipped download? It is really only a matter of time, right?

Once the Occulus Rift goes viral next year, there are going to be hundreds of add-ons and accessories springing up to meet the needs of all the new games that we will be seeing. It is maybe a little too early to predict exactly what will be available and when, but I do have a few ideas of what will be on my preliminary wish list. Some kind of omni-directional treadmill seems like a likely contender, and perhaps control panel with some kind of hot dog tray harness. If I am going to be playing *Pacific Rim*-type mecha games, then a good solid dashboard is going to be essential.

Open Source Book Scanner

I would give my left arm for a linear book scanner, but I am simply not technically minded enough to deal with some of these early open source models that are available at the moment. I need something a bit more user friendly than the Pizza Box Grumble type seen in *Mr. Penumbra's 24 hour Bookstore.* My CD collection has now gone completely digital, as have all my DVDs. I still have a great many out-of-print, non-fiction books that I cannot bear to part with, as I might never find most of them again, so it is probably about time that I find a scanner that can turn them all into PDFs and mobi files.

Figure 79. A linear book scanner

I really like Google's open source linear scanner, but the fact that it costs around $1,500 in parts, and I have to assemble it myself is enough to scare me off. I am sure that I could pick up a couple of cheap digital cameras and a vacuum cleaner if there was a good printable frame design. Hopefully, as the price of 3D scanners falls, so will book scanners, so that eventually I will have access to something really cool such as a Japanese BFS-Auto robotic system that can digitize books at over 250 pages per minute, with high-speed, fully-automated page flipping, real-time 3D recognition of the flipped pages, and high-accuracy restoration to a flat document image.

Figure 80. BFS-Auto book scanner

Robots

I have already talked extensively about the impact of automata technology, but I have not really said very much about the revolution that is already taking place in the robotics field. Until very recently, only the very largest corporations and university labs could afford to invest in robotics research, but that is now changing very quickly. One good example is the Poppy droid that has been introduced by the Inria Flowers Lab. This is an advanced lightweight humanoid robot made with 3D printed limbs and a variety of cheap motors and electronics, but costs only $10,000. I know that is still a lot of money for most of us, but in the field of advanced robotics, it is practically peanuts. In addition, the Poppy is open source and so its development is likely to be much faster than examples like Asimo, which has been the prized project of just a handful of top researchers.

Figure 81. Poppy - the world's sweetest droid

I predict that 3D printing is going to drop kick development in this field into a completely new realm. Modern smart phones will make powerful electric brains for the next generation of droids, while convergences in miniaturisation, bio-mimicry, and drone tech ensure that advanced and breakthroughs come at an unprecedented pace. It will not be long, for example, before we see semi-autonomous CNC bots dominating ice carving competitions. The long term goal of the robo football league is to challenge and beat a professional team of humans by the year 2050. I will go out on a limb and predict that this will take place as early as 2025, if not before. After all, soccer players are extremely limited specialists with precious little multi-tasking requirements. This is a field where the top players and managers do not even need to be able to read and write to reach the highest paid levels of the sport. Anybody that has seen a DARPA Big Dog at full gallop must realize that even the most accomplished professional athletes will have little chance in competing against the robots sportsmen of tomorrow.

If you have been watching the field, there has been a flurry of interesting robots hitting the scene in the last twelve months. Some of these, such as the Robugtix T8 bio-inspired octopod robot, were little more than wirelessly controlled gag giant spiders, but the fact that it contained twenty-six motors and was made up of 3D printed parts was certainly a taste of things to come. Even so, $1,350 was still a pretty high price to pay for scaring the bejeesus out of all your closest female relatives.

Figure 82. Robugtix T8

With its panoply of mini-weapons including a dart launcher, ball blaster, and disc launcher, the Spider Tank Mark 6 fully articulated robot would have been great for intimidating small pets and annoying noisy infants, but with a Kickstarter goal of $350,000, there was never that much chance of it being fully funded. It is a shame that the project was priced so high, as the deluxe kits complete with all three weapon attachments and an extra set of "explodo armor" were only $99. Not bad at all considering the complexity of the robot.

Figure 83. Spider Tank Mark 6

Myself, I am waiting for an affordable snakebot. My prediction is that this type of robot will be able to cope with the widest variety of environments from underground tunnels to controlled glides among the treetops. Biological snakes occupy a wide variety of ecological niches, ranging from arid desert to tropical jungle to open oceans. Abandoning limbs and developing elongated spines has proved an effective survival strategy and many generations have evolved since the early prototypes, until we now have untethered designs with their own artificial intelligence and sensing capabilities.

The complex segmentation drive system is easily controlled with just a simple joystick but we still have a great deal to learn about navigating and traversing the world in a very different fashion to traditional bipeds. Most of all, I want to have a robot that is so useful that it will be called upon for specialized emergency missions. Many people have a pet dog, but how many of those mutts have their own hot line, so that the authorities can call upon them for specialized search and rescue missions? I figure that if I am going to have a robot then it should at least be capable of providing a public service when needed. These could be tasks like locating flood victims or sniffing out earthquake survivors, both of which are all too common events in my part of the world.

Figure 84. Beware of the venomous snakebot

I am keenly following the bio-tensegrity snake experiments of Brian Tietz, a NASA Space Technology Research Fellow from Case Western Reserve University's BioRobotics lab, who has been using tensegrity motion to traverse a variety of complex terrains, in the same way that a real snake functions. With the right kind of design, a couple of these beauties would be even more effective sentries than a pack of Rottweilers. Even pit bulls and Dobermans are susceptible to doped steak, whereas I would challenge anybody to even approach a menacing pair of autonomous AI anacondas, let alone get past them. Maybe the image of a Hydrobot in coil attack mode from the Terminator Salvation show might be the shape of things to come?

For more details of snakebots, I highly recommend Dr. Gavin Miller's book *Neurotechnology for Biomimetic Robots*.

http://www.snakerobots.com/

For a more general outlook of robot technology, I enjoy the everything-robotic blog, by the Robot Report, which provides good coverage of topical and interesting aspects in the robotics industry. http://www.everything-robotic.com/

Delivery Drone and Network Base Station

For the magical $100, I want to be able to print off my own drone and base station, and become one of the first providers on the "matternet" or drone network. Despite the negative connotations widely attached to drones, a number of companies are trying to set up a short haul logistics drone delivery service, built on an open protocol. The network might be almost non-existent at first, but it is just like fax machines or email addresses, the more that are created, the more useful the service becomes. In the longer term, these could become very useful in creating a new transportation infrastructure, and I am personally very much looking forward to seeing Bruce Sterling's Maneki Neko gift economy becoming a reality.

The cost of building just one mile of single lane road is about $1 million. For that price, we could have hundreds of privately owned drones and base stations doing quick and cheap deliveries. It is estimated that 80 percent of e-commerce packages are below 2 kilograms (4.5 pounds) which is perfect for the current generation of unmanned copters. Drones are able to fly at heights of up to four hundred feet for around ten miles, which would work out at around $0.25 a kilo per ten miles. What is more, they are at least twice as efficient as road traffic over short distances, because they can travel as the crow flies. The landing pads come complete with solar battery chargers and are based on an open source decentralized P2P network.

I realize that there are a few issues to iron out such as crash liability, inclement weather, local ordinances, and the fact that in some places rednecks are already trying to shoot anything that hovers out of the sky, but I am sure that they can be overcome. I am quite happy to become one of the earliest adopters and see this explode in a similar fashion to the web. After all, it was geeks like us with shelves full of modems and expensive T-1 lines that were some of the earliest Internet providers. Once the system is fully functioning in the developed world, then I am looking forward to seeing a global network of delivery drones, allowing for large-scale coordination and transportation of goods to places that are inaccessible due to lack of development. I want to see cheap generic medicines zipping out to rural villages in sub Saharan Africa or seeds and seedlings crossing the otherwise inaccessible valleys of the Himalayan foothills.

Kite Generator

For a while now, I have been researching small home wind generators, everything from horizontal carousels to high efficiency Darrieus rotors. As yet, I have not been able to find anything with an advanced level of fluted complexity that is worthwhile printing. Instead, I have become very interested in a robotic kite-powered generator set up. Google X—the secretive research and development arm of the search giant—recently bought out Makani Power, the designers of fully autonomous robot kites, bearing power-generating propellers, and has previously invested $15 million in the company, so I am assuming that they must have made some kind of major breakthrough.

Figure 85. Makani Airborne Wind Turbine

Actually, these are more like turbines mounted on tethered airplanes rather than kites, but even so, if they have a robust, uninterruptable combination of a flying wing and a wind energy harvester then that is something that I would be very interested in printing and installing. In a standard wind turbine, the outermost part of the propeller blade generates most of the energy, with the rest of the structure acting essentially as dead weight. By designing a flying wing that can hover under its own power, Makani's approach has cut the weight by roughly an order of magnitude. The device can operate in slow as well as high-speed winds, and the fact that it is a tethered plane design means that it automatically copes with heavy gusts. I think that this kind of breakthrough technology will take a while to come down to $1,000 let alone $100, but when it does I can imagine our energy generation problems being solved almost overnight.

Figure 86. The Altaeros AWT

I have been watching developments in this field quite closely, and for a long time was very optimistic about the work being conducted by Altaeros Energies and their airborne wind turbines (AWT) that use lighter-than-air technology adapted from tethered aerostats. Although the subscale prototype is only 35 feet in diameter, at just 350 feet altitude it can produce more than twice the power generated at conventional tower height. The whole thing can be deployed and recaptured in a fully automated cycle. The Makani tethered unmanned aircraft autonomously climbs to altitude of 1,000 feet where it produces power at half the cost of a conventional wind turbine, using 90 percent less material. It can also handle sudden shifts in wind speed and direction, with the 28 meter span, 600 kW commercial version capable of delivering energy at an unsubsidized cost competitive with coal. It will be very interesting to see what restrictions are put on home users by organizations such as the FAA. Domestic airborne wind systems could quickly become unwelcome competitors for the big utility providers, and it is likely that they will lobby intensely to retain their monopoly positions.

Observation Drone

Whenever I travel, I always carry a pair of binoculars to make sure that I can extend my field of vision as far as possible. What is the point in traveling half way around the world unless you are going to try and see everything possible? I have a very nice PLA officer issue pair that were a gift, but what I am looking forward to is a virtual observation drone as a replacement. Basically, these are lightweight semi-autonomous remote controlled planes, equipped with high quality zoom lenses. The on-board accelerators take care of the flying, while the user dons a small pair of goggles so that he or she can have a pilot's aerial point of view. At the moment these are a bit bulky, but it will not be long before a fully integrated set, including wing, controller, and glasses comes down to the size of my binoculars. Just imagine what a boon such an item would be while out hiking in remote areas. My personal trekking preference is for limestone karst areas of the kind found in South Eastern Europe and South East Asia. Pilgrim philosopher Xu Xiake described these areas best when he documented his thirty year exploration of China's most sacred mountains. Again and again he was confronted by "massive, labyrinthine heaps of rock, towering wavelike into crests or busting out like petals, dizzying in their effect as they jostle and surge toward the sky!"

Figure 87. The opium trails of the Guangxi karst plateau

"Imagine a series of quaintly shaped hillocks littering a landscape that is also pockmarked with deep depressions," explained seventeenth-century French explorer Francis Garnier. "No valleys or mountain ranges. No general sense of direction. The streams flow to all points on the compass. Every step would have led us up against some impossible piece of terrain."

I really enjoy the challenge of this kind of topography, especially the ancient opium trading routes that stretch all the way from Yunnan and Guangxi down to Hong Kong. Trekking these forgotten routes is laborious and time consuming, but with an observation drone I could easily check to see if the route ahead was treacherous stone crevasses or relatively easy mule trails. I could explore mountain grottos high above me and descend into the deepest collapsed caves that litter an already difficult terrain. Best off all, I would be able to capture some of the most spectacular routes on a media that would finally do justice to the area. Photographs of the area are impressive, but they always fail to capture the scale and intricacies of the geography.

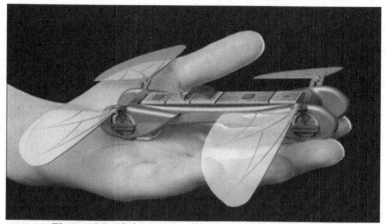

Figure 88. Alpha Dragonfly Micro Aerial Vehicle

Although I am impressed by the Alpha Dragonfly Micro Aerial Vehicle that was so well funded on Indiegogo, their technology still seems a little immature. At $250 the price is good, but I would like to see a couple more generations evolve into a more robust open source model that is more suited to virtual flying and aerial recon. Even so, the Dragonfly is a fantastic step in the right direction.
http://www.indiegogo.com/projects/robot-dragonfly-micro-microaerial-vehicle

About the Author

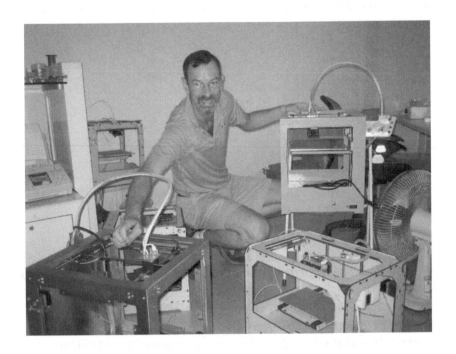

Christopher D. Winnan is a full-time travel writer, seasonally following the very best of the Asian weather, from the blazing sunshine of the Himalayan Plateau, to the snowbird beaches of Southern Thailand. Somehow he manages to squeeze in a surprisingly wide range of projects in between writing commissions. He is currently preparing for another trip to Myanmar, where he will be contributing to a popular American guide book, as well as location scouting along the Burma Road for a number of prominent Mainland investors. He is a qualified permaculture designer, using his specialized knowledge to pinpoint opportunities to which few other people can even gain access. As this particular volume goes to press, he is headed further south, continuing his research on a long-term project that will eventually become a guide book about the Best Exotic Marigold Lifestyle.

The author can be emailed at:
christopherdwinnan@gmail.com.

Other books by Christopher D. Winnan
3D Printing: The Next Technology Gold Rush (Kindle & Paperback Edition)

88 Easy Ways to Improve Your English (Longman and Shaghai Foreign Language Press)
Frommers' China (Frommer's Complete Guides)
Yunnan Province (Bradt Travel Guides)
Intercontinental's Best of China (Intercontinental Travel Guides)

Forthcoming in 2014
A Buyer's Guide to the Wholesale Markets of Guangzhou
Around the World in Eighty Documentaries

Attributions

With so many people to thank for their generous assistance, it is difficult to know where to begin. Firstly, I would like to offer my gratitude to all those people who granted me permission to use their images. These were very useful in illustrating many of the futuristic concepts included in this book. Secondly, my thanks to all those who helped with research, inspiration, and valuable feedback. Most especially, I want to thank the 3D printing pioneers featured in the "What to Print" chapter, but also the following people: Joris Peels, Melba Kuman, Matthew Li, Matt Gardner, Royce Hobbs, Hannah Jones, Karen Reynolds-James, Eva Wolf, Sam Boss, Professor Marcia Pointon, Chen Xingyuan, Zhang Weihong, Zhang Jiangshi, Jon Buford, James Griffiths, Keith Lyons, and John Alexander Stewart.

Special thanks goes to artist extraordinaire Andrei Lacatusu, for his amazing 3D printer image that graces the front cover.

Disclaimer

The information provided in this book is for educational purposes only. It is based on my interpretations of the past and current research available. The author or publisher does not accept any responsibilities for any liabilities or damages, directly or indirectly, resulting from the use of this book.

CPSIA information can be obtained at www.ICGtesting.com
Printed in the USA
LVOW01s1722160414

381977LV00019B/939/P